pg. 40   www. fx triggers . com

Forex Conquered

Founded in 1807, John Wiley & Sons is the oldest independent publishing company in the United States. With offices in North America, Europe, Australia, and Asia, Wiley is globally committed to developing and marketing print and electronic products and services for our customers' professional and personal knowledge and understanding.

The Wiley Trading series features books by traders who have survived the market's ever-changing temperament and have prospered—some by reinventing systems, others by getting back to basics. Whether a novice trader, professional, or somewhere in-between, these books will provide the advice and strategies needed to prosper today and well into the future.

For a list of available titles, visit our Web site at www.WileyFinance.com.

Forex Conquered

High Probability Systems
and Strategies for
Active Traders

JOHN L. PERSON

John Wiley & Sons, Inc.

Published by John Wiley & Sons, Inc., Hoboken, New Jersey.
Published simultaneously in Canada.

Wiley Bicentennial Logo: Richard J. Pacifico.

For general information on our other products and services or for technical support, please contact our Customer Care Department within the United States at (800) 762-2974, outside the United States at (317) 572-3993 or fax (317) 572-4002.

Wiley also publishes its books in a variety of electronic formats. Some content that appears in print may not be available in electronic books. For more information about Wiley products, visit our Web site at www.wiley.com.

Library of Congress Cataloging-in-Publication Data:

Person, John L.
  Forex conquered : high probability systems and strategies for active
traders / John L. Person.
    p. cm. — (Wiley trading series)
  ISBN 978-0-470-09779-3 (cloth/cd-rom)
1. Foreign exchange market.   2. Foreign exchange futures.   3. Stocks—Charts, diagrams, etc.
4. Investment analysis.   I. Title.
  HG3851.P47 2007
  332.4'5—dc22   2006037000

Printed in the United States of America.

10 9 8 7 6 5 4 3 2 1

To Mary, my partner, best friend, and wife of twenty years; time has gone by, but it seems like it has been a short yet not so strange trip with you at my side.

Contents

Preface

F or the most part, day and swing traders use all forms of market analysis to identify opportunities from specific chart patterns that demonstrate frequent reoccurring results. They need to trade in active time
periods, using trend lines and moving averages, both of which are a form of
trend line analysis; these will help in certain market conditions. We will go
over a different set of moving averages than what is normally written about;
this will help identify conditional changes in the market, thereby giving
forex traders a better edge. We will also incorporate and show you how to
calculate support and resistance levels from such mathematically based
models as pivot point analysis and other means, such as Fibonacci corrections and extensions, to identify opportunities and drive trading decisions.

These are the methods I will be covering in this book to help you form
a trading plan based on specific rules and conditions for trading the forex
market. This trading book should help you learn the methodology of the
best and most effective trading techniques to harness and capture consistent results in the forex market. Consider this like market analysis on
steroids. This book combined with the compact disc (CD) should help you
learn in the most effective fashion. By rereading and continually studying
this material, these study tools will help you change the way you trade and
leave you with a specific set of rules on when to enter a position; how to
identify a trade setup, a trigger, or entry execution order; and how to effectively place a stop and know when to exit a trade without hesitation. Most
successful traders live by the adage, *Buy low and sell high*; really great
traders also know when to *buy high and sell even higher*.

The best traders in the world also take advantage of short selling,
which is one aspect that draws so many skilled traders to the forex market;
they can sell short at extreme price highs and buy back at lower prices.

Whatever your method is, the results need to be profitable or your career as a trader will be cut short. Whether you are a position trader, a swing
trader, or the more popular day trader, the key to profits is to try to capture
a portion of a price move in order to generate a positive cash flow (make
money). A trader's search for discovering a method that generates con-

sistency in positive results is the primary goal and should be a continuous learning event. There is one common feature among successful traders, and that is that many of them are prepared before trading and have a formulated game plan.

The techniques in this book can be applied to other markets, but this specifically targets the forex market. I will teach you a trading system so that you develop your own personal program and then follow that plan. Using these techniques should help you to effectively anticipate a potential resistance or support level that will give you an edge in the market for both entering and exiting positions. Blending the strengths and characteristics of candlestick chart pattern recognition with pivot point analysis is what I have been teaching private investors, professional traders, and other leading educators. Many new methods have been introduced to traders, but the one constant is human emotional behavior. In order to master trading, people need to control their emotions. After all, the markets are simply a reflection of these emotions. Fear of losing money causes market prices to head lower as people sell; and fear of missing an opportunity causes market prices to move up as greedy people buy, trying to catch a free ride. As a forex trader, you are looking at technical analysis to help capture profits from a movement in price. Therefore, it is imperative that you understand how and when a market moves and what signals or patterns give you a clue for a directional price move. There are consistently recurring patterns and these are what I plan to share with you in this book. I will also discuss methodologies on trade management and risk management to help you when an inevitable trading loss occurs.

I will disclose how to use time-tested tools such as the Elliott wave theory to help you determine where prices are in a given cycle. We will go over a system based on pivot point analysis and disclose how to effectively use Fibonacci analysis, which is a system based on the theory that prices rise or fall by specific percentages after reaching a high or a low. I will also discuss two very popular indicators, stochastics and the moving average convergence/divergence (MACD), to demonstrate which one interacts best with pivot point support and resistance levels that can produce maximized returns for an automated trading system. I will not only teach the system and include the code but also share the results with you. I believe that a trader who possesses knowledge of the key concepts in technical analysis will have superior advantage over a trader who is simply depending on computer- or software-driven trading signals. My goal in writing this book is to give you an edge from the most powerful trading tools I have come across in my 26 years as a trader.

JOHN L. PERSON

Acknowledgments

I want to thank Pamela van Giessen and Jennifer MacDonald of John Wiley & Sons, who helped me get this book project off the ground and published. Another individual who deserves a big round of applause is Mary Daniello, also from John Wiley & Sons. Thank you for going over the top in making sure the production schedule was pushed back so I could get this book completed in time.

I would also like to thank Glen Larson and Pete Kilman from Genesis Software for testing my theories and helping me develop my trading library on their software; a big thumbs up to TradeStation and, in particular, Stanley Dash. With these two charting software companies, traders will be set in the best possible direction for seeking success in their trading careers. And many thanks to my wife Mary who worked hard on programming the pivot point and Fibonacci calculators—your work did not go unnoticed.

J. L. P.

Disclaimer

The information contained herein is believed to be reliable but cannot be guaranteed as to reliability, accuracy, or completeness. John Person, Inc., John L. Person, will not be responsible for anything that may result from one's reliance on this material or the opinions expressed herein. There is significant risk of loss trading forex, stocks, futures, and options. Trading may not be suitable for everyone, and you should carefully consider the risks in light of your financial condition in deciding whether to trade futures, options, and forex. Further, you assume the entire cost, loss, and/or risk of any trading you choose to undertake; therefore, only genuine risk funds should be used. Past performance is not necessarily an indication of future performance. You may sustain a total loss of the initial margin funds and any additional funds that you deposit in your account to establish or maintain a position in the forex market. No representation is being made that any person will, or is likely to, achieve profits or losses similar to those shown in this book. In fact, there are frequently sharp differences between hypothetical performance results and the actual results subsequently achieved by any particular trading method. Hypothetical performance results have many real limitations; one of which is that limitations of hypothetical performance results are generally prepared with the benefit of hindsight. In addition, hypothetical trading does not involve financial risk, and no hypothetical trading record can completely account for the impact of financial risk in actual trading. There are numerous other factors related to the markets, in general, or to the implementation of any specific trading program that cannot be fully accounted for in the preparation of hypothetical performance results and that can all adversely affect actual trading results.

CHAPTER 1

The Business of Trading Money

WHAT IS FOREX?

Foreign currency is simply money valued against one currency or another, in most cases the U.S. dollar. Simply put, a forex trader is simultaneously buying one currency and selling off another. Money, after all, is what makes the world go 'round. There will always be demand and activity in this product. How to successfully trade this market or any market requires proper education of the vehicle in which you are trading and knowledge of the basic fundamentals and technical analysis tools. One also has to be fairly savvy in technology, as forex trading is virtually all done online through the Internet. Conquering the forex market and mastering success in trading absolutely requires identifying and learning how to avoid a multitude of pitfalls more than it does identifying trading opportunities. In fact, most professional traders will tell you that it is not any specific trading methodology or trading system that makes successful trades; rather it is the discipline and patience needed to master and to stick to their trading rules and to remain controlled in their overall trading methods. In order to win at trading, you must manage risks and understand that there will be lots of losing trades. Remember that success takes time, but mostly it requires consistency in how you seek, execute, and exit positions. If you want to conquer the forex market and wish to learn which technical tools will serve you best, then this is the right book for you.

My goal in this book is to present an easy yet comprehensible set of trading techniques and reliable trading tactics that you can apply in everyday trading circumstances. These techniques should help you identify frequently reoccurring trading opportunities. Yet to better enhance these techniques, I will cover why it is important to develop and maintain a systematic approach based on historical data that is back-tested either visually or by the aid of a computer or trading software program. The signals and methods can be applied for long and short positions. Forex has no restrictions on selling short, so these trading methods will improve and increase your trading opportunities because you can trade both long and short strategies. Imagine a trading product that allows you 24-hour access so you can apply techniques that will set your stop-loss levels, profit objectives, and various order types (such as contingency orders and trailing stops) to maximize your performance. This is what the forex market offers, including flexible leverage and commission-free trading.

WHY TRADE FOREX?

As I stated one moment ago, there will always be demand and supply for money. Democracy, capitalism, and the American dream have led people to seek fortunes. The problem is that many folks who rushed into a venture or an investment saw these dreams diminish as they got in either too late or too early or were just poorly informed. Looking back in recent history, manias such as the "tech wreck" and the stock market bubble financially ruined many people. And there were the innocent victims who invested in Enron, AT&T, and other such companies. I am not talking about speculators; I am referring to employees of those companies who had their retirement savings invested with their employers. Lately, we see weakness and a potential for a bubble to burst in the real estate market. Perhaps you are invested in a second home or know someone who made a killing buying and selling fixer-uppers. The term "flippers" was popular as FSBO (for sale by owner) signs were planted in the front lawn of houses across the United States as eager investors were enticed to flip the property and make a fast buck. If you were in the game early on, you did well. If you got in the game late and are holding onto excess inventory, then you are at risk.

In late June 2006, many investors were left holding the bag on excess inventory—they bought a housing unit (condo, town home, or home) to turn around and sell for a profit but, due to such market conditions as an excess supply of homes for sale, cannot sell the property. Most of their cash or past profits may be tied up in the investment. Even worse, they may be overextended in credit from their bank. These are the folks who will be exposed to major financial disaster. To make matters worse, the Federal Reserve (the Fed) raised interest rates once more, for a record-breaking 17 consecutive hikes. That brought the Fed Funds interest rate to 5.25 percent. The prime lending rate shot up to 8.25 percent. That put the fixed rate for a 30-year mortgage up to 6.62 percent (actual mortgage rates depend on your credit score, down payment, etc.). What this did in effect was to bring on higher borrowing costs, which slowed the housing market even more.

As of October 2006, both new and existing home sales have continued to slow. Higher mortgage rates had been expected to slow the housing market, and they finally started showing their effects. Just to show you, mortgage rates went up roughly 125 basis points since the same period starting from 2005. So when the reports came in from June 2006, new home sales edged down 3.0 percent to an annual rate of 1.131 million. New home sales were down 11.1 percent on a year-over-year basis. The graph in Figure 1.1 shows the rise in mortgage rates and the decline in new home sales.

It did not stop there either; existing home sales slowed with supplies rising. Existing home sales edged down 1.3 percent in June 2005. Existing home sales at that time were down 8.9 percent on a year-over-year basis. Supply became even more of an issue for existing homes than for new homes as inventory of unsold existing homes rose in June 2006 to 6.8 months from 6.4 in May 2006. That set a supply figure at a nine-year high. Figure 1.2 shows the same trend: As rates moved up, sales declined.

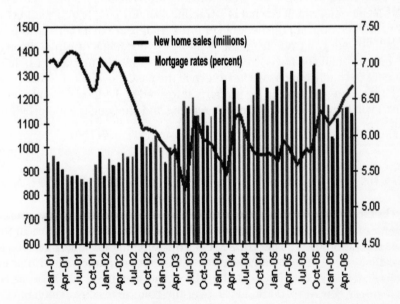

FIGURE 1.1   New Home Sales versus Nationwide Average Mortgage Rates

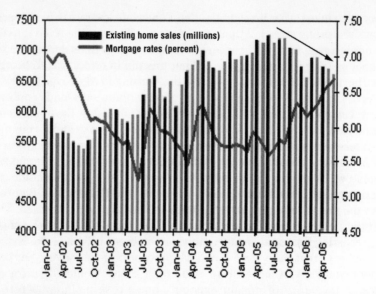

FIGURE 1.2   Existing Home Sales versus Mortgage Rates

This slowdown has many investors looking to maintain a means to generate an income, which is what is attracting so many people into trading the forex market. Some of the benefits of forex trading are that there is no traveling involved, you trade from the comfort of your home or office through the Internet, and you have virtually 24-hour access to the market. Yes, there are risks to trading; but as we have seen in the past, most investments come with risk. You just need to be properly informed and educated, and that is what I want you to achieve through reading and studying the material presented in this book.

FOREX OR FUTURES: WHICH IS RIGHT FOR YOU?

The Foreign Exchange (FX) is one of the fastest-growing investment arenas today. Large institutional investors and hedge funds are big players in the forex market; and in the past three years, the Foreign Exchange market had an estimated 50 percent increase in volume. Some had credited this increase to the large activity created by the online currency trading for the retail investor. The forex market is an over-the-counter market, which means that there is no main exchange or clearinghouse. This is contrary to the futures markets which offer futures trading in "open outcry" and electronic access; which is transparent pricing through a trading platform. This enables one to see the bids/asks and size, otherwise known as the "depth of market" (dome).

In this book, we will be looking at the different aspects of trading the currency markets, including the advantages and disadvantages of trading the forex market. In addition, you will learn how to use other resources to make better decisions on when to enter or exit your forex positions. Trading the forex offers leverage, leverage that the individual controls. Through the use of margin, an individual investor has the choice to increase or decrease leverage through various means. Most currency firms offer 100 times leverage on a regular size account; compare this leverage to the leverage offered to the average equity investor, and you can see why many traders are more attracted to trading the forex. As mentioned previously, leverage in the forex market can also be customized to the individual trader, which means that a trader can choose to lower or eliminate leverage while trading foreign currencies.

FOREX: THE ATM OF THE INVESTMENT WORLD

Foreign Exchange currency trading, otherwise known as the forex market, offers a completely different investment asset class that offers leverage and virtually unrestricted access 24 hours a day. Forex trades virtually around the clock from the Asian market open on Sunday night until the U.S. market close on Friday afternoon. One of the attractions from an individual trader's perspective is that there is this constant access to make a trade. In other words, in every transaction, a trader is long one currency and short the other. A position is expressed in terms of the first currency in the pair. For this reason, currencies are always traded in pairs; for example, if you have purchased euro and sold U.S. dollars, it would be stated as a euro/dollar pair. With a volume of over $1.5 trillion daily, the Foreign Exchange market is the largest and most liquid financial market in the world—more than three times the aggregate amount of the U.S. equity and Treasury markets combined. This means that a trader can enter or exit the market at will in almost any market condition with minimal execution risk. Due to the sheer size of liquidity, a continuous supply-and-demand driven product (we all use and need money), and the accessibility of trading make many professional traders consider the forex market like a bank's automatic teller machine (ATM).

The forex market is so vast and has so many participants that no single entity, not even a central bank, can control the market price for an extended period of time. Unlike other financial markets, the forex market has no physical location, no central exchange. It operates through an electronic network of banks, corporations, and individuals, trading one currency for another. The lack of a physical exchange enables the forex market to operate on a 24-hour basis, spanning from one zone to another across the major financial centers.

HARNESS THE POWER OF LEVERAGE

The forex market allows traders to control massive amounts of leverage with minimal margin requirements; some firms offer as much as 100-to-1 leverage. For example, traders can control a $100,000 position with $1,000, or 1 percent.

Obviously, leverage can be a powerful tool for currency traders. While it does contribute to the risk of a given position, leverage is necessary in the forex market because the average daily move of a major currency is about 1 percent, while a stock typically sees much more substantial moves in excess of 10 percent. When trading in the forex arena, the use of leverage is pretty much considered similar to an interest-free loan from your broker. It enables a trader to use as much as 200-to-1 leverage. This translates to having $500 in margin while controlling a $100,000 position in the market, or 0.5 percent of the position value. This is considerable leverage that can work in favor of as well as against an online forex trader. Once again, leverage can be seen as a free short-term credit allowance, just as it is in the futures markets, allowing traders to purchase an amount of currency exceeding that of their account balance. As a result, traders are exposed to an increased level of both risk and opportunity. Due to the nature of the leverage in the forex markets, positions are normally short-lived. For this reason, entry and exit points are crucial for success and must be based on various technical analysis tools. While fundamental analysis focuses on what should happen, technical analysis is based on what has or is happening at the current time.

Identifying the overall trend, whether it is short term or long term, is the most elementary element of trading with technical analysis. A weekly or monthly chart should be used to identify a longer-term trend, while a daily or intraday chart must be used for examining the shorter-term trend. After determining the direction of the market, it is important to identify the time horizon of potential trades and to apply those strategies to the appropriate trend. Therefore, the techniques covered in this book are highly effective in trading the FX markets. Technical analysis techniques will be your "bread and butter"; they will help you master and generate profits in the forex market.

Technical analysis is the study of historical prices in an attempt to predict future price movements. There are two basic components on which technical analysis is based: (1) prices and (2) volume. With the proper understanding of how these two components exploit the impact of supply and demand in the marketplace, combined with a stronger understanding of how indicators work, especially when combining candle charts and pivot analysis, you will soon discover a powerful trading method to incorporate in the forex market.

PLAY BOTH SIDES: LONG OR SHORT

If one wants to take advantage of a price decline, one of the advantages that the forex market has over equity markets is that there is no uptick rule as exists in the stock market; short selling in forex is similar to that in the futures market. By definition, when a trader goes *short*, he is selling a currency with the expectation that the price will drop, allowing for a profitable offset. If the market moves against the trader's position, he will be forced to buy back the contract at a higher price, resulting in a loss on the trade. There is no limit to how high a currency can go, giving short sellers an unlimited loss scenario. Theoretically, a short seller is exposed to more risk than a trader with a long position; however, through use of stop orders, traders can mitigate their risk, regardless if long or short. It is imperative that traders are well disciplined and that they execute previously planned trades, as opposed to spontaneous, spur-of-the-moment, emotionally driven trades. There are obvious benefits to short selling. This aspect of the forex market allows traders to profit from declining markets. The ease of selling contracts before buying them first is in contrast to typical stock trades. Market prices have a tendency to drop faster than they rise, giving short sellers an opportunity to capitalize on this phenomenon. Similarly, prices will often rally gradually with increasing volume.

As prices begin to reach a peak, trading volume will typically taper off—a signal to short sellers to initiate a trade. When a reversal does occur, there will typically be more momentum than for the corresponding up move. Volume will increase throughout the sell-off until the prices reach a point at which sellers begin to back off. The concept here is represented in detail in this book and is a powerful tool for swing and position traders. Even day traders will benefit from knowing volume analysis. It is important to know where to get the daily volume information and how to apply this information to foreign currency trading. I will share this with you shortly.

HEADLINE TRADES

The BBC commonly refers to the British Broadcasting Corporation; but in the forex market, it is trader's nomenclature or slang for the Big Boys Club:

banks, brokers, and corporations. And there is a fourth group: large hedge
funds. Each one has made its mark in history using foreign currencies. Two
milestone trades made headline news. These are the famous curency
trades, both of which took advantage of taking short and long positions.
Let's look at the hedge fund world when famed financier George Soros
"broke" the Bank of England. He placed an estimated $10 billion bet that
the British pound would lose value, and he won the bet! How about Daim-
lerChrysler, the parent company of Chrysler and Mercedes Benz; it report-
edly made more money in the forex market that it did selling cars! Imagine
explaining to your boss that you made more money hedging and trading foreign currencies than doing what you do best, building cars.

Another milestone event is as recent as early 2005. This involved Warren Buffett the founder of Berkshire Hathaway (the fourteenth-largest
U.S. company, according to the July 4, 2006, issue of *Fortune* magazine).
When the financial media was pounding out news stories that the dollar
was in trouble, Warren made a statement that he was heavily short the U.S.
dollar. Unfortunately, once he made that announcement, the dollar gained
value and rallied for most of 2005. If you did not do your own research or
homework and blindly followed his advice, things did not turn out so well
for you.

In the remainder of 2005, the dollar moved higher against most major
currency pairs. What turned the market around? Some of the events that
drove the dollar higher were dictated by monetary policy as the Federal Reserve continued to raise interest rates. Then there were economic, geopo-
litical, and political developments on the domestic front that influenced
the dollar's value. For starters, the Homeland Investment Act (HIA) was
passed. The HIA is part of the 2004 American Jobs Creation Act and was intended to entice U.S.–based multiconglomerate corporations to bring
money back into the United States. The window of opportunity for companies to take advantage of the HIA benefits prompted companies to increase
the pace at which funds are repatriated to the United States. Since companies had only until the end of 2005, many analysts suspected that companies would rush to repatriate foreign profits by year's end and that there
would then be a high dollar demand to convert foreign currencies. Geopo-
litical issues arose during the summer of 2005 when there were riots in
France as a result of less support for the euro currency. That contributed to
a very poor market sentiment and a lack of confidence in the euro. This was
grounds for foreign investors to make a flight to financial safety, selling
their currency to buy U.S. dollars. The tone was essentially dollar positive
and euro negative, which is a result of a change in political views and shows
how consumer sentiment can have a negative effect on a currency. I said
earlier that technical analysis will be your "bread and butter" for profiting
in the forex market; but you still need to be aware of fundamental develop-

ments, economic reports, and the times when these reports hit the newswires. As this section shows, fiscal policy changes can drive markets in new directions.

What may have contributed to the dollar rally in 2005 and hurt Mr. Buffett's position was the fact that other players may have been preying on his position. Berkshire Hathaway, Inc., is without a doubt a high-profile player. So when Warren Buffett announced he was going to cut back speculative positions against the U.S. dollar after losing profits due to surprising dollar strength, the buying to cover his shorts boosted the dollar. Keep in mind that Mr. Buffett had bet that the dollar would continue losing ground, as it did in 2004; he felt the massive U.S. current account deficit would be dollar negative. But instead, monetary policy dictated otherwise, as the Federal Reserve continued to raise interest rates. That was helping to drive demand as the interest rate differentials widened. In its third-quarter report in 2005, Berkshire Hathaway said it had cut its foreign-currency exposure from $21.5 billion to $16.5 billion. That was a significant amount of selling foreign currencies and buying U.S. dollars.

As you can see from the Dollar Index weekly chart in Figure 1.3, on a

FIGURE 1.3 U.S. Dollar Index Contract (monthly bars)
Used with permission of GenesisFT.com.

year-to-year basis, the dollar did make an outstanding run. However, that rally fizzled out in 2006. Also, keep in mind the dollar was at a high of 120.80 back in 2002; so depending on where Mr. Buffett was shorting the dollar, he could still be in a lucrative or profitable position. When I was wrapping things up for this book, the Dollar Index had managed to decline near the multidecade lows, and investor sentiment remained longer-term negative on the dollar. In addition, if you look at the longer-term price direction dating back since the inception of the Dollar Index contract, the Dollar Index is in a descending or declining channel.

The focus of this example is how shifts in monetary and fiscal policies can and do dictate price swings in the market, as happened in 2005 and 2006. Furthermore, foreign currency trading has become an acceptable asset class and valuable trading vehicle for the large multinational corporations. Just for your knowledge, the July 4, 2006, issue of *Fortune* magazine listed the top-10 largest U.S. corporations as ExxonMobil, Wal-Mart, General Motors, Chevron, Ford Motor, Conoco Philips, General Electric, Citigroup, American International Group, and International Business Machines. Funny that 30 percent of the top-10 businesses consisted of energy companies. I found this intriguing; Microsoft was ranked number 50 and Intel number 51. Who was number 100, you ask? John Deere. I think you can see the trends of investment flows and which sector is the leader as represented by the amount of a company's revenue growth. In 2006, the leader was British Petroleum!

Back in late 1999, money poured into technology stocks. In late 2003 and 2004, money poured into home builders. Then in 2005 and 2006, money poured into energy stocks, and not just for short-term trading but also for long-term investment opportunities in exploration and research and development for new oil fields and infrastructure repairs of pipelines and refineries. The most important terms to remember here are *money flow* and *sector leaders*. Following money flows, sector leadership among corporations can help you to determine where we are in a business cycle. We will talk about how these two concepts are important factors to monitor when trading foreign currencies. The relationships between how and where money is being made and which industry it is being made in directly impact foreign currency values and can help you in your trading decisions.

Money flows into one sector and out of another. If consumer demand is in technology, as was the case in the middle to late 1990s, then the U.S. dollar is strong. If demand changes to commodity-based products, such as crude oil, gold, and construction materials, the Aussie and Canadian dollars will appreciate. Australia and Canada are both producers of such commodity products as gold and lumber; and since Canada has vast reserves of tar sands, its currency benefits from higher crude oil prices.

THE PRIVATE BANKERS' CLUB HAS NOW TURNED PUBLIC

In the past, currency trading was exclusively accessible for individual speculators through the futures industry, whereas the spot marketplace in the banking arena was for the private bankers' club, the privileged few. This has all changed now, and the competition is fierce. The industry has expanded from what was an exclusive club of proprietary hedge fund traders, corporations, banks, and large institutions. Just to give you an idea of who the competition is that takes part in the forex arena, here is the list of the top five banks in the United States as of July 4, 2006, according to *Fortune* magazine. This is in order of capitalization: Bank of America, JP Morgan, Citigroup, Wachovia, and Wells Fargo. This does not include foreign banks or pension funds who participate in trading. Forex is no longer exclusive to the major trading firms, such as Goldman Sachs, Mitsubishi, Merrill Lynch, and Morgan Stanley. Now it is available to any and all individual traders who want to participate. You have 24-hour access in this market from your home or office right off your desktop or laptop computer.

Forex trading is considered the behemoth of the investment world, with more than $3.5 trillion in currency trading taking place per day, according to the Bank for International Settlements. There is more daily volume in the forex market than in all of the U.S. stock markets combined. There is no doubt that that is one reason why foreign currency has become so popular. Also, the market has liquidity; has favorable trading applications, such as the ability to go long or short a position; and has a tendency to trend well. Chart watchers love the currency market because it trades well based off technical analysis studies.

FOREX TRADES EASILY

The forex market offers traders free commissions, no exchange fees, online access, and plenty of liquidity. Unlike the futures products, the forex market uses *standardized contract values*, meaning that full-size positions are valued at 100,000. The one main element that has attracted investors was and is the commission-free trading. Plus, most forex firms require less capital to initiate a start-up account than a futures account. In fact, investors can open accounts on their debit and/or credit cards; and the practice still exists of online payments through PayPal.

Some firms offer smaller-size *flexi-accounts* that allow traders to start applying their skills at technical analysis with as little as $500. And there is also the *mini-account*, which allows individual investors to adjust their positions by not having too big a contract value per position, as they can add or scale into more or fewer positions to adjust the level of leverage according to their account size. This means that smaller-size investors are not excluded from trading because they can participate with mini-contracts. What is great about this feature is that a new trader or an experienced trader who is testing a system can trade the market with real money, rather than simply paper trading; the new traders can benefit from the actual experience of working with money and will be able to see how they handle the mental or emotional side of trading. People are emotionally driven. Fear, greed, and anxiety can wreak havoc on people's psyches. Therefore, practice trading with smaller leverage will not make you rich immediately; but it will help you hone your trading skills and help you develop confidence in your methods and execution skills.

Having real money on the line certainly helps people to learn about their emotional makeup. This is one great way to overcome the fear and greed syndrome that many traders seem to battle. Another excellent quality that forex mini-accounts have is that smaller-size traders can afford to trade multiple lots for scaling out of trades in order to let a portion of their contracts ride for a longer, more-profitable trade and still capture profits on a partial exit.

Another attraction is that most forex companies offer free real-time news, charts, and quotes with state-of-the-art order-entry platforms; some even have automated order-entry features, such as "one cancels the other" and "trailing stops." All of these tools and order entry platforms come at no additional charge to the trader. This market is a pay-as-you-go concept because there are no commissions—you simply pay a premium, or a higher spread, to buy and a higher spread to sell. Most forex dealers take the other side of your trade. You do not have direct access to the interbank market, as it is called. Because the forex market is decentralized, it is possible that five different companies are showing five different prices all at the same time within a few points (or PIPs, as they are called). Most forex traders are short term in nature, meaning they are quick-in-and-out players. Day trading in the forex market is beneficial for these traders due to the fact that there are no commissions, but the PIP spreads can and do add up.

 IMPORTANT FEATURE

Flexi or mini forex accounts can be set up by an individual. The main benefit is that you can control the leverage and use smaller lot sizes, which enable you to trade multiple contracts that will allow you to scale into and out of a trade at various price points.

PAY THE SPREAD

Forex prices, or quotes, include a *bid* and an *ask*, similar to other financial products. The bid is the price at which a dealer is willing to buy and traders can sell a currency. The ask is the price at which a dealer is willing to sell and traders can buy a currency. In forex trading, unlike futures or equities, one has to pay a PIP (percentage in points) spread on entering and on exiting a trade. The *PIP spread* is the point difference between the bid and the asking price of the spot currency price. This can vary between two and six PIPs, depending on the volume and the popularity of the cross currency.

A typical example is the euro (EUR) versus the U.S. dollar (USD). We will see a bid price on the EUR/USD of 1.2630 and an asking price of 1.2633, which means you are paying a three-PIP spread. The spread essentially works like this. You place a buy on the EUR/USD at 1.2633, but you won't see breakeven on the trade until the price moves to 1.2633 bid. If you are trading a mini-account, you will see a $3.00 deduction for your trade profit on entry. Once the price moves to 1.2633 bid, then your account comes out of the red and into the black. In an exotic cross such as the euro versus against the Japanese yen or the New Zealand dollar versus the Japanese yen, you might pay a higher bid-ask spread of 6 to 12 PIPs. You need to check with your forex dealer for the listing of PIP spreads per preset crosses and pairs trades.

WHAT ABOUT INTEREST?

If you want to hold a position for several days, a rollover process is necessary. In the spot forex market, all trades must be settled within two business days at the close of business at 5 P.M. (Eastern Standard Time, EST). The only fee involved here is the interest payment on the position of currency held. At times, depending on the position, you can receive an interest payment as well. This is where the term tomorrow/next (Tom/Next) applies. It refers to the simultaneous buying and selling of a currency for delivery the following day. As with futures, the forex market is now regulated to an extent and comes under the scrutiny of the self-imposed regulators, such as the National Futures Association after the Commodity Futures Trading Commission (CFTC) Modernization Act passed in 2002; but since there is no centralized marketplace, many forex dealers can and do make their own rules and policies. Because forex dealers are in the business to make money and to provide a service for traders, some firms will charge interest on your account but not make an interest payment to your account

unless you meet certain financial requirements. Again, because these dealers are in the business to make money, I have heard stories that some
will even increase the interest charge by more than double the going rate;
and if they do give a credit offer, the rate will be below what the market is
really at.

Since most traders in forex are short term in nature, by settling up or
closing out their positions by 5 P.M. (EST), they are not generally concerned
with the interest rate charge aspect. Also, unless they have serious positions on (over $1,000,000 value), the interest charge will be minimal anyway
and not something that should distract from the job at hand, which is trading. My advice is this: Do your homework when looking for the right dealer
to trade through and ask questions regarding interest charge policies when
holding positions for several days.

IS THERE GOING TO BE A NEW KID IN TOWN?

Yes, there is going to be a new kid; and by the time this book is published,
the name and place will be FXMarketSpace. This entity represents a col-
laborative effort between two foreign currency industry leaders: Reuters
and the Chicago Mercantile Exchange (CME).

This venture is expected to launch in 2007. What it will do is facilitate
spot trading transactions on six major currencies against the U.S. dollar:
the euro, the Japanese yen, the British pound, the Australian dollar, the
Swiss franc, and the Canadian dollar. Four cross-currency pairs will also be
supported. FXMarketSpace intends to add more products in forwards and
options at a later date. Since the forex market has changed dramatically
over the past few years, many players, such as hedge funds and commodity
trading advisors who manage money, have entered the market with a new
set of needs, one of which is order anonymity.

This concept will be the first over-the-counter FX trading platform to
offer central counterparty clearing and full trade anonymity. FXMarket-
Space will also be accessible through multiple portals, giving its users
unprecedented breadth of access to its trading platform. These characteristics are expected to increase participation and to enhance liquidity in
the forex market. FXMarketSpace combines the central counterparty
model and clearing function of the Chicago Mercantile Exchange with the
global distribution network and direct processing capability of Reuters. It
is supported by one of the best matching and clearing technology programs and offers industry-leading matching-engine capabilities provided
by the CME.

Who Is Reuters?

Reuters is the leading provider of news, financial information, and technology solutions to institutions, businesses, and media worldwide. Founded in 1850, Reuters has always been committed to delivering information using the best available technology. In 1992, Reuters pioneered electronic trading services and established its presence with the launch of Reuters Dealing (originally D-2001, now Dealing Direct), an electronic peer-to-peer trading platform. Since then, the Reuters platform, in its formative and subsequent versions, has provided a catalyst for forex trade-volume growth by significantly reducing both execution speed and transaction costs.

FXMarketSpace

This venture will offer participants unprecedented choice of access to its platform through a variety of means including CME's i-Link API, Reuters Dealing 3000 and Reuters 3000 X-tra desktops, Reuters standard transactions, API Select Independent Software Vendors (ISVs), and portals of participating clearing member firms. FXMarketSpace is targeted to meet the explosive growth in demand for currency transactions by banks and other financial institutions, including traditional asset managers, proprietary trading firms, leveraged funds, currency managers, hedge funds, and commodity trading advisers (CTAs). It is designed to provide increased price transparency, to introduce trading anonymity, and to heighten forex market accessibility. These three features will attract more players, which in turn will increase market liquidity and market efficiency for the next generation of forex traders. All market participants will be able to trade against the same set of firm, executable prices. The central counterparty clearing model provides for full anonymity and eliminates the need for bilateral credit lines to support trading activities. The company's matching host provides increased transparency through both a five-level depth of book display with bid/offer quantities and detailed "time and sales" information. Firms may utilize the existing CME telecommunications hubs to facilitate their connections to FXMarketSpace, providing improved speed of access while reducing costs. Hubs are currently located in London, Amsterdam, Dublin, Paris, Milan, Gibraltar, and Singapore. Customers may utilize either their existing Reuters infrastructure or secure Internet connections to access the market.

FXMarketSpace will reduce counterparty risk by being the buyer to every seller and the seller to every buyer by employing CME clearinghouse functionalities. If you bought this book to learn about the trading opportunities in the forex arena or even if you are a seasoned trading pro, look to learn some of my techniques. Keep your eyes and interest open on this new venture for currency trading; it promises to revolutionize the way we trade. It is like combining the best of futures and the spot forex market. Perhaps as it develops the centralized marketplace, we will have access to spot forex volume and will not need to worry about capturing that data from the futures market.

WHY TRADE THE SPOT FOREX MARKET?

From all the financial instruments traded, forex is believed for a number of reasons by many professional traders and analysts to be one of the best-suited markets to trade using technical analysis methods. First, it is well-suited because of its sheer size in trading volume; according to the Bank for International Settlements, average daily turnover in traditional Foreign Exchange markets amounted to $1.9 trillion in the cash exchange market and another $1.2 trillion per day in the over-the-counter (OTC) Foreign Exchange and interest-rate derivatives market as of April 2005. Second, the rate of growth and market participants in forex trading has increased some 2000 percent over the past three decades, rising from barely $1 billion per day in 1974 to an estimated $2 trillion per day by 2005. Third, since the market does not have an official closing time, there is never a backlog or "pool" of client orders parked overnight that may cause a severe reaction to news stories hitting the market at the U.S. bank opening. This generally reduces the chance for price gaps. Currencies tend to experience longer-lasting, trending market conditions than do other markets.

These trends can last for months, or even years, as most central banks do not switch interest rate policies every other day. This makes them ideal markets for trend trading and even breakout systems traders. This might explain why chart pattern analysis works so well in forex trading. With such widespread groups playing the game around the world, crowd behavior plays a large part in currency moves; and it is this crowd behavior that is the foundation for the myriad of technical analysis tools and techniques. Due in part to its size, forex is less volatile than other markets. Lower volatility equals lower risk. For example, the Standard & Poor's (S&P) 500 Index trading range is between 4 percent and 5 percent daily, whereas the daily volatility range in the euro is around 1 percent. Trading veterans know that markets are interdependent, with some markets more heavily influenced by certain markets than others. We covered some of these relationships looking at futures and certain stocks and how interest rates move equity markets and currencies. We will learn in coming sections how to detect hidden yet repeating patterns that occur between these related markets. Forex is the ideal market for the experienced trader who has paid his or her "trading tuition" in other markets. Forex is by far the largest market in dollar volume. At times it can be less volatile; experiences longer, more accentuated price trends; and does not have trading commissions as we discussed. However, there are no free lunches. Traders must use all the trading tools at their disposal; the better these fundamental and technical tools, the greater their chance for trading success.

While intermarket and other relationships are often complex and difficult to apply effectively, with a little high-tech help, traders and investors can enjoy the benefits of using them without having to scrap their existing trading methods.

FOREX VERSUS FUTURES MARKET

The futures market through the International Monetary Market (IMM) of the Chicago Mercantile Exchange has many benefits as well. Founded in 1898, CME is the leader in the FX futures arena, accounting for 96 percent of all currency futures contracts traded on a worldwide basis. The Chicago Mercantile Exchange pioneered this segment by offering the world's first financial futures contracts on seven foreign currencies in May 1972. Since that time, it has continued to expand its reach in FX by introducing new products, expanding its customer base and leveraging the market leading technology found in CME Globex®, its proprietary electronic trading platform. The exchange handles over a billion contracts valued at more than $638 trillion on an annual basis. It is a public company; and as of August 18, 2006, the stock (CME) was trading at 461.35. Amazing, considering that when this stock was first released in its initial public offering (IPO) in December 2002, it was trading at under 40 per share! The history of the exchange and the innovator of the IMM, Leo Melamed, who brought foreign currency trading to life, is legendary. It has allowed investors, large and small, to trade foreign currencies exclusively for nearly 25 years before the explosive growth of spot forex was available. As with any product, there are strengths and weaknesses. I wish to share with you the facts so you can determine which investment vehicle suits your taste and trading style.

First, you should know the symbols for the individual futures currencies as quoted against the U.S. dollar. There are just minor differences between spot forex and futures symbols, as shown in Table 1.1.

Note that futures trade in quarterly cycles; and to differentiate between the various contract months, futures have universal symbols for each of the different contract months. December is "Z," March is "H," June is "M," and September is "U." Here is what you would use with a charting or quote ven-

TABLE 1.1 Symbols for Futures and Forex Quoted against the U.S. Dollar

Currency	Futures Symbol	Forex Symbol—Nickname
Euro currency	EC	EUR/USD—Euro
British pound	BP	GBP/USD—Cable
Japanese yen	JY	USD/JPY—Yen
Australian dollar	AD	AUD/USD—Aussie
Canadian dollar	CD	USD/CAS—Loonie
Swiss franc	SF	USD/CHF—Swissy

dor to get a futures contract quote on a June 2007 euro currency—ECM7. On some quote and charting services, the current year or the next contract month going forward would be assumed and understood. The quotes symbols for the different expiration months and various contract sizes of the futures markets are confusing, but you can quickly learn these variables.

At times, the futures arguably have tighter "spreads" between the bid and the asking prices; plus there is no interest charge or rollover fee every other day. In addition, the futures markets offer options for longer-term traders. There are transactions costs that apply per round turn; but if the brokerage commission exchange, regulatory, and transaction charges are less than the PIP spread in forex, an active speculator would be given a better cost advantage using the futures markets instead of the forex spot market. For example, let's compare a trade in forex on a contract value similar in size to one on the futures exchange. Use the example of a euro futures contract on the CME with a contract size of USD125,000 worth of euros, where each tick or PIP would be 12.50 in value. If the commissions and related fees are $10, which is the average charge by most brokerage firms, that is your transaction cost per round turn. That is $5 to buy and $5 to sell out of the position. Keep in mind that the contract value is 25 percent higher than a full-size forex position, too. If a day trader in forex trading in a 100,000 full-lot-size contract pays two PIPs on every transaction of a position, this trader would be charged $20 per round turn transaction. The futures arena also has other interesting features and products; one is the U.S. Dollar Index® contract traded on the New York Board of Trade. It is computed using a trade-weighted geometric average of six currencies. It trades virtually around the clock; the trading hours are from 7:00 P.M. to 10:00 P.M., then from 3:00 A.M. to 8:05 A.M., and then from 8:05 A.M. to 3:00 P.M. Unlike the forex, there are daily limits on the price movement, with 200 ticks above and below the prior day's settlement, except during the last 30 minutes of any trading session, when no limit applies. Should the price reach the limit and remain within 100 ticks of the limit for 15 minutes, new limits will be established 200 ticks above and below the previous price limit. The chart in Figure 1.4 shows a breakdown of the six currencies and their respective

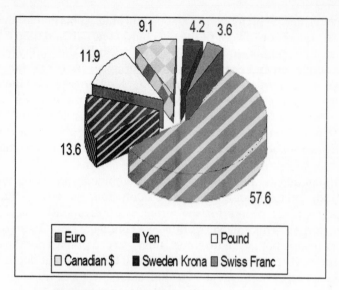

FIGURE 1.4 Currencies and Their
Respective Average Weights

weights on the average. The top four include the euro, which is the heaviest weight with 57.6 percent; then the Japanese yen with 13.6 percent; then the British pound with 11.9 percent; and the Canadian dollar with 9.1 percent. The Swedish krona is only 4.2 percent and the Swiss franc 3.6 percent.

FOREX ANALYSIS IS SIMPLER

From an analytical point of view, tracking the forex market is a much simplified trading vehicle when compared to the futures products. One reason is due to the uniform contract sizes. In the forex market, the standard lot size is $100,000. The tick, or PIP, value varies in the futures products based on the contract, and the contract size varies on the different currencies. For example, the euro is $125,000, and the tick value is $12.50 per point; the Canadian dollar is $100,000, and the tick value is $10 dollars per point. The British pound futures have a contract value of $62,500, which makes each tick worth $6.25. The yen is worth $125,000, so every point is valued at $12.50; but it is quoted inversely to the cash market. For instance, the futures is quoted at 0.8610, and at the same time the spot forex would be bid at 116.50 and offered at 116.54. Forex traders do not have to deal with what is known as rollover. Every quarter in the futures markets, there is an expiration of the contracts. The rollover period takes place in the second week of every June, September, December, and March. It is at that time that you need to convert or roll out of the old contract month and then into the new month or next expiration contract going forward. Commodity markets can cause confusion and can create errors during a rollover period. Often times, when I was a frequent guest on CNBC, Joe Kernan hated the crude oil market because it rolled every month. Generally there was a $2 premium from one month to the next; so in early November 2006, crude fell to just $55.00. But when the front contract month expired and the next rolled over, prices were quoted $2 a barrel higher. The same scenario exists for currencies; however, the rollover is every three months.

The first notice day and last trading day combined with the options expirations can hinder trading and cause confusion; there are situations where traders place orders for the wrong contract months during this "switching period." This rollover period gets confusing even for an old pro like me; but if you know what to expect, then you can prepare for the event. We have not covered this topic yet (which will be covered in depth in the next few chapters), but the greatest technical tool for forex trading is *pivot point analysis*. It is based on a mathematical formula to predict future support and resistance target levels. If you are calculating pivot points for the futures markets, you already know that you need to constantly switch your analysis from the expiring contract to the new contract month. This can cause "gaps" in your analysis. Take, for example, the rollover that occurred in March 2006. On March 7, the March futures contract was still trading and was quoted at 0.8485. The June futures contract had become the lead month and was quoted at 0.8597. That would mean that there was a gap of over 100 PIPs due to what is called the *basis*—the difference between the cash market today and the futures contract for delivery in June. The basis includes what is known as the *carrying costs*.

As a trader, I would need to adjust my numbers and analysis for this gap or start backtracking prior sessions to accommodate for the price differences. It is done every quarter; and, believe me, it is a royal pain. So not only do you have to be careful placing the right contract, but you need to know the various margin requirements, the right expiration dates, the contract values, and the value of each tick (point). I am not going to give you the "let's turn lemons to lemonade" line here; futures rollover is a pain in the neck.

To summarize, the benefits of trading the spot forex market outweigh trading the futures markets from many perspectives. If you acknowledge that paying the PIP or spread for your trades is not cutting into your profits, especially since you do get free charts, news, and order execution privileges, then trading in the spot forex market is better than the futures markets. Granted, most forex dealers trade platforms and charting capabilities are not high-powered systems but they do allow a beginner to execute trades without additional software expenses. The analytical tools such as volume analysis and open interest studies combined with the CFTC *Commitment of Traders* (COT) report data can and should be integrated for spot forex trading. If you can learn to merge the benefits of both worlds, then perhaps one of the best short-term trading vehicles is the spot currency market known as forex.

GEM OF A BENEFIT IN FUTURES

One of the best features of the futures markets is that they have listed options; and because these are futures products, they also have the access of the transparency on how many options on the futures contracts are available to buy and how many options on the futures contracts are offered to sell. This book, *Forex Conquered*, is designed to give you specific trading plans on all aspects of foreign currency trading opportunities. I feel that there are many, many choices; and yet so few people are aware of them. Options are just one futures trading vehicle, and many forex traders have had only limited exposure to options. Therefore, I want to introduce you to what they are and how you can benefit from them in your trading career. To start with, there are two types of options: a call and a put. And there are two kinds of positions for each call and put: a buyer and a seller, or an option writer.

A buyer or long option holder of a call has the right but not the obligation to be long a futures position at a specific price level, for a specific period of time and for a specific price called the *premium*. A buyer or long option holder of a put has the right but not the obligation to be short a futures position for a specific price that is paid by the buyer at a specific price level and for a specific period of time. For option buyers, the premium is a nonrefundable payment, unlike a margin requirement for a futures contract where it is a good-faith deposit. Premium values are subject to constant changes as dictated by market conditions and other variables, such as time decay and the distance between the underlying value of the market and the strike price of the option. One more factor that determines an options value is the *volatility rate*, which is based on price fluctuations in the activity on the underlying futures market. The wider and faster the price movements are, the higher the volatility level is; and a higher volatility rate will help increase the options value.

There are other variables that are used to calculate an options value, such as interest rates and demand for the options itself. For instance, if you bought a call option and if the underlying futures market is moving up toward your strike price, then the option's premium value may increase, because option writers or sellers will want more money and buyers will have to pay more for the premium of the option. This is an example of an increase in demand for the option as a direct result of the market's expectation of the movement in the price direction.

One of the first things to know about buying options in futures is that you do not need to hold them until expiration. Option buyers may sell their position at any time during market hours when the contracts are trading on the exchange. Options may be exercised at any time before the expiration date during regular market hours by notifying the broker. Usually one exercises in-the-money options; this is called the *American style* of option exercising. It is called the *European style* of option exercising when the option can only be exercised on the day the option expires.

A seller or option writer of a call or put grants the option buyer the rights conveyed from that option. The seller receives a price that is paid by the buyer, that is, the premium. Sellers have no rights to that specific option except that they receive the premium for the transaction and are obligated to deliver the futures position as assigned according to the terms of the option.

A seller can cover his or her position by buying back the option or by spreading off the risk in other options or in the underlying futures market if market conditions permit. A buyer of an option has the right to either offset the long option or exercise his option at any time during the life of the option. When a trader exercises his option, it gives the buyer the specific position (long for calls and short for puts) in the underlying futures contract at the specific price level as determined by the strike price. Options are generally exercised when they are *in the money* (ITM)—the strike price is below the futures price for a call option and above the futures price for a put option.

 HOT TIP

The Chicago Mercantile Exchange, as of July 31, 2006, started trading European-style options on the British pound, the Canadian dollar, and the Swiss franc; futures contracts; and euro and Japanese yen contracts. These options, if in the money, are automatically exercised at expiration. European-style options are used by most options traders in the OTC FX markets. Because there is no risk of early exercise, they are often priced lower than American-style options. European-style options on CME FX futures are traded electronically, virtually around the clock, from Sunday afternoon to Friday afternoon on the CME trading platform and Monday morning through Friday afternoon on the trading floor.

There are three major factors that determine an option's value, otherwise known as the premium.

1. *Time value*—the difference between the time you enter the option position and the life the option holds until expiration. An option that has more time value is worth more than an option that is soon to expire, all things being equal. The term *wasting asset* is applied to an option because the closer the time comes to the option's expiration, the less the option is worth.

2. *Intrinsic value*—the distance between the strike price of the option and the difference to the underlying derivative contract. If an option's strike price is closer to the underlying futures contract, it will be more expensive than an option that is further away. The term used is a call option, which gives the buyer the right, not the obligation, to be long the market. A call option will cost more if the strike price is closer to the actual futures price. The reverse is true for put options. A put option will be more expensive if it is closer to the derivitive market price. These two examples are considered to be out of the money (OTM), because neither is worth exericising. (An in-the-money option is referred to when the strike price is below the futures for a call option and above the futures for a put option.)

3. *Volatility*—the measure of historical price changes. Volatility accounts for the pace of price change. In periods of violent price moves, options will command high premium values. Volatility is calculated by the magnitude of a market's past price move and current market condition.

Let's review some examples and at the same time help review what we have covered as forex and futures relate to each other. Keep in mind that the value of a futures contract is $125,000 worth of euros, the initial margin requirement as of August 29, 2006, is $2,835, and the maintenance margin is $2,100. These are subject to change without notice and are set by the individual exchanges.

Option Strategy Exercise

On August 29, 2006, at 12:00 P.M. (EST), the forex spot euro currency was at 127.67. At that precise moment, the December futures contract was at 128.49. Reference the *basis*, which is the price difference between where the spot market is valued and where the futures price is traded. That difference is 0.82 points. The 130.00 strike price for the December euro currency call option, which expires on December 8, 2006, has a shelf life of 101 days until it expires. The premium was quoted at 1.67 points. Each point is worth $12.50, so the value or cost of that option would be $2,087.50. At expiration, the December futures contract price would converge to represent what the spot forex market price would be.

The basis would narrow as futures becomes the cash market. For you to just break even, as this was an out-of-the-money call option at expiration, the spot and futures markets would need to be at 131.67. That is the point value of the premium added to the strike price of the option (130.00 + 1.67 = 131.67). That's the bad news. The good news is that if the market price moved within the first 30 days after you purchase the out-of-the-money call option, then the value would theoretically increase by 0.17 percent, which was determined by the "delta," one of what is called the "Greeks." It is a calculation that helps options traders to determine prices for option premiums.

By the same token, an out-of-the-money put option with a strike price of 125.00 was valued at 85 points or $1,062.50 (85 × 12.5 = $1,062.50). The 125.00 put option was out of the money by 349 points (125.00 − 128.49 = 3.49).

Applying the Strategy

First, if you are outright bullish on the euro and thought the dollar would decline to new all-time lows, the best strategy for unlimited rewards and limited risk would simply be to buy a long-term call option, which in the example using the 130 December strike would be less money and defined risk to the premium you paid, $2,087.50. Second, if you thought the dollar would rally and the euro would decline with the same risk/reward parameters, then using the OTM 125 put option would be a good consideration because your maximum risk would be the premium you paid, $1,062.50.

There are many combinations of option plays with various names, such as "strangles and straddles." Using options allows you a whole new world of opportunities other than long/short outlooks in a specific time frame. Table 1.2 shows the spread between the strikes and the actual cash or spot market; they are roughly equal to each other, with the call at a 233-point-spread difference to the spot and the put at a 267-point-spread difference to the spot. Only the futures markets has the big point spread difference; and remember, as we get closer to expiration, the futures becomes the cash market, and the basis narrows with time. Therefore, another strategy called a *strangle* would be, if you thought the price of the euro was going to stay in a range between 125 and 130, to sell (or write) both the call and the put options. This way you would receive the premium of both the call and the put. You would have changed your risk parameters because writing options have limited profit potential with unlimited risks and your margin requirements would increase as well.

TABLE 1.2   Pricing Options

130 Call Option	125 Put Option
167 points, or $2,087.50	85 points, or $1,062.50
233-point spread to spot	267-point spread to spot
151-point spread to futures	349-point spread to futures

However, by writing the call and the put options, you would collect a combined 252 points (167 for the call and 85 points for the put), or $3,150.00 ($252 \times \$12.50 = \$3,150.00$). The margin required would be twice the amount of one position since there are two contracts minus the premium collected, or $2,520.00. Once again, the margins can change; and if the underlying market makes an adverse move sharply above 130.0 or well below 125.00, you have unlimited risk exposure. But let's check one aspect out: If the market does move above 130.00 at expiration, you have a break-even price of 132.52. If the market declines, your break-even level would be 122.48.

If you had no clue which way the market would move but felt there was going to be a massive breakout one way or another, particularly in the time horizon of the three-month shelf life of the December option, then employing what is called a *straddle* would limit your risks while allowing you to participate. A straddle occurs when you buy the 130 call and the 125 put. In this case, you would need to pay out $3,150.00, which is the amount of the two premiums. Keep in mind that your breakeven at expiration would be 132.52 on the upside and 122.48 on the downside. So at expiration, anything above or below those levels would start to accrue profits.

In the Money

Using the same variables as in the preceding example, a 125.00 call option would be considered in the money since the futures market was at 128.49. This call option has an intrinsic value that is the difference between the strike price and the underlying market of 349 points ($125.00 - 128.49 = 3.49$). That leaves a balance of 94 points given for the time premium value. Notice that the 130 call option was entirely out of the money and has more time premium value built into the option. Sometimes it pays to buy in-the-money options versus out-of-the-money options.

Collar, Not Choke, the Market

For a dollar bear or a euro bull, here is one of my favorite option strategies. It is a hedge strategy using both options and the underlying market, which under the right circumstances can work very effectively as far as risk-to-

TABLE 1.3 Option Price Comparisons

130 Call Option	125 Put Option
Collect 167 points	Pay 85 points
82-point credit	185-point risk/315-point reward

reward ratios and money management tactics are concerned. The opposite position can be implemented as well if you are bullish the U.S. dollar and bearish the euro. Let's examine a bullish collar strategy for longer-term traders. This strategy allows you to participate in a limited move with limited risk and still lets you sleep at night. If you trade the spot forex market, you will need two accounts: a forex account and a futures account. Forex traders who take a long position in the spot euro currency market with a full $100,000 lot size position will need to add $25,000 worth of mini lots to be equal in capitalization size with one futures contract. First, you want to enter the options side by selling the 130 call option and then buying the 125 put option. Once your order is filled, then enter the long position. You will collect premium from the short call option, which you will use to finance the put option. You are collecting more premiums from the call side and will have a credit, as Table 1.3 shows.

Also keep in mind that this is not an equally weighted position due to the basis difference between the spot and the futures markets; but as time passes, remember that the futures will line up with the spot market. If you are long the spot euro at 127.67, keep in mind that the futures market was at 128.49. But as you know, on any given day, generally both the cash and the futures will move in tandem, with a gradual decay in the futures market's basis. The key here is that you have protection to the downside calculated at expiration of 185 points; your maximum reward is 315 points. This is close to a one-to-two risk/reward ratio.

In order to make the collar strategy worth executing, you generally want to collect a premium or get a credit on the strategy or, at the very least, not pay out-of-pocket money on the options side. Since these are options on a futures contract, you will be charged a commission; therefore, you will need to check rates and margin requirements with different futures brokers. Futures brokers cannot lower the margin that the exchange sets, but they can increase the amount. So you need to do your homework. As far as options are concerned, they do have great benefits from the aspect of simple speculating on a directional price move to the use and application as an insurance vehicle, which is what we refer to as a hedge. As a foreign currency trader, certainly expanding your knowledge of these features and benefits can enhance your trading opportunities on various time frames, especially longer-term horizons. Using options to hedge positions into long holiday weekends, before government reports (such as the monthly unemployment number), or before Federal Open Market Committee (FOMC) meetings can help protect your account during violent adverse price moves, especially when they are short-lived. It is one aspect of trading with which all traders and investors should become more familiar.

TRADING CURRENCY STOCKS?

Foreign currency trading is not just for gamblers or hungover commodity traders. It really has become a respected asset classification and is extremely popular with professionally managed trading entities and hedge funds. Foreign currency is so hot that major players are taking it to the extreme. How so? Well, there is now what is called exchange traded funds (ETFs) on foreign currencies. The first to be introduced was the Euro Currency Trust (FXE). On the first day of trading, the Euro Currency Trust had over 600,000 shares trading hands.

Advantages and Disadvantages

As with any product, there are advantages and disadvantages to ETFs. One is that this vehicle has an annual expense of 0.4 percent of assets. If that amount is not enough (the interest rate is below the 0.4 percent expense ratio), then the sponsor can withdraw deposited euros as needed, which could diminish the amount of euros each ETF share represents. The currency ETFs are linked to the spot price versus the U.S. dollar. The obvious strategy to make money in these vehicles is to see the value move in the desired trade direction (you can buy and sell short) and to cover the interest charge less the trust expenses.

The benefactor or the depository for the ETF is JP Morgan Chase Bank. This product is structured as a grantor trust, and Bank of New York is the trustee. Here is how JP Morgan will make money: It will maintain two euro-denominated accounts in London, a primary account that will earn interest and a secondary account that will not earn interest. JP Morgan will not be paid a fee for its services to the ETF. It will instead generate an income or accept the risk of loss based on its ability to earn a spread on the interest it pays to the trust by using the trust's euro position to make loans in other banking situations. To be sure, JP Morgan has an advantage of floating money, so I would not worry that it will put itself in a position of extreme risk. As it has control over granting lending rates, I do not think that anyone will expect that the trust will pay the best available interest rate back to the

ETF so it will lock in a profit. The bank is in the business of making money. The best feature for individual investors for using an ETF is that it allows one to accumulate exposure without excessive leverage in the euro currency for a long-term position play. It can also be used as another means to hedge forex transactions. Each share of the ETF will represent 100 euros plus accrued interest. Under the guidelines of an ETF, it is acceptable to trade the short side without the uptick rule. Also, ETFs are listed on exchanges and trade throughout the day like individual securities. Since it is a tradable vehicle, unlike the forex market, it does charge a commission, which needs to be paid to a brokerage firm, to buy or to sell ETF shares.

Downside Risk

One of the downside risks to U.S. shareholders is that these ETFs are not insured by the Federal Deposit Insurance Corporation (FDIC), according to documents filed with the Securities and Exchange Commission (SEC). Also, interest on the primary account accrues daily, with rates based on the most recent Euro Overnight Index Average (EONIA), minus 0.27 percent that is paid monthly. The rate can change over time, according to the prospectus from Rydex; so there is no fixed rate or cost. This is a minor consideration; but for a large hedge fund, this could make a difference to an individual investor looking to take advantage of a long-term investment play. I hardly think this will cause a major change in the value of the investment.

For the record, the ETF's net asset value (NAV) is based on the Federal Reserve Bank of New York noon buying rate and expressed in U.S. dollars. And as you can imagine, the true influence on the value of this product is the same group of variables that affect the spot currency markets. Therefore, I believe that combining traditional technical analysis with the futures data, such as the *Commitments of Traders Report*, Volume and Open Interest studies, can greatly enhance the performance of longer-term investors over time. In June 2006, Rydex released six additional curency ETFs. So if you want to hedge or speculate that the U.S. dollar is strengthening or weakening against major foreign currencies and like the idea and concept of ETFs, now there is a pretty good inventory of product to choose from. The new currency ETFs trade on the New York Stock Exchange (NYSE) uner the symbols shown in Table 1.4.

To summarize, each unit represents 100 shares. You can sell short without the uptick rule that exists in stocks. ETFs allow a longer-term trader with limited risk capital to participate in an opportunity against the U.S. dollar versus major currency markets. Trading hours are during the U.S. equity markets' session—9:30 A.M. (EST) until 4:00 P.M. (EST). If you want to

TABLE 1.4 ETF Symbols on the NYSE

Currency	Symbol
Euro currency	FXE
British pound	FXB
Japanese yen	FXC
Australian dollar	FXM
Canadian dollar	FXA
Swiss franc	FXF
Swedish krona	FXS

read more on the subject of currency ETFs, especially about the risks, charges, and expenses on these products visit www.rydexfunds.com.

DIVERSIFICATION THROUGH TRADING PERIODS

So far, we have introduced you to various products to take advantage of foreign currency markets through the spot forex and futures and now through exchange traded funds via the stock market. Many traders and investors need to incorporate *diversification* into their arsenal of investments. Many believe the best means to diversify is through investments that have little to no correlation with each other with reserve cash balance, such as stocks, bonds, real estate, commodities, forex, and cash parked in a certificate of deposit (CD) or government Treasury bill (T-bill).

If you have a passion for currency trading, then in order to utilize diversification to the extreme, consider your overall allocation of your investment strategies within this sector. Depending on your time constraints, you may only be able to participate to a limited extent in day trades during the European session or early morning U.S. hours as economic numbers are released. As such, you should also have devotion toward holding positions as they go into a strong trend mode and should carry a position for more than a few days. This is known as a *swing trade*. Then, if you want to really capture a longer-term market trend, finding the right vehicle and strategy will allow you to hold a longer-term position. Let's define what I consider the three important time periods and classifications of a trade.

1. *Day trade*—1 minute up to 24 hours.
2. *Swing trade*—2 days to 10 days.
3. *Position trade*—10 days to 1 year or longer.

Day traders can use the forex or futures markets for small price swings. Swing traders can also use the forex and futures markets but can also implement an option strategy, such as a long call or a long put. This is a good consideration if you want to take advantage of establishing a position ahead of a major economic report, such as the Monthly Jobs number or a central bank meeting where you expect an interest rate adjustment to create a price shock in the market. For longer-term position trading where you would want to take advantage of a fundamental policy change or a technical trading program, you have several doors open to you besides just trading spot forex. You can implement an options strategy as an outright trade or use options as a hedge to reduce your risk exposure, which in turn can reduce your margin requirements. Also, you can invest in an ETF and gradually add positions without excessive risk exposure; and because ETFs have no time decay element, such as options on futures, you can really hold onto a position for a very long time. In a perfect world, I would say that a trader's time factor would limit him or her to a percentage breakdown to allocate resources to trading forex as I indicate in Figure 1.5—25 percent to day trading, 40 percent to swing trading (since a majority of significant market moves happen over a period of 3 to 10 days and then enter in a consolidation period), and 35 percent to position trading (to account for slow periods, time off, and vacations).

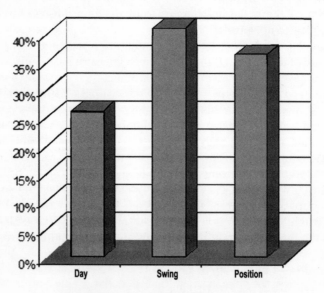

FIGURE 1.5   Allocation of Resources

Which Currency Tracks What and Why?

As Figure 1.4 showed, the most popular or heavily weighted currency against the dollar is the euro. There are several considerations and nuances that each individual currency tracks, as each not only is affected by the U.S. dollar but also is manipulated by its own country's economic and political influences. From a historic perspective, let's examine the top-five major currencies and what influences their values:

1. *The Euro.* The euro was first introduced to world financial markets as a currency in 1999 and was finally launched with physical coins and banknotes in 2002. The European Union is composed of these member countries: Austria, Belgium, Greece, Germany, France, Ireland, Italy, Luxembourg, the Netherlands, Portugal, and Spain. The largest members are considered socialist countries; and as a result, these countries tend to run the largest governmental budget deficits. The European Central Bank (ECB) dictates monetary policy and puts more emphasis on inflation concerns than it does on economic contraction. We have seen in the past where the ECB would rather maintain steady interest rates in periods of slower economic growth than lower rates and risk igniting inflationary pressure. As a result, the ECB is less likely to frequently adjust rates.

2. *The Japanese Yen.* The Japanese economy depends on sales of export. For the most part, Japan is a net importer of raw material goods, especially crude oil. Japan's economic machine hinges on foreign demand for their manufactured goods. Their main customers are the U.S. consumer and Europe. One of the biggest concerns that faced the Bank of Japan (BOJ) in the 1990s was deflationary pressures. This compelled the BOJ to keep what was known as a zero-interest policy to help reignite its economy. In turn, it also artificially kept the value of the yen low as many savvy investment funds made billions of dollars in what is known as a carry trade—one entity would borrow cheap money at nearly zero interest, export those funds to another country, and park them in a higher-interest-bearing account. This transaction prompted selling of yen to buy the currency in which those funds were to be invested or parked. U.S. Treasury notes and bonds as well as German bunds were the target of these transactions. As a result, the yen would trade lower against the U.S. dollar and the euro. Therefore, trading the yen/euro cross pair is a viable market to trade. One more consideration when focusing on factors that can influence the yen's value is that China is one of Japan's competitors. Since China also artificially floats its currency, the yuan, against the U.S. dollar, China's monetary policy also weakens or can put downward pressure on the yen's value.

3. *The British Pound.* The Bank of England (BOE) is in charge of dictating monetary policy in the Unted Kingdom. One of the main influences on Britain's economy is oil production in the North Sea. Money may make the world go round, but energy keeps it running. With that said, you will see in history that as oil prices rise, the British pound also tends to follow suit. However, oil supplies are dwindling in the North Sea, and Britain is using more and more natural gas. As of August 2006, Britain was Europe's biggest consumer of natural gas, and it is continuously increasing imports of the fuel to make up for declines in crude oil production. As a result, natural gas prices in Britain have risen an average of 60 percent from 2005 through 2006. It is now reliant on natural gas and susceptible to economic risk exposure if there are outrageous price spikes in the cost of that product. As of 2004, Britain became a net importer of natural gas. If natural gas prices spiral out of control, this factor can influence consumer spending or can create a surge in inflationary pressure; and that would justify action by the Bank of England to change monetary policy. This scenario could influence the value of the British pound. The pound is also sensitive to economic developments of its European neighbors. Therefore, trading the cross of the euro against the pound is a very liquid trading relationship.

4. *The Canadian Dollar.* The Canadian dollar is often referred to as the "loonie." The French equivalent of loonie is *huard*, which is French for *loon*, the bird that appears on the face of the Canadian one dollar coin. The Bank of Canada (BOC) sets monetary policy as it is the central bank for that country. Back in November 2000, the BOC adopted the system of eight meetings each year, in which it announces whether it will change its interest rate policy, just as in the United States. Canada is rich in natural resources, especially crude oil. The primary source of Canada's growing crude oil supplies are vast oil sands reserves. Oil sands production, which exceeded the 1 million barrels per day (b/d) plateau late in 2003, is forecast to more than double by 2015 to almost 2.6 million barrels per day. With 175 billion barrels of reserves, it is the second-largest petroleum deposit in the world. Since the United States is Canada's biggest client, as oil prices rise, the value of the Canadian dollar will be supported in value.

5. *The Swiss Franc.* The Swissy, as it is called, is considered the safe-haven currency, as it is backed by gold. The Swiss National Bank makes monetary policy decisions based on events that impact the value of gold as they influence the value of the currency. Factors that influence the Swiss franc are inflation, excessive economic growth or periods of economic contraction, and periods of political instability. The

Swiss franc tracks the value of the euro; but during periods of European upheaval, as occurred in 2004 when there existed dissention among members of the European Union, the Swiss franc will outperform the euro.

Fundamental News Drives the Markets

Traders who are new to forex can take comfort in knowing that analyzing and forecasting exchange rate movements does not rely solely on macroeconomic factors, the "big picture" issues. These are concepts for which information is readily available but that are not so intuitively grasped by the masses. Currency traders who are looking to capture big moves in exchange-rate movement definitely should focus on the fundamentals and the understanding of what drives interest rate differentials between various countries. The currency pairs are traded especially when attempting to assess the value of currencies.

Traders need to be aware of several key elements and events that can cause currency values to move. For one, the adjusting of interest rates by central banks is a major factor that moves markets. These decisions are based on many concerns, such as international trade flows, investment flows, the health of individual country's economies, and inflation worries. The opposite concern, as has been the case for Japan for over a decade, is deflation. These are the same factors that can and do influence moves on the stock and bond markets.

Our civilization has evolved into a very complex international capitalistic environment. Some governments intercede to help benefit their economies through government support programs, as had been the case in China. China had artificially supported its currency, the yuan, to move in relationship with the U.S. dollar. Then we have multinational conglomerate corporations, whose money flow needs can and do influence short-term price swings in currencies. Throughout these developments, it has become increasingly difficult to target one single effect on the value of a currency in the short term, especially one weighted against the U.S. dollar. Take for example what happens in an economic business cycle. Money flow moves where there are better opportunities either from the perspective of attractiveness on rate of return or from a safety issue in uncertain times. Huge investment funds can move money to higher-yielding interest-earning instruments, namely bonds, or to foreign stocks. When major hedge funds see better opportunities from one country to another, they have the resources to move quickly with limited restrictions. These shifts in trading strategies also cause short-term moves in currency values.

Historically, when we see signs of economic changes taking place, money flows in the equity markets move from one sector to another as the economic business cycle goes into an expansion mode, then into a contraction, and then back into an expansion mode. Foreign investors may wish to take part in these changes as well, therefore increasing capital flows to the United States, which will have a short-term supportive boost for the dollar. As of the middle of October 2006, what we were possibly entering would have been considered an early-stage economic contraction. There were many factors at play that would lead to that conclusion. For starters, the Federal reserve had raised interest rates by 0.25 percent 17 consecutive times over a two-year period, bringing the federal funds rate to 5.25 percent. It concluded its interest-rate-hiking campaign based on concerns that it might choke off liquidity, bringing more risks to economic growth than the risks of inflation. That was a pretty good tip-off that the economic expansion phase just might moderate. As a result of increased interest rates, even the housing market turned south, as we discussed previously (see Figures 1.1 and 1.2). We had been in a longer-than-normal economic expansion period, starting from early 2003 through mid-2006. With this said, it was at the time considered a "long in the tooth" recovery (lasting more than 40 months), especially after the economic contraction period that followed 9/11/01.

Treasury Yield Relationship to Currencies

With the Federal Reserve interest-rate hikes and escalating energy prices taxing the American consumer, it is no wonder we were expecting a contraction. Some argued with the longer-term yields on Treasury bonds inverting in relationship to shorter-term maturities. This gave even more reasons to suspect a more-than-moderate slowdown might occur. Based on historical standards, when interest rates on the long end of the yield curve are below those of shorter-term maturities, we have entered into recessionary periods. The word *recession* was being tossed about by many leading analysts as a result of this reoccurring. As of August 21, 2006, the yield on the 10-year note was at 4.84, and the yield on the 2-year note was at 4.87. Figure 1.6 plots the yield on the various Treasury maturity issues. As you can see, the yield on the 10-year note dips below that of the 2-year note and creates the inversion.

An investor or a foreign central bank can park money into a short-term instrument and receive close to a 5 percent return without risk. That is one feature that will attract foreign capital flows and help support the dollar. This effect will occur until better opportunities evolve elsewhere. As a forex trader, you want to monitor yields on a global scale or events or reports that may impact these rates.

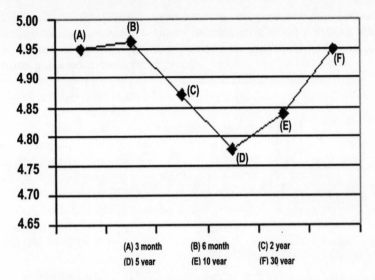

FIGURE 1.6 Yield on Treasury Notes, as of August 21, 2006

ECONOMIC CONDITIONS CLUES TO WATCH FOR

- Inverted yield curve gives warning of an economic slowdown. — *long term debt has lower interest rate than short term debt*
- Flat yield curve signals economic recovery.
- Steep yield curve signals economic expansion.

Lessons Learned from Energy Prices

We can benefit with the knowledge from where energy prices are, especially crude oil. As prices rise, oil-producing countries increase their wealth. However, oil-consuming nations are at a disadvantage, and the increased cost of fuel can contribute to a recession, as occurred in the United States in the 1970s. If you think about it, higher fossil fuel prices actually act like a taxing effect on consumers. However, after a prolonged price appreciation, to reflect the higher energy costs, producers eventually need to raise prices in their finished goods and services to maintain a decent profit margin and not absorb the burden of higher energy costs. Who pays the price? You and I, the consumer, and that is inflationary. Crude oil prices hit an all-time high close at $78.40 per barrel on July 14, 2006 (see Figure 1.7), due to global demand and fighting in the Middle East. Tensions flared between Israel and Lebanon. Fears arose when many suspected Iran and Syria

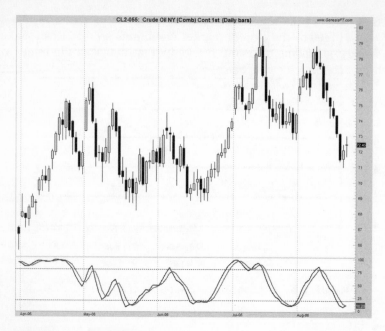

FIGURE 1.7   Crude Oil Prices
Used with permission of GenesisFT.com.

were backing Hezbollah with supplies, fears that Israel would take action to stop the weapon shipments. The markets were on edge as that region was deteriorating by the minute. If that was not enough, Iran was threatening to continue with its nuclear program, despite UN resolutions to have them stop enriching uranium. Iran's Supreme Leader Ayatollah Ali Khamenei was quoted as saying, "Iran would press ahead with its pursuit of nuclear energy," thus indicating it would not follow requests or directions from the United Nations. President Bush was quoted as saying we are in "challenging times" in a speech made on August 21, 2006. This was in reference to the global war on terrorism. This strongly impacted crude oil prices, as did the geographical location of Iran and the Straits of Hormuz, where oil cargo vessels sail to the Western world.

Imagine how sensitive the area was with reports that Iran was "testing" surface-to-sea missiles. There are two points I want to bring to your attention: (1) We want to look at the impact higher energy prices have on the dollar versus the currency of oil-producing countries, such as Canada and Britain. (2) We can determine from history that with higher energy prices, the United States is susceptible to recessionary pressures, which put further pressure on the dollar.

As a trader, I want access to as much relevant information as possible to give me clues to the overall market conditions so that I can make a more-educated trading decision. If I know that higher crude prices will weigh on economic development, I need to ask myself how can I profit from that situation. Based on a widely accepted business-cycle flow chart, we see business sectors that perform better under certain market conditions. As we enter a late-stage economic expansion (as I believe we entered in mid-2006), energy markets make a move, as do basic materials, as building is going like gangbusters. Then as higher interest rates slow consumer spending and credit costs a little more, we see money moving into safer issues, such as consumer staples and utilities. This occurs as consumer confidence declines in the economy, and people rein in spending. Technology is weakest during an economic contraction period as capital spending dries up. Figure 1.8 defines the various stages of the business cycle. At the top of the pyramid, when we are in the middle to late expansion period, we see energy as one of the top money sectors. As the economy slows, demand for fuel declines; people are more cognizant of their spending habits and start conserving.

Now to confirm that we were, in fact, in a period of contraction, we would look to see if these similarities were reflected in the various stock index performances. If we were entering a period of economic contraction,

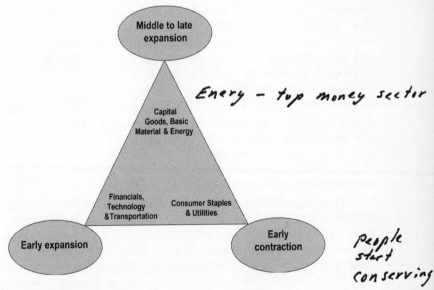

FIGURE 1.8 Stages of the Business Cycle

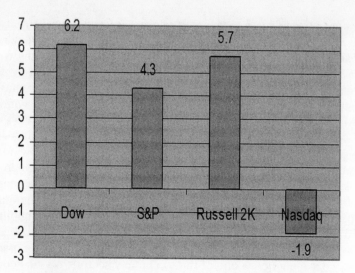

FIGURE 1.9   Year-to-Date Gain, 12-31-2005 to 8-18-2006

the Dow Jones Industrial Average, which represents 30 of the top blue-chip stocks, many of which offer dividends, might outperform the other indexes. We would certainly expect the Dow to outperform the Nasdaq. Let's examine Figure 1.9. This graph shows the year-to-date gain from December 31, 2005, through August 18, 2006. The Dow outperformed all the major stock indexes during that seven-and-a-half-month period. Notice the negative return on the Nasdaq? The key word here is *negative*. That implies that businesses, investors, and consumers are not positive on the economic outlook here in the United States. That does not bode well for the U.S. dollar. What we would look for as a clue that the dollar has bottomed would be for a period of economic expansion led by the technology sector. Until we see signs that the economy reenters a new business cycle, the U.S. dollar might just as well remain under pressure.

As we look ahead to the 2008 presidential election, this period may redefine an economic expansion. So watch for signs as technology leads the way. This may attract foreign investment flows, and the dollar may bottom at that time. Longer-term and short-term position traders can profit by watching for resurgence in the U.S. economy and confidence in the dollar. Eventually, it will reign supreme again. If the U.S. economy continues to grow, and if inflationary pressures build, then the Fed will probably continue to raise rates. This action will help support the dollar's value.

GEOPOLITICAL EVENTS

Like all markets, the currency market is affected by what is going on in the world. Key political events around the world can have a big impact on a country's economy and on the value of its respective currency. Turmoil, caused by labor strikes and terrorist attacks, as we have witnessed in this new millennium, can cause short-term price shocks in the currency markets. Terrorist attacks seem to have played more havoc on the energy markets than on the currency markets in 2006, but we need to be aware of any lasting economic impact these heinous acts have before we react by forming an opinion and placing a trade. We have heard the term *flight to safety*, indicating that traders are moving money from one country to another, thereby causing shifts in currency values. These events need to be monitored by forex traders as well.

Monetary and Fiscal Policy

When central banks act, it is called *monetary policy*. Other factors controlled by government decisions are referred to as *fiscal policy* changes, which are controlled by political concerns. Such changes can be linked to a change in specific laws, the changing of the guard, so to speak, such as how a new leader can and certainly does influence currency values. If a new leader is voted into office and does not have the confidence to run a country effectively, then we can see money leaving a country, which causes a decline in value of that currency. Therefore, these two points are major concerns for which forex traders should watch.

1. Economic conditions, including outlook on interest rates and inflation.
2. Fiscal policy changes and political leadership.

These factors have a long-term impact, which makes forex attractive to trade due to the long-term trending conditions established by central bank decisions based on these factors. Forex also offers investors some diversification, necessary as protection against adverse movements in the equity and bond markets.

Let's go over what you and I will see on a day-to-day basis through reports and news events and apply what is otherwise known as *fundamental analysis*—the study of tangible information in order to anticipate supply and demand flows. Several events can directly affect the outcome of supply. For example, changes in interest rates from country A would make its currency less valuable compared to the currency of country B where one would receive a higher rate of return on money invested. This would certainly reduce the demand for country A's currency. That is a prime example of a supply/demand–driven event.

How about trying to decide or to anticipate if there is a change in the strength or the weakness of an economy? This is where we really need to pay close attention to specific reports. For starters, a report showing a country's employment rate might reveal what the potential for future household disposable income is. It would give analysts and economists an idea of how much spending could occur due to the number of people working. Another aspect of fundamental analysis may be the ability to follow and understand the political scene on both an international and a domestic level.

If the European Central Bank meets and announces that it will raise interest rates in a surprise move, this will have an immediate impact on the value of the euro and, inversely, the U.S. dollar. If values of these currencies shift abruptly and severely, then products that are imported and exported would be priced differently. Ultimately, this could cause a ripple effect on the prices of goods and services. It is important to understand and to interpret what the potential outcome might be in the markets you are trading when these special reports are released. For a fundamental trader not to know what day or time a report is released could be hazardous to his financial health. At the very least, even if you are a veteran trader or a beginner, it cannot hurt to be aware of the main fundamental factors that might affect the markets you are trading. You should be aware of what could happen before most reports are released. That is why news services put out what time current events and special reports are coming out. Publications like *Barron's Weekly*, *Investor's Business Daily*, or the *Wall Street Journal* will most likely show you what you will need to know to stay in tune with the markets. Most forex dealers also provide special calendars that include the date and times that most major economic and agricultural reports are released. A calendar of events is also available free of charge at www.fxtriggers.com. Trading is not an easy venture, and there is one bit of advice that I wish you would follow: Be aware of the day's current events if you are in the markets. Knowing about a major report before it is released is sometimes better only because you have a chance to eliminate a surprising adverse market move. You could always make an adjustment to your position before a report is released.

Another reason you want to follow the developments on the economy is because it usually dictates how various equity markets and financial products will perform. The stock market likes to see healthy economic growth because that equates to better or substantially larger corporate profits. The bond market prefers a slower sustainable growth rate that will not lead to inflationary pressures. By watching and tracking economic data, analysts and investors will be better able to stay in tune with the markets and their investments. Moreover, foreign capital flows may increase if U.S.

instruments are higher-yielding than those abroad. We want to track the value of these instruments because that can give us a clue that there will be a shift in currency values.

Understanding what fundamental events dictate the markets at a given time may give you better insight to trade a currency based on the price direction of these financial products. The terms *yield maturity*, *rates*, and *prices* are all relevant in forex trading.

Playing the Carry-Trade Game

Each foreign currency has a central bank that issues an overnight lending rate. This is a prime gauge of a currency's value. In recent history, low interest rates have resulted in the devaluation of a currency. Many analysts assume this is a function of the *carry-trade strategy*, employed by many hedge funds. This is a trade where one buys and holds currencies in a high-yielding interest rate market, such as the United States, and sells or borrows money from a foreign country where the currency is in a low-yielding interest rate market, such as exists in Japan. There is a significant risk exposure to this investment, which requires large capital, or a highly leveraged position from an exchange-rate fluctuation.

Understanding Treasuries: Yield and Price

When I discussed the inverted yield curve and pointed out the discrepancy between the 10- and 2-year notes as shown in Figure 1.6, I wanted to further explain how these instruments work and the relationship to forex. Let's first define what a Treasury bond is and how it works and is priced out. U.S. Treasury bonds (T-bonds) are by all definitions a loan. Taxpayers are the lenders. The U.S. government is the borrower. The government needs money to operate and to fund the federal deficit, so it borrows money from the public by issuing bonds.

When a bond is issued, its price is known as its "face value." Once you buy it, the government promises to pay you back on a particular day that is known as the "maturity date." They issue that instrument at a predetermined rate of interest called the "coupon." For instance, you might buy a bond with a $1,000 face value, a 6 percent coupon, and a 10-year maturity. You would collect interest payments totaling $60 in each of those 10 years. When the decade was up, you'd get back your $1,000. If you buy a U.S. Treasury bond and hold it until maturity, you will know exactly how much you're going to get back. That's why bonds are also known as "fixed-income" investments; they guarantee you a continuous income and are backed by the U.S. government. There are also the concepts of *yield* and *price*. That is what confuses most investors. It is very simple: When yield goes up, price goes down; and vice versa.

Treasury Bonds, Bills, and Notes

The U.S. government issues several different kinds of bonds through the Bureau of the Public Debt, an agency of the U.S. Department of the Treasury. Treasury debt securities are classified according to their maturities:

- Treasury *bills* have maturities of 1 year or less.
- Treasury *notes* have maturities of 2 to 10 years.
- Treasury *bonds* have maturities greater than 10 years.

Since there are more equity traders in the investment world than there are forex traders, this investment area may attract more participants. If the equity markets are forecast to generate normal to even subnormal returns based on a historical standard for 2006 and beyond, then the appetite for making money may attract the individual investor to trade in the Treasury and forex markets.

WHICH REPORTS ARE MORE IMPORTANT THAN THE OTHER?

I want you to know that whether you are a beginner or an advanced trader, it is important to know what to look for and how certain reports may affect the price behavior of the markets. Figure 1.10 shows what I see as the major focuses of economic reports here in the United Statees and what is in my opinion the order of importance. My selection holds true in all business cycles. The number-one focus should always be to read and to listen to what the voting members of central banks are looking at and on what they are basing their decisions to adjust interest rates. That makes sense, right? So the releases of their FOMC meeting announcements are important, as well as the minutes of their last meeting. The minutes are released within two weeks of the last FOMC meeting. In Figure 1.10, I have two small branches from the FOMC meetings: One is the Beige book; heighten your awareness of this, as it is released two weeks prior to a Fed meeting. The other is the Federal Reserve districts business surveys; these reports will show the underlying strength or weakness of everything from business credit conditions to the health of the consumer debt to income ratios.

You and I want to watch the reports and speaking engagements of the voting members of the FOMC. Generally, they will give clues as to what their intentions are and what their concerns are. One series of reports is the Fed's Beige book, and the other reports are the individual Fed district business surveys, such as the Philadelphia Fed survey. Then we trickle down

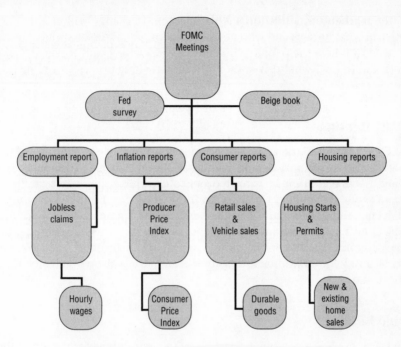

FIGURE 1.10   Economic Report Reference Chart

the flow chart reading from left to right and see the employment situation; in good times, we should see a low employment level with moderating wage costs. In hard times, we should see high unemployment rates. When times are good, as in the period through 2005 when the nation's unemployment level was under 5 percent, we need to be aware of ugly inflationary pressures; so forex traders need to focus on these inflation reports, such as the Producer Price Index and the Consumer Price Index. After that, taking a look at the financial health of the consumers is key to determining the continued strength or weakness of the economy. After all, if they have no more spending cash or are maxed out on their credit cards, we can anticipate a downturn in the retail sector, right? If the consumer stops shopping for clothes, electronic products, home design products, cars, or appliances, which we consider durable goods, then that won't be good for the economy and the Fed would be expected to stop raising interest rates or to possibly *lower* rates.

Here is a great example of why we want to pay attention to Fed speakers. When newly appointed Chairman Ben Bernanke took over, he had a private conversation with Maria Bartiromo, anchor of CNBC, one weekend. When she revealed his thoughts in an exclusive interview on national

TV, the markets responded in such a way that Bernanke will be more selective in what he says and who he talks to at private functions! Once again, we need to follow the people who make the decisions, and we need to listen to and to read what drives their decision-making process for adjusting interest rates.

FOMC Meetings

The Federal Open Market Committee consists of the seven governors of the Federal Reserve Board and five Federal Reserve Bank presidents. The FOMC meets eight times a year in order to determine the near-term direction of monetary policy. Changes are now announced immediately after FOMC meetings. There are a few accompanying statements the Fed may make after it announces any adjustments in interest rates. One statement is if the economy is at risk for economic weakness, or the other is if the economy is at risk for inflationary pressures. And there is always a chance for a neutral stance.

Beige Book

The Beige book is a combination of economic conditions from each of the 12 Federal Reserve regional districts. Truthfully, the report is aptly named the Beige book due to the color of its cover. This report is released usually two weeks before the monetary policy meetings of the FOMC. This report on economic conditions is used at FOMC meetings, where the Fed sets interest rate policy. These meetings occur roughly every six weeks. If the Beige book portrays an overheating economy or inflationary pressures, the Fed may be more inclined to raise interest rates in order to moderate the economic pace. Conversely, if the Beige book portrays economic difficulties or recessionary conditions, the Fed may see the need to lower interest rates in order to stimulate activity.

EMPLOYMENT REPORTS

The unemployment rate is a strong indicator of a country's economic strength. When unemployment is high, the economy may be weak and its currency may fall in value. The opposite is true as well. Many economists look for answers to the question "What is a country's full employment capacity level?" That knowledge will give clues to the peak in productivity and economic output. That also helps determine a country's capital flows and is, therefore, good information for currency traders to follow for longer-term trend identification. The unemployment rate measures the number of unemployed as a percentage of the nation's workforce. Nonfarm payroll employment tallies the number of paid employees working part time and or full time in the nation's business and government sectors.

There are several components that are also included in the employment report. One is the average hourly work week; that figure reflects the number of hours worked in the nonfarm sector. Another component is the average hourly earnings; it shows the hourly rate that employees are receiving. There are two versions of this report. One is a weekly report that is released every Thursday morning; and the other, the more influential report, is the monthly figure that is usually released on the first Friday of every month. The fear when we are at or near "full employment is that employers might have to pay overtime wages to their existing workforce and use higher wages to bring in new workers from the competitor. This action can raise labor costs because of a shortage of workers. This leads to wage inflation, which is bad news for the stock and the bond markets. Federal Reserve officials are always on the lookout for inflationary pressures. In August 2006, the monthly employment report showed a less-than-expected increase in new jobs. This gave a hint to traders that the Federal Reserve might halt its interest-rate-hiking campaign. That so-called campaign took the Fed funds rate from 1.0 percent to 5.25 percent with a record-setting 17 consecutive interest-rate adjustments. When the market thought the Fed was done due to the potentially weakening jobs market, the dollar fell sharply and foreign currencies exploded in value in short order. The British pound chart in Figure 1.11 shows a 15-minute time period, one of my favorite time periods to watch for trade signals. The bullish indicators, as represented by the triangles that are pointing up, generated buy signals before the report was released (the construction and theories behind this particular trading system will be discussed throughout this book) and would have given an extremely profitable trade. The explosive behavior of the market's reaction was due to the sentiment that the Fed would change its interest-rate policy from a tightening mode to a neutral watch-and-review mode.

One other method I utilize is trading like or similar markets, which is often referred to as trading *tandem* market relationships. In a situation that reveals a major change in interest-rate policy, such as a surprise in the employment growth or a contraction in the United States, we should see the dollar move against the entire spectrum of currencies. Call it a second-dimension confirmation technique.

Figure 1.12 shows the euro currency. Utilizing the same time period as in Figure 1.11, a 15-minute chart, we have similar buy signals generated before the report. It was the internal technical condition of the market on not one but two "like" or tandem markets that signaled that a change might take place in the value of these currencies.

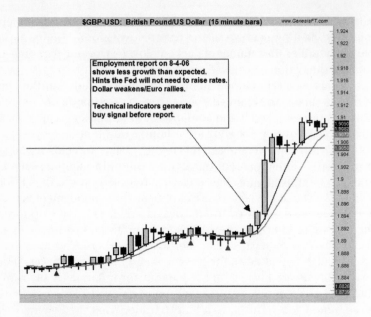

FIGURE 1.11 British Pound Explodes on Employment Report
Used with permission of GenesisFT.com.

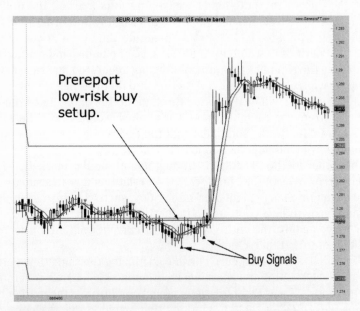

FIGURE 1.12 Euro/U.S. Dollar (15-minute buy signals)
Used with permission of GenesisFT.com.

As the charts show, a major change in fact did take place; the euro rocketed to the upside, generating over a 170-PIP profit per position in less than one hour. If you examine the two charts closely, you can see that while they both generated buy signals, both were at or near their pivot point support levels; but the trend in the British pound before the report was in an upward direction and the trend in the euro was in a declining mode.

What is interesting about this observation is that some traders were bound to be selling prior to the report, possibly because they were unaware that a significant report was due out or that it was an important enough event to warrant attention or because they were not looking at the same specific technical techniques that we will be covering in this book.

TRADING BEFORE REPORTS

Here are the major reports that have created dramatic and violent price swings in currencies. I want you to have a good understanding of what they mean so you can relate possible shocks to the markets when and if they are dramatically changed from what is expected before the reports' release.

- *Employment Cost Index* (ECI). This is a measure of total employee compensation costs, including wages, salaries, and benefits. The ECI is the broadest measure of labor costs. The employment cost index helps analysts determine the trend of the direction of employers' cost of having employees. This can give economists a clue whether inflation is perking up from a cost-of-doing-business standpoint. If a company needs to pay more to hire qualified workers, then the cost of doing business increases. This reduces profit margins. Companies usually raise their prices to consumers if their costs increase, and that is where the inflation theme plays out.
- *Producer Price Index* (PPI). This is a measure of the average prices paid by producers for a fixed basket of capital and consumer goods. The PPI measures price changes in the manufacturing sector. Inflation is a general increase in the prices of goods and services.
- *Consumer Price Index* (CPI). This is a measure of the average price level of goods and services purchased by consumers. Monthly changes in the CPI represent the rate of inflation. The consumer price index is the most widely followed indicator of inflation in the United States. Just knowing what inflation is and how it influences the markets can put an investor ahead of the game. Inflation is a general increase in the price of goods and services. The relationship between inflation and interest rates is the key to understanding how data like the CPI influence the markets. Higher energy prices, manufacturing cost increases, med-

ical costs, and imbalances in global supply and demand of raw materials and food products all weigh on this report. Take the price of gasoline we pay at the pumps. If gas prices escalate to the point where it costs $30 to fill up a car, or $60, or even $100, as was the case in 2006, consumers will have less spending money for other items. Even weather can be a factor on short-term changes on food. What would be the cost of tomatoes at the grocery store after a damaging freeze in California or in Georgia—$3 or $4 per pound? It has occurred. Think of the restaurants that serve salads and lose revenue, let alone the farmer whose crop is destroyed. This all plays a part in the CPI number. The core rate is the inflation number that excludes the volatile food and energy components.

- *Gross Domestic Product* (GDP).   This is the broadest measure of aggregate economic activity and accounts for almost every sector of the economy. Analysts use this figure to track the economy's performance because it usually indicates how strong or how weak the economy is, and that helps predict the potential profit margin for companies. It also helps analysts gauge whether the economy is accelerating or slowing down. The stock market likes to see healthy economic growth because that translates to higher corporate profits.

- *Industrial Production and Capacity Utilization Rate.*   This is a measure of the physical output of the nation's factories, mines, and utilities. The capacity utilization rate reflects the usage of available resources and provides an estimate of how much factory capacity is in use. If the utilization rate gets too high (above 85 percent), it can lead to inflationary pressures. Industrial production shows how much factories, mines, and utilities are producing. Since the manufacturing sector is estimated to account for one-quarter of the economy, this report can sometimes have a big impact on the stock and financial markets' movement.

- *Index of Leading Indicators.*   This report is a composite index of 10 economic indicators that typically lead overall economic activity. The Index of Leading Indicators helps to predict the health of the economy, such as recessions and economic expansions.

- *International Trade.*   This measures the difference between imports and exports of both goods and services. Changes in the level of imports and exports are an important tool that is used to gauge economic trends both here and overseas. This report can have a profound effect on the value of the dollar. That in turn can help or hurt multinational corporations whose profits overseas can diminish when they convert their funds back to the United States, especially if the U.S. dollar is overvalued. Another valuable aspect of this report is that imports can help indicate demand for foreign goods here in the United States and exports may show the demand for U.S. goods in overseas countries.

- *Institute of Supply Management* (ISM) *Index* (formerly the National Association of Purchasing Managers [NAPM] Survey). This survey is a composite diffusion index of national manufacturing conditions. Readings above 50 percent indicate an expanding factory sector. The ISM Index helps economists and analysts get a detailed look at the manufacturing sector of the economy. Since manufacturing is a major source of strength for the economy and can reflect the nation's employment condition, this report is very important to watch.
- *Factory Orders.* This reports the dollar level of new orders for manufacturing durable and nondurable goods. The data from this report shows the potential that factories will be increasing or decreasing activity based on the amount of orders they receive. This report provides insight to the demand not only for hard goods, such as refrigerators and cars, but also for nondurable items, such as cigarettes and apparel.
- *Productivity and Costs.* Productivity measures the growth of labor efficiency in producing the economy's goods and services. Unit labor costs reflect the labor costs of producing each unit of output. Both are followed as indicators of future inflationary trends. Productivity growth is critical because it allows for higher wages and faster economic growth without inflationary consequences.
- *Consumer Confidence.* This is a survey or a poll of consumers' opinions regarding both their present conditions and their expectations regarding their economic conditions. Five thousand consumers across the country are surveyed each month. The theory here is that the level of consumer confidence is directly related to the strength of consumer spending. Consumer spending accounts for two-thirds of the economy. If consumers are confident that times are good, spending is likely to remain stable or even to increase. If consumer confidence is weak, then more times than not consumers save and do not spend money. This shift in spending habits can help or hurt the developments in the economy from durable goods sales to home or car purchases. If consumers are not confident, then they are less likely to purchase those big-ticket items.
- *Personal Income and Spending.* Personal income is the estimated dollar amount of income received by Americans. Personal spending is the estimated dollar amount that consumers use for purchases of durable and nondurable goods and services. This economic number is important because if consumers are spending more than they make, eventually the spending will stop, thus causing a downturn in the economy. Another aspect to consider is consumers who save, maybe in-

vesting in the markets, and that can increase the value of stock prices. In addition, it can also add liquidity to the banking system if the money goes to savings or money market accounts.

- *Durable Goods Orders.*   These reflect new orders placed with domestic manufacturers for immediate and future delivery of factory-made products. Orders for durable goods show how busy factories will be in the months to come as manufacturers work to fill those orders. The data provides insight into demand for things like washers, dryers, and cars and also takes the temperature of the strength of the economy going forward.
- *Retail Sales.*   These measure the total sales at stores that sell durable and nondurable goods. This can reveal the spending habits of consumers, and the trend of those spending "sprees" can more often than not influence analysts' expectations for future developments to the economy.
- *Construction Spending.*   This report shows analysts the amount of new construction activity on residential and nonresidential building jobs. Prices of such commodities as lumber are sensitive to housing industry trends. In addition, business owners usually will put money into the construction of a new facility or factory if they feel confident that business is good enough to validate an expansion.
- *Housing Starts.*   This is a measure of the number of residential units on which construction is about to start. The backbone of the U.S. economy is construction. Think about this: When you purchase a new home, you probably also purchase durable items, like refrigerators, washers and dryers, furniture, and lawn care products. This is known as a ripple effect throughout the economy. Think of all the jobs produced from construction to factory and transportation and even to communication and technology that goes into the building and financing and furnishing of a new home. The economic commerce is substantial, especially when there are a hundred thousand or more homes built in a month around the country. At the very least, the data from housing starts can help project the price direction for the sector of stocks in homebuilders, mortgage banks, and appliance companies. It used to be that lumber and copper futures prices were dramatically affected by the Housing Starts figure. However, since the development of prefabricated and new construction materials, especially fiber optics and plastics (PVC is used for plumbing rather than copper), lumber and copper are now less sensitive to the building industries' trends.
- *Mortgage Bankers Association Purchase Applications Index.*   This is a weekly index of purchase applications at mortgage lenders. This is a good leading indicator for single-family-home sales and housing construction. It provides a gauge of not only the demand for housing but

also economic momentum. Each time the construction of a new home begins, it translates into more construction jobs and income, which will be pumped back into the economy.

- *New Home Sales.* This is the number of newly constructed homes with a committed sale during a month. The level of new home sales indicates housing market trends. This provides a gauge of not only the demand for housing but also economic momentum. People have to be feeling pretty comfortable and confident in their financial position to buy a house. Furthermore, this narrow piece of data has a powerful multiplier effect throughout the economy and, therefore, across the markets and your investments. By tracking economic data such as new home sales, investors can gain specific investment ideas as well as broad guidance for managing a portfolio. Each time the construction of a new home begins, it translates to more construction jobs and income, which will be pumped back into the economy. Once the home is sold, it generates revenues for the home builder and the realtor. It brings a myriad of consumption opportunities for the buyer. Furniture and large and small appliances are just some of the items new home buyers might purchase. The economic ripple effect can be substantial, especially when a hundred thousand new households around the country are doing this every month. Since the economic backdrop is the most pervasive influence on financial markets, new home sales have a direct bearing on stocks, bonds, interest rates, and the economy in general. In a more specific sense, trends in the new home sales data carry valuable clues for the stocks of home builders, mortgage lenders, and home furnishings companies.
- *Existing Home Sales.* This is the number of previously constructed homes with a closed sale during the month. Sales of existing homes (also known as home resales) are a larger share of the market than new homes and indicate housing market trends. This provides a gauge of not only the demand for housing but also economic momentum. People have to be feeling pretty comfortable and confident of their own financial situation to buy a house. Analysts follow economic data such as home resales because this generates a tremendous economic ripple effect. Even for existing homes, buyers may purchase new refrigerators, washers, dryers, and furniture.
- *Consumer Credit.* This report measures consumer credit that is outstanding. Since one of U.S. consumers' pasttimes is to "charge" goods and services to their credit cards, the overall changes in consumer credit can indicate the condition of individual consumer finances. On one hand, economic activity is stimulated when consumers borrow within their means to buy cars and other major purchases. On the other hand, if consumers pile up too much debt relative to their income lev-

els, they may have to stop spending on new goods and services just to pay off old debts. That could put a big dent in future economic growth. The demand for credit can also have a direct effect on interest rates. If the demand to borrow money exceeds the supply of willing lenders, interest rates rise. If credit demand falls and many willing lenders are fighting for customers, they may offer lower interest rates to attract business.

- *Business Inventories.* Alan Greenspan watched this report; you should become familiar with it as well. This report shows the dollar amount of inventories held by manufacturers, wholesalers, and retailers. The level of inventories in relation to sales is an important indicator for the future direction of factory production.

- *Consumer Confidence.* There are several such surveys that gauge consumer attitudes; one is the Conference Board, and another is the University of Michigan. These reports reveal both the present situation and expectations regarding economic conditions. The level of consumer confidence is generally assumed to be directly related to the strength or weakness for consumer spending. Generally speaking, the more confident consumers are about their own personal finances, the more likely they are to spend. Think of how you act and feel as a "consumer." If you have money in the bank and feel confident that your job is secure, buying an extra gadget or splurging on a night out usually won't be trouble, right? But if times are tough, then the purse strings get pulled in, correct?

 HOT TIP

Get a calendar of events; check it every day to find out which reports will be released and at what time. Also be aware if there are scheduled speakers, such as heads of central banks, the president, or voting members of the FOMC. Make sure you converted these report release times for the time zone in which you live and trade. That way you will be prepared and not hit with an unexpected news-driven, price-shock event.

WHEN IS THE BEST TIME TO TRADE?

Forex traders use fundamental analysis as described earlier to identify trading opportunities by analyzing economic information for a longer-term perspective. Short-term traders should also understand which reports can cause a shift in currency markets and know when they are released.

Knowing the best times to trade the markets will help you nail down when a potential trade may materialize. The pie chart in Figure 1.4 showed that the largest percentage value traded against the U.S. dollar was the euro; therefore, that suggests that one of the highest-volume time periods would be when the European session opens. The central place of foreign currency dealings is in London, where the second-most-active trading volume occurs (the U.S. session being the first). Therefore, London is where there are likely to be large-range swings in the market granting day traders an opportunity to profit. That session begins at 3 A.M. (EST) and goes until 11:30 A.M. (EST). So a euro to U.S. dollar (EU/USD) or euro to British pound (EU/BP) or British pound to U.S. dollar (BP/USD) pair would be an appropriate selection to trade during the European session. The U.S. session opens at 8 A.M. (EST), which overlaps the European session; these two sessions combined generate the bulk of trading activity. Most major U.S. economic reports are released at 8:30 A.M. (EST); and, as expected, the currency markets generally react off those reports. This offers traders the opportunity to trade off violent price spikes when economic news is released, especially when the news is a surprise.

Once the U.S. markets close at 5 P.M. (EST), the currency markets are available to trade; but it is not until the Asian session opens at 7 P.M. (EST) that markets will experience potential price swings as volume levels rise. During the Asian session, traders would want to focus on the Australian dollar and the Japanese yen and the trade opportunities offered by the USD/JY or the USD/AUS or the cross pair trading the JY/AUS dollar. Notice that the Asian markets overlap the European session as well, so the Japanese yen versus the euro cross (JY/EU) is a popular pair to trade. Table 1.5 shows the time zones on which you want to focus when trading spot forex markets.

Forex Traders Can Benefit from Futures Data

Forex traders can integrate futures data to help in trading decisions, such as taking a trading signal based on chart patterns in the futures and trans-

TABLE 1.5 Trading Times for Forex

Trade Session	Eastern Time	Greenwich Mean Time
Asian open	7:00 P.M.	23:00
Asian close	4:00 A.M.	08:00
London open	3:00 ~~P.M.~~ *A.M.*	07:00
London close	*11:30* ~~11:00~~ A.M.	15:30
U.S. open	8:00 A.M.	12:00
U.S. close	5:00 P.M.	21:00

lating it into a trading trigger signal in a forex market. Spot FX and futures
trade in tandem, and any price difference is called the "basis"; both FX and
futures generally trade, pricewise, equally on a day-to-day basis (within a
few PIPs). As we discussed previously, forex markets are decentralized, so
there is not a collective database to measure two distinct studies, such as
volume and open interest. These are important tools, so let's review the basics. If you are just using your FX dealer's trading platform for charts and
quotes, you will not be able to get the volume and open interest information. However, you need only end-of-day data, and you can search the Internet for end-of-day charting data for futures markets. If you do subscribe
to a charting software company, then it can add end-of-day charts for nothing or a very nominal monthly charge.

Volume

At this point, it is important to define what the *volume figures* are that you
can receive and analyze in the forex market. The volume for forex pairs represents the number of transactions or ticks and not true trade-size activity.
Forex does not have actual trade-size information because there is not a
central marketplace to tabulate and send the information out to traders.
The true definition of *volume* is the number of trades for all the total contract months of a given future's contract, both long and short, combined.
For example, the futures foreign currency markets trade on quarterly expirations—the March, June, September, and December contract months. The
volume will represent the total for all the trades in each contract month.
Most technical analysts believe that volume is an indicator of the strength
of a market trend. It is also a relative measure of the dominant behavior of
the market. Here is a further explanation; volume is the measurement of the
market's acceptance or rejection of price at a specific level and time. There
are several theories and so-called rules when using volume analysis on
price charts; the first one is that if a market is increasing in price and the
volume is increasing, then the market is said to be in a bullish mode and can
indicate a continued move in the direction of the trend.

   The exact opposite is true for a declining market. However, if a substantial daily market price increase or decrease occurs after a long steady
uptrend or downtrend, especially on unusually high daily volume, it is
considered to be a "blow off top or bottom" and can signal a market turning point or trend reversal. Here are some guidelines to use when using volume analysis.

- Increasing volume in a rising price environment signals excessive buying pressure and could lead to substantial advances.

- Increasing volume in a falling price environment might signal a continual fall in prices or a prolonged bearish trend.
- Decreasing volume in a rising price environment may indicate a plateau and can be used to predict a reversal. Especially when prices make a higher high such as occurs with divergence patterns, a decline in volume with a rise in prices is extremely bearish.
- Decreasing volume in a weaker price environment shows that fresh sellers are reluctant to enter the market and could be a sign of a trend reversal.
- Excessive volume in a high price environment indicates that traders are selling into strength and often creates a price ceiling.
- Excessively low volume in a low price environment indicates that traders are buying on weakness and often creates a floor of support.

I want you to study the chart in Figure 1.13; it shows the trends that occurred in the Japanese yen futures contract. If you recall, earlier in the book, I gave an example of the confusing aspect of the quotation of yen futures contracts versus spot forex contracts. Figure 1.13 shows what I was referring to. The futures contracts are quoted yen to dollar, FX is quoted dollar to yen. Let's go over how to interpret the data, and then I will explain

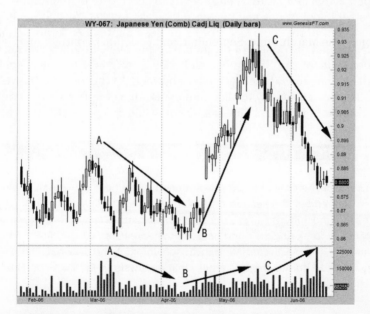

FIGURE 1.13 Japanese Yen Trends (daily bars)
Used with permission of GenesisFT.com.

how you will apply that information to the forex market. Looking at the chart from left to right, the first trend (point A) condition is down. The corresponding volume levels are also trending lower. This indicates that, with the decreasing volume in the weakening price environment, new sellers are reluctant to enter the market and that a reversal is imminent. As the market bottoms in late April (point B), the sharp price increase is followed with a rise in volume, indicating prices can sustain an advance. Finally, when the high of the move has formed (point C), it is made with a large bearish engulfing candle pattern. The trend reverses as sellers enter the market and longs liquidate their positions. Notice that this new downtrend is on increasing or rising volume, which alerts you that a substantial move is in the works.

Two Flaws in Volume

As with life or any aspect of trading, nothing is perfect. Collecting and analyzing volume is no exception, especially in the futures markets. The first flaw is that the data is delayed by one day. You can get real-time tick volume, which shows how many times a price level was traded, but not real-time contract size volume; the exchanges do not post this information until the following day. There is a huge difference in the two concepts. The second flaw is that as a futures contract month gets closer to expiration, it converges with spot prices and becomes the cash market. At that point, it no longer is a "futures" contract. For example, a September futures contract expires around the middle of the month by late August traders moving their positions out of the September and rolling over into the next contract month, which would be a December contract. As this occurs, the volume levels start to artificially decline in one month as the further-out contract month starts to increase. This can be confusing and generate false signals.

 HOT TIP

Stay ahead of the crowd! I have a solution and can help you possibly beat the system! Remember the section on the currency ETFs? They trade in real time; they track almost identically to the spot currency markets (perhaps even better compared to forex dealers); and because they are listed on the New York Stock Exchange, they report real-time transaction volume! The drawback here is that they only trade during the U.S. equity market session—9:30 A.M. (EST) to 4:00 P.M. (EST).

Let's examine this principle of using volume analysis from the euro ETF (FXE) versus the futures market, which is shown in Figure 1.14. The

FIGURE 1.14   Euro Currency Trust (daily bars)
Used with permission of GenesisFT.com.

first thing that should pop out at you is the fact that the ranges of each bar
(or, in this chart, the candles) are comparatively smaller than the ones in
Figure 1.15, which is a spot forex euro currency. This is because the euro
ETF only trades during the U.S. equity market session. However, if you
compare the price points as shown at point A and point B on both charts,
you will see that the lows and the highs are almost exactly the same. The
volume analysis is easily tracked, and you do not have to account for the
rollover effect that exists in the futures markets. This is a continuous market. You can easily see where the market declines in price on declining volume; and as a reversal forms into an uptrend, it is accompanied with an
increase in volume. This again is a very healthy sign that the trend may
maintain more upward momentum. The increase in volume helps amplify
the magnitude of an increase in the value of the euro.

Armed with this information, you can make better decisions for staying
on the long side of the market if you are a day trader. As a swing trader, you
may wish to exploit the potential for a serious price advance. If you are a
position trader, you can develop a solid trading plan with various choices in
strategies or trading vehicles.

Figure 1.15 shows that at point A, we broke below a previous swing
low. Some traders may have looked at that as a sign of continuing weakness
in prices. However, with the aid of volume analysis, the price decline was

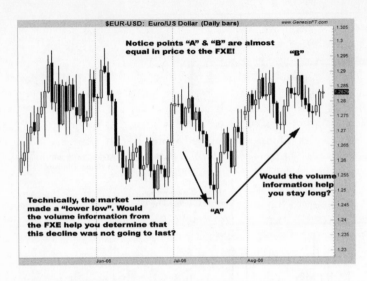

FIGURE 1.15   Euro/U.S. Dollar (daily bars)
Used with permission of GenesisFT.com.

on sharply declining volume. That was indicating that sellers were running out of steam and that a price reversal was imminent. The very low marked by point A shows a very strong reversal engulfing/piercing candle pattern. That was a confirming clue that the price decline had ended. If you have knowledge on the technical analysis theory and combine the use of several indicators, such as price and volume studies, you will increase your probability of success.

Open Interest

Open interest reveals the total amount of open positions that are outstanding and are not offset or delivered on. Remember that in futures trading, this is a zero-sum game: For every long, there is a short; or for every buyer, there is a seller. The open interest figure represents the longs or the shorts, but not the total of both. So when examining open interest, the general guidelines are that when prices rise and open interest increases, this reveals that more new longs have entered the market and more new money is flowing into the market. This reflects why the price increases. Of course, the exact opposite is true in a declining market. Chartists combine both the price movement and the data from volume and open interest to evaluate the condition of the market. If there is a price increase on strong volume and open interest increases, then this is a signal that there could be a continued trend advance. The opposite is true for a bear market when prices decline. Also, if prices increase, volume stays relatively flat or little changed, and open interest declines; this then reflects a weakening market condition. This is considered to be a bearish situation because if open interest is declining and prices are rising, then this shows that shorts are covering by buying back their positions rather than new longs entering the market. That would give a trader a clue that there is a potential trend reversal coming. Here is a guide as to how to identify an opportunity when there is a major top or bottom in the spot forex markets using this information: When observing a continued *long-term* trend in a spot forex currency in order to spot a *climaxing market condition* or reversal of the trend, whether it is in an uptrend or a downtrend, clues to watch for:

- Prices start to fluctuate with wider-than-normal daily price swings or ranges, or are in an extremely volatile condition.
- Prices move against the trend accompanies unusually strong volume and a decline in open interest.

The market is getting ready to turn or reverse the trend.

In Figure 1.16, the graph is a futures euro contract with the volume and open interest study. The bar graph represents the volume with the open interest overlaid by plotting a line measurement.

Notice after the peak in prices, the volume started to dry up (decline).

FIGURE 1.16 Euro (daily bars)
Used with permission of GenesisFT.com.

Open interest started to decline confirming a top was in place. This was a warning that a trend reversal was forming rather than a small correction. Therefore, spot forex traders would more clearly recognize that selling rallies and/or looking to take sell signals at resistance would be a more fruitful and profitable course of action, due to the bearish volume and open interest signals that the futures markets provided.

INSIDER TRADING INFORMATION: *COMMITMENTS OF TRADERS* REPORT

There is one more piece of information that spot forex currency traders can "borrow" from the futures industry; it is the Weekly Commodity Futures Trading Commission's *Commitments of Traders* report. The primary purpose for this report is to monitor trading activity and to have a tight surveillance program in order to identify situations that might pose a threat of a market or price manipulation and, therefore, allow traders to take appropriate action.

The CFTC market surveillance staff closely monitors trading activity in the futures markets in order to detect and prevent instances of potential price manipulation. Some consider this "insider trading" information because every week we get to take a look at which investor group is taking which side of a trade. There are many studies and books written on the subject. (Larry Williams was a pioneer on the subject. Also, it was covered in my first book *A Complete Guide to Technical Trading Tactics* (Wiley, 2004), on pages 162–165.) As a veteran trader for over 26 years, I have used this information to capture many significant moves in the markets. In the sample shown in the table in Figure 1.17, there are several categories. The first is the Non-commercial, which lists all large professional traders or entities, such as hedge funds, commodity trading advisers, commodity pool operators, and locals on and off the exchange floors. It includes any trading entity that hits a reportable position limit; for instance, in the CME, in 2006, the limit for currencies was 400 contracts.

The next category of importance is the Commercials, which includes banks and institutions or multinational conglomerate corporations looking to hedge a cash position. The long and short open interest shown as Nonreportable positions is derived by subtracting total long and short reportable positions from the total open interest. Accordingly, for Nonreportable Positions, the number of traders involved and the Commercial/ Non-commercial classification of each trader are unknown. This balance of positions is assumed to be the small speculators. If you look at the first column under Non-commercials, you see the breakdown of how many long po-

CFTC Commitments of Traders Report - CME (Futures Only)

```
BRITISH POUND STERLING - CHICAGO MERCANTILE EXCHANGE              Code-096742
FUTURES ONLY POSITIONS AS OF 04/11/06                   |
------------------------------------------------------------| NONREPORTABLE
       NON-COMMERCIAL     |   COMMERCIAL    |    TOTAL      |   POSITIONS
----------------------------|-----------------|-----------------|----------------
 LONG  | SHORT  |SPREADS |  LONG  | SHORT  |  LONG  | SHORT  |  LONG  | SHORT
-------------------------------------------------------------------------
(CONTRACTS OF 62,500 POUNDS STERLING)                  OPEN INTEREST:      79,127
COMMITMENTS
 16,971   22,595        0   42,536   37,687   59,507   60,282   19,620   18,845

CHANGES FROM 04/04/06 (CHANGE IN OPEN INTEREST:         -244)
  2,956   -2,104        0   -6,352    5,470   -3,396    3,366    3,152   -3,610

PERCENT OF OPEN INTEREST FOR EACH CATEGORY OF TRADERS
   21.4     28.6      0.0     53.8     47.6     75.2     76.2     24.8     23.8

NUMBER OF TRADERS IN EACH CATEGORY (TOTAL TRADERS:       64)
     17       19        0       16       17       33       36
```

FIGURE 1.17   CFTC *Commitments of Traders* Report—CME (futures only)

sitions versus short positions are held. The next line shows the changes from the prior week; this is important information because you will be able to see if these guys unloaded some of their positions or added to them from one week to the next. The line under that tells you what percentage of long and shorts is held, and the last line shows how many traders control longs or shorts. The information is gathered as of the close of business every Tuesday by each of the clearing brokerage firms and is turned over to exchange officials, who then report the information over to the regulatory body know as the CFTC. This information is released on Friday afternoons at 3:30 P.M. (EST). Before acting on a decision based on this information, it is critical to know if there was a major price swing from Tuesday's close to the time the information was released because positions may have changed hands.

CAN YOU MAKE MONEY FROM THIS INFORMATION?

There is always a chance to make money; the key is to be able to afford not to be too heavily leveraged if the market moves further than anticipated. This report is like an insider information report. It acts like a true consensus of who literally "owns" the market. A forex trader can use this data to determine if market participants are too heavily positioned on one side of the market in a long-term trend run. It is generally the small speculator who is left holding the bag. I mean, let's face it, money moves the market;

and the banks and large professional traders are a bit savvier when it comes to their business. After all, one would think a bank has a good idea of the direction interest rates are going to go in once a central bank meeting occurs, right?

Suppose the small speculators are showing a nice short position of, say, at least two longs for every one short. If the Non-commercials are net long and the Commercials are net long, chances are that the small speculators will be wrong. I am looking for imbalances in markets that have been in a trending market condition for quite some time, and therefore I can develop a game plan and start looking for timing clues to enter trades accordingly. Keep in mind that the Commercials can and sometimes are not right; they are not in the market to time market turns. They are hedging their risk exposure in a cash position. Therefore, the Non-commercials, or professional speculators, in the short term are considered the smart money. Here are some general guidelines to follow:

- If Non-commercials are net long, Commercials are net long, and the Nonreportable Positions category is net short by at least a two-to-one margin, look at buying opportunities. In other words, go with the pros.
- If Non-commercials are net short, Commercials are net short, and the Nonreportable Positions are net long by at least a two-to-one margin, look at selling opportunities.
- If Non-commercials are net long, Commercials are net short, and Nonreportable Positions are neutral, meaning not heavily net long or short, look at buying opportunities. Stick with the smart money, the bank and institutions category.

Let's put the theories to the test combining volume with the *Commitments of Traders* data by studying the chart in Figure 1.18. This is the British pound futures contract; the chart pattern resembles a rounding bottom or an inverted head-and-shoulders formation (both of which we will cover in the following chapters). The CFTC report was released on the close of business on April 14, 2006. With the information at hand, we can determine that the Commercials (banks and institutions) were net long the market, the large speculative Non-commercials were net short, and the Nonreportable small speculators were net long. Granted, these are not heavily weighed numbers—we don't see a tremendous imbalance like a two-to-one ratio of net shorts versus net long in the small speculator category—but we do see a two-thirds grouping of net longs led by the Commercials and the Nonreportable small speculators. The Non-commercials are the only ones net short and needing to buy back their shorts. If we integrate our newfound knowledge of using volume studies, we can determine that prices are rising with an increase in volume. This signals a

FIGURE 1.18   British pound (daily bars)
Used with permission of GenesisFT.com.

healthy market condition for the bulls. It signals that buyers are entering the market, not just a small short covering rally. In early May, we see a small consolidation pattern called an ascending triangle form; and as prices break out to the upside, the volume levels are increasing as well, indicating continued strength and a strong bullish trend.

Now let's look at the spot forex market as shown in Figure 1.19. Examining the low in April, a candle shows a hammer pattern that formed in both the spot forex and the futures markets. Then, taking the information from the CFTC *COT* report released on that Friday, we know Commercials were net long. In addition, we see the increase in volume, as shown in the futures chart in Figure 1.16. This helped clearly identify that higher prices were accompanied with rising volume. This is a very healthy sign that a major price move could be underway. Here is an example of where digesting the information on volume with *COT* data could help you make the decision to diversify your trading approach with a long-term position. From what we have covered in this chapter, you could go long an outright spot forex British pound or could enter in a mini-lot position. You could use a futures option strategy or could invest in the British pound ETF (FXB). Several techniques that we will go over in this book are trend-line breakouts from wedge patterns and the Defcon III trading signals that alert to long entry as indicated with the little triangles shown in Figure 1.19. The

FIGURE 1.19   British pounds/U.S. Dollar (daily bars)
Used with permission of GenesisFT.com.

factual data revealed in the CFTC *COT* report is tremendously important information; and, best of all, it is easy to access and free.

IMPORTANT WEB SITE INFORMATION

To access the CFTC *COT* reports, go to this link:
http://www.nationalfutures.com/CFTC_Reports.htm

CHAPTER 2

Pivot Point Analysis, Filtering Methods, and Moving Averages

T his chapter describes in full detail the principles behind the mathematical calculations that determine pivot point support and resistance levels, as well as the rationale behind the psychological impact that drives traders to make decisions around these levels. I break the chapter into separate sections to explain how pivot point analysis can be applied for short- and long-term trading and how it specifically applies to the spot forex market. Each investment vehicle has its own nuances, such as trading session hours, time periods in which volume flows change, contract sizes, and decimal-point placement so that you know how to correctly calculate the pivot point levels. First, you need to know the foundation of the methodology of pivot point analysis so you can apply it to the specific markets of interest that you are trading. My goal is to inform you how to:

- Predict price ranges in a given time period.
- Use the pivot point as a moving average.
- Build a trading system based on the pivot point.

The power in using pivot point analysis is that the strategy works in all markets that have established ranges, based on significant volume or on a large group of collective participants. After all, the current market price equals the collective action of buyers and sellers. Pivot point analysis is a robust, time-tested, and, best of all, testable form of market analysis. This means that you can back-test to see the accuracy of this trader's tool's predictive analysis. The really unbelievable aspect of pivots is who uses them.

However, many novice traders feel compelled not to learn about them because they seem complicated. I will dispel that myth.

PIVOT POINT ANALYSIS

This is the best "right side" of the chart indicator, as I like to call it, due to its predictive accuracy. Pivot points are based on a mathematical formula originally developed by Henry Wheeler Chase in the 1930s. Chester W. Keltner used part of the formula to develop the Keltner Bands as described in his book, *How to Make Money in Commodities* (Keltner Statistical Service, 1960).

However, it was really Larry Williams who was credited with repopularizing the analysis in his book *How I Made One Million Dollars . . . Last Year . . . Trading Commodities* (Windsor Books, 1979). Don Lambert, the creator of the Commodity Channel Indicator (CCI) uses the pivot point formula that makes the CCI work.

In my first book, *A Complete Guide to Technical Trading Tactics* (Wiley, 2004), I illustrated many trading methods that one can apply using pivot point analysis combined with candlestick patterns, including the advantage of trading using multiple time frames, or what is know as a confluence of various target levels based on different time periods. This chapter will highlight those techniques as well as explain how to incorporate the pivot point as a *moving average* trading system and how to filter out and narrow the field of the respective support and resistance numbers and will divulge various formulas that are popular today.

As I said, pivot points are a mathematical formula designed to determine the next time period's range based on the previous time period's data, which includes, the high, the low, and the close or settlement price. One reason why I believe in using these variables from a given time period's range is that it reflects all market participants' collective perception of value for that time period. The *range*, which is the high and the low of a given time period, accurately reflects all market participants' exuberant bullishness and pessimistic bearishness for that trading session. The high and the low of a given period are certainly important, as they mirror human emotional behavior. Also, the high is a reference point for those who bought out of greed, thinking that they were missing an opportunity. They certainly won't forget how much they lost and how the market reacted as it declined from that level.

The opposite is true for those who sold the low of a given session out of fear they would lose more by staying in a long trade; they certainly will respect that price the next time the market trades back at that level, too. So the high and the low are important reference points. With that said, the pivot point calculations incorporate the three most important elements of the previous time period: the high (H), the low (L), and, of course, the close (C) of a given trading session. First, let me give you the actual mathematical calculations, and then I will go over what each level represents.

- Pivot point—the sum of the high, the low, and the close divided by three.

$$P = (H + L + C)/3$$

- Resistance 2 (R-2)—pivot point number plus the high minus the low.

$$R\text{-}2 = P + H - L$$

- Resistance 1 (R-1)—pivot point number times two minus the low.

$$R\text{-}1 = (P \times 2) - L$$

- Support 1 (S-1)—pivot point number times two minus the high.

$$S\text{-}1 = (P \times 2) - H$$

- Support 2 (S-2)—pivot point number minus the high plus the low.

$$S\text{-}2 = P - H + L$$

Some analysts are adding a third level to their pivot calculations to help target extreme price swings that have occurred on certain occasions, such as a price shock resulting from a news event. I have noticed that the spot forex currency markets tend to experience a double dose of price shocks because they are exposed to foreign economic developments and U.S. economic developments that pertain to a specific country's currency. This tends to make wide trading ranges. Therefore, a third level of projected support and resistance was calculated.

- Resistance 3 (R-3)—the high plus two times (the pivot minus the low)

$$R\text{-}3 = H + 2 \times (P - L)$$

- Support 3—the low minus two times (the high minus the pivot)

$$S\text{-}3 = L - 2 \times (H - P)$$

or

$$R\text{-}3 = P - S\text{-}2 + R\text{-}1$$

$$S\text{-}3 = P - R\text{-}2 - S\text{-}1$$

There are other variations that include adding the opening range, which, in this case, would involve simply taking the sum of the high, the low, and the open, and the close and dividing by four to derive the actual pivot point.

$$P = (O + H + L + C)/4$$

Since there is no formal closing and opening range, forex traders can use the N.Y. bank settlement as the close at 5 P.M. (EST) and assign the next day's session open as 5:05 P.M. (EST).

The following list shows what these numbers represent, how price action reacts with these projected target levels, how the numbers would break down by order, what typically occurs, and how the market can behave at these levels. Keep in mind that this is a general description, and we will learn what to look for at these price points to spot reversals in order to make money. I must stress that it is important to look at the progressively higher time period's price support or resistance projections; for example, from the daily numbers, look at the weekly figures; and then from the weekly numbers, look at the monthly numbers. The longer the time frame, the more important or significant are the data. Also, it is rare that the daily numbers trade beyond the extreme R-2 or S-2 numbers; and when the market does, it is generally in a strong trending condition. In this case, we have methods to follow the market's flow, and we will cover them in more detail in the next few chapters. Remember, pivot point analysis is used as a guide; these numbers are not the holy grail. By focusing on just a few select numbers and learning how to filter out excess information, I eliminate the analysis paralysis from information overload.

- *Resistance Level 3*—This is the extreme bullish market condition generally created by news-driven price shocks. The market is at an overbought condition and may offer a day trader a quick reversal scalp trade.
- *Resistance Level 2*—This is the bullish market price objective or target high number for a trading session. It generally establishes the high of a given time period. The market often sees significant resistance at this price level and will provide an exit target for long positions.
- *Resistance Level 1*—This is the mild bullish to bearish projected high target number. In low-volume or light-volatility sessions or in consolidating trading periods, this often acts as the high of a given session. In a bearish market condition, prices will try to come close to this level but most times will fail.
- *Pivot Point*—This is the focal price level or the mean, which is derived from the collective market data from the prior session's high, low, and

close. It is the strongest of the support and resistance numbers. Prices normally trade above or below this area before breaking in one direction or the other. As a general guideline, if the market opens above the primary pivot be a buyer on dips. If the market opens below this level, look to sell rallies.

- *Support Level 1*—This is the mild bearish to bullish projected low target number in light-volume or low-volatility sessions or in consolidating trading periods. Prices tend to reverse at or near this level in bullish market conditions but most times fall short of hitting this number.
- *Support Level 2*—This is the bearish market price objective or targeted low number. The market often sees significant support at or near this level in a bearish market condition. This level is a likely target level to cover shorts.
- *Support Level 3*—In an extremely bearish market condition, this level will act as the projected target low or support area. A price decline to this level is generally created by news-driven price shocks. This is where a market is at an oversold condition and may offer a day trader a quick reversal scalp trade.

Weekly and monthly time frames can and should be utilized as well as the daily numbers you may be used to or have heard about in the past. To understand how price moves within the pivots, begin by breaking down the time frames from longer term to shorter term. As traders, we should begin with a monthly time frame, where there is a price range or an established high or low for a given period. This range, with its price points, is what we as traders should be looking for. Here is how I utilize the range in my research. There are approximately 22 business days, or about 4 weeks, in each month. Every month there will be an established range—a high and a low. There are typically five trading days in a week. Now consider that in one day of one week in one month, a high and a low will be made. It is likely that this high and low may be made in a minute or within one hour of a given day of a given week of that month. That is why longer-term time frames, such as monthly or weekly, should be included in your market analysis. In the world of 24-hour trading, the most popular question I get from those studying and using pivot points is, "What are the times that you derive the high-low-close information?" There are many different people telling many different stories. Here is what I do and what seems to work the best for me. For starters, just keep things simple, and apply some good old-fashioned common sense. If the exchanges and the banking system use a specific time to settle a market, then that is the time period that should be considered for a "close." They should know those are the rules that make money move. I want to follow the money flow and be on the same time schedule as the banks and institutions, so here are a few pointers:

- Use the 5 P.M. (EST), New York bank settlement close to determine pivots.
- For the weekly calculations, take the open from Sunday night's session and use the close on Friday.
- For the monthly calculations, take the opening of the first day of the month and the close from the last day of the month.

Which Method Is Better? You Decide!

In Figure 2.1, we have a good representation of how the R-3 down to the S-3 levels would line up based on a previous session's high, low, and close data. Included are where the midpoint numbers would line up. As you can see, this presents 13 price points to monitor. For most traders, including myself, this is simply information overload. Using these 13 levels for each day, week, and month would put 39 trading support and resistance numbers on your chart for each trading day. This much data to process may cause analysis paralysis. Granted, you may be right in stating you picked the top or the bottom of each trading session, but it is impractical or highly unlikely that you can trade effectively using that information. I am not saying that at times it may help having the midpoints or R-3 or S-3 target levels in front of you; but I believe in keeping things simple and less is better.

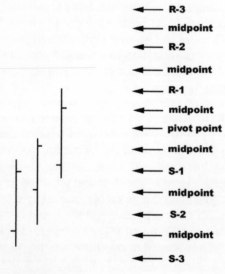

FIGURE 2.1

Figure 2.2 shows a spot FX euro/U.S. dollar with only the daily support and resistance levels from R-3 down to S-3, including the pivot point (PP) and the pivot point moving average (MA). Imagine adding the weekly and monthly numbers. No wonder new traders have a hard time using pivot point support and resistance lines. There is so much information that it can cause confusion and analysis paralysis. In addition, most of these levels will not come into play for you to trade off in any given time period, so wouldn't it be better to have a filtering method to cut the excess information off of this screen? That is exactly what this chapter will explain.

Here is how I personally use pivot point analysis with my filtering method, which effectively helps me narrow the field down to select either the high and/or the low of a given trading session. Sometimes this works to project both the high and the low consistently with amazing accuracy. Look at Figure 2.3, and you will see the same market with my filtering method automatically calculating the projected target resistance and support numbers with the moving average and the actual pivot point. The only difference here is that I narrowed the chart to include the prior few days' sessions so that you can see how the market almost fits the projected support and resistance numbers, which are automatically calculated and displayed on the charts each day.

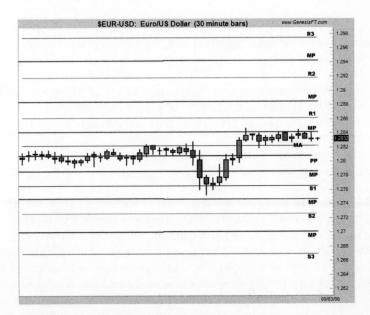

FIGURE 2.2 Euro/U.S. Dollar (30-minute bars)
Used with permission of GenesisFT.com.

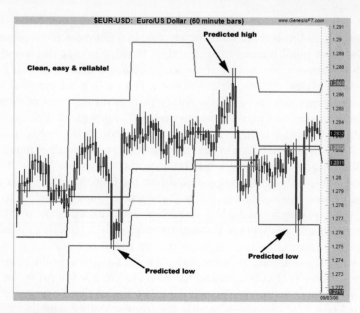

FIGURE 2.3   Euro/U.S. Dollar (60-minute bars)
Used with permission of GenesisFT.com.

I believe in keeping things simple because trading requires split-second decisions. Therefore, it is important not to be burdened with information overload. Remember:

- Pivot point calculations help determine when to enter/exit positions.
- Pivot points help as leading price indicators for traders.
- Pivot points are used to project support and resistance or actual highs and lows of trading sessions.
- Pivot points help confirm other technical methods.
- Daily, weekly, and monthly time frames should and can be used.

Remember these issues: In every week, there are five trading days. In every month, there will be an established range, in other words, a high and a low. In one day of one week in one month, a high and a low will be made. It is likely that the high and the low may be made in a minute or an hour of a given day of a given week in that month; that is why longer-term time frames, such as a monthly or weekly analysis, should be used. Pivot point analysis relies on specific time frames in determining support and resistance levels for that timing element only and infers that the analysis or calculations for the prior day will not be applicable *in most cases* two, three, or four days later. The same principle goes for the weekly and monthly calculations; so at the end of that time period, new data must be recalculated.

Filtering the Numbers

- Take the R-1 and the S-1 initially from all time frames for your analysis, especially in low-volume consolidating trading sessions.
- The pivot point can be used as an actual trading number in determining the high or the low of a given time period, especially in strong bull or bear market conditions.
- In a bearish market, the highs should be lower and the lows should be lower. In this case I use the actual pivot point up to the R-1 for resistance and the S-2 for support targets.
- In a bullish market, the highs should be higher and the lows may be higher than those for the preceding time period. I use S-1 up to the pivot point and the R-2 for targeting the potential trading range.

 IMPORTANT TIP

When using the pivot point numbers, watch out for the prior time periods that have had unusually small ranges (narrow-range days). These sessions will project smaller ranges for support and resistance numbers for the next time frame. Therefore, be aware of potential breakouts of those narrow-range target numbers. In this situation, you want to monitor the next-higher time frames, such as weekly or monthly numbers. The opposite is true on unusually wide-range days; the calculations will give you exaggerated support and resistance numbers. In this situation, watch for the market to be contained between the R-1 and the S-1 for the next trading session.

If in a given trading day the market goes through my daily target numbers, the importance of the weekly and even monthly numbers is what gives me an indicator for the next major target levels of support and resistance. I use the actual pivot point for many things; for example, it is important to understand that it can be used as an actual trading number in determining the high or the low of a given time period, especially in strong bull or bear market conditions. In an extremely bullish market condition, the pivot point can become the target low for the trading session. This number represents the true value of a prior session. In an uptrending market, if the market gaps higher above the pivot point, then a retracement back to the pivot will attract buyers. Until that pivot point is broken by prices trading below that level, traders will step in and buy the pullback. The opposite is true in an extremely bearish market condition; the pivot point will act as the target high for the session.

If a news-driven event causes the market to gap lower after traders take time interpreting the information and the news, generally prices come back up to test the pivot point. If the market fails to break that level and trade higher, sellers will take action and start pressing the market lower again. Technically speaking, in a bearish market, the highs should be lower and the lows should be lower than in the preceding time frame. If they are, then to help me filter out unnecessary information or excessive support and resistance numbers on my charts, I use the actual pivot point up to the R-1 number for resistance; and then I target the S-2 for the potential low or for that time period's trading range.

As you can see in Figure 2.4, if I determine that the market is bearish and if I understand the relationship of the geometric distance of the resistance and support targets, I can eliminate the R-2 number, since in a bearish environment we should see a lower high. If I am looking for a lower low, then I can eliminate the S-1 support number as well; and now I have reduced the field to just three numbers. If I apply the same methodology on a daily, a weekly, and a monthly chart now, instead of 39 numbers, I am now working with just 9 numbers. Once again, I am not using the numbers to place orders ahead of time (even though you could); I use the numbers as a guide.

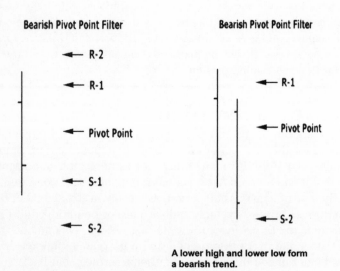

A lower high and lower low form
a bearish trend.

FIGURE 2.4 Bearish Pivot Point Filters

These numbers work very well and often act as a self-fulfilling prophecy because so many institutions and professional traders use them. Many have different-size positions on; and some traders may not wait for the exact number to hit and may start scaling out of positions (as I do), and as you should also. With this method, you can use these numbers as exit areas on your trades. As Figure 2.5 depicts, in a bullish market environment, by definition, you may agree that the highs should be higher and the lows should be higher than those of the preceding time period. When I have determined that we are in a bullish trend, I target the S-1 up to the pivot point for the low of the session and the R-2 for targeting the high; and that will give me an idea of what the potential trading range will be.

When the market goes through the projected daily target numbers, I then use the next time periods to give me the next reliable price objective. That is where the significance of the weekly and monthly numbers comes into play.

There are several methods to use to help determine whether a market is bullish, bearish, or neutral. One method is an open/close indicator. If after a prolonged uptrend prices close below the open (black candles: C < O) after at least two or three consecutive sessions, and there is a close below prior lows, then you will know the market internals have switched from bullish to bearish or from uptrend to a consolidation phase. Therefore, you could choose the R-1 to the pivot point to target the high of the next session down to the S-2 number.

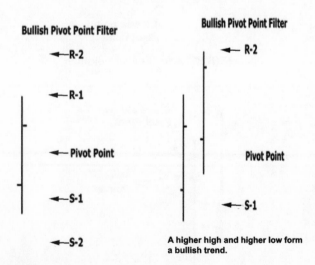

FIGURE 2.5 Bullish Pivot Point Filters

Another method, which is more in line with my moving average methodology, is if on a daily, weekly, or monthly time period, the close is below the prior time period's close and if the current close is below the open and closes below the pivot point, then the next time period should be considered as a bearish trading session. In Figure 2.6, the square boxes represent the value of that time period's pivot points.

If the market closes below the session's open, below the prior session's close, and below the pivot point, then the next time period would be considered a bearish trading session. In this case, I would consider the next time period's pivot point up to the R-1 for a targeted high and the S-2 for a targeted low.

The opposite would be true for a bullish consideration. In Figure 2.7, if the market closed above the open, above the prior session's close, and above the pivot point, then I would target the next trading session range from the S-1 up to the pivot point to the R-2 resistance target level.

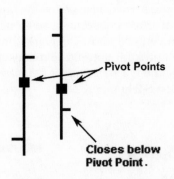

FIGURE 2.6　Bearish Indication

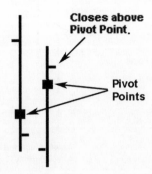

FIGURE 2.7　Bullish Indication

77

The Advantage of Confluence

Time is an essential element in trading. Many times, traders are correct in their predictions for a top or a bottom in a market; but their timing is off, which results in a loss. Many analysts were calling for a top or for the bubble to burst in the stock market in 1999. In that situation, not demonstrating patience would have resulted in dramatic loss of profit potential or, worse, actual losses due to selling short tech stocks too early. How about economists' predictions of a housing bubble back in 2004 and their expectations for a decline in real estate prices? As of February 2006, that has not happened. I can go on and on about examples when prognostications were correct but timing was wrong, resulting in a financial loss. As I stated earlier, pivot point analysis relies on both time and price specifics in its calculations to project future support and resistance levels.

By incorporating various time frames, such as daily, weekly, and monthly price data, the trader can take advantage of price areas that coincide with the different time periods. These price clusters will repel the market's advance in an uptrend or act as support by causing prices to reverse in a downtrend. This clustering or confluence of more than one time period is an awesome event and can translate into a very lucrative setup. The more confluences or corroborating numbers there are that target a general area, the more significance there is for that specific targeted price level. Pivot calculations work to pinpoint almost exact times and prices for trades in various markets and can be used to validate other analyses. Remember this phrase: "There is always strength in numbers!" When several pivot numbers line up, there is a great potential for a reaction from these levels. This knowledge, combined with identification of the shift in momentum by recognizing and acting on strong triggers, increases the probability of a successful trade. One reason for using various time periods (day, week, month) for your pivot point analysis is that it incorporates and reflects three different groups of traders: short-term day traders, intermediate-term swing traders, and long-term position traders, who are generally higher-capitalized, trend-following hedge funds.

Figure 2.8 shows the daily, weekly, and monthly pivot point numbers drawn across the chart; this gives a trader the heads-up that the market may reach an unsustainable extreme or oversold market condition. Just by looking at the graph, one can see that the market has been in a prolonged downtrend. Generally, the market may stop its descent at a confluence support zone, and then you would want to wait for a shift in momentum to trade a potential price reversal. As the market starts to give clues that a bottom is near, you can determine a low-risk entry since a bottom has been defined. What would not be known is how high the market's reaction will be from this target level of support. This is where the section on candle

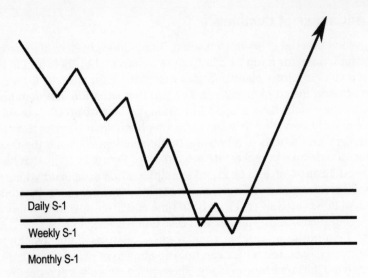

Daily S-1

Weekly S-1

Monthly S-1

FIGURE 2.8 Confluence of Pivot Support

charts will play an important role in helping to determine the strength of the trend reversal.

Let's examine the chart in Figure 2.9, which is a 60-minute chart from July 19, 2006, on the spot forex euro currency versus the U.S. dollar. The monthly S-1 target low was 125.16, the weekly S-2 lined up in close proximity at 125.01, and the daily S-1 was 124.63.

The actual low was 124.55! Looking at the market's reaction, we see a strong value area in which the market embarked on a stellar rally. The confluence of pivot support numbers gave one of the best and only predictive support targets. Therefore, it should be noted that the longer-term numbers should be watched carefully for clues not only for trading opportunities to enter positions, but also as a warning that the current trend could be exhausted and potentially reverse. At the very least, even though you may not have established a long position, you certainly would have been alerted not to sell short at the lows or at this confluence of pivot support target numbers.

I want to dissect this trade a bit further and switch to a daily chart to show you when, at times, you can implement these confluences with candle chart patterns and milk what might turn out to be a simple day trade into a nice swing trade. Figure 2.10 zooms in on the low that occurs on that Wednesday, July 19, 2006, when the daily chart shows the euro took off in a three-day run. July 21, 2006, was a Friday; so as a trader, if you can learn to spot these high-probability value areas or confluence of pivot point support targets, more times than not, when you have a secondary confirming

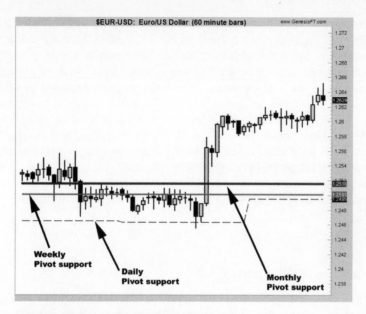

FIGURE 2.9   Confluence of Pivot Support
Used with permission of GenesisFT.com.

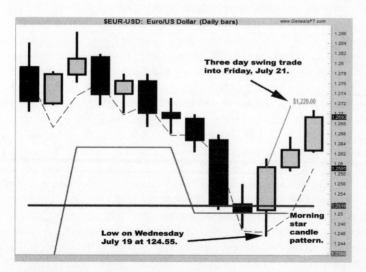

FIGURE 2.10   Profiting from Confluences
Used with permission of GenesisFT.com.

element (such as the three-candle pattern like the morning star formation), you can milk a trade for more than you think by letting the trade mature and following along with the position. Trailing your stop-loss or stop-profit orders and setting either a profit target or a time target (such as exiting the trade before Friday's close so as not to leave yourself exposed to surprise risks through the weekend), will get you ahead of the game as these lineups occur. If you bought to go long on the close on July 19 or on the open, which would be considered 5:05 P.M. (EST) on Thursday, and then by holding that trade until Friday's close, which is approximately 5:00 P.M. (EST). By identifying longer-term time period pivot support targets that are in play, you can determine that there could be more room for prices to appreciate. By monitoring the positions and managing the trade with trailing stop techniques, you can let these trades "breathe" or allow to mature into big trend plays, which is where you really can rack up some juicy profits.

Confluences Work at Tops

We have all heard in the field of technical analysis that what works for some patterns or signals is not applicable for all situations. However, the power of pivot point confluences does work at market tops and also works to indicate bottom reversals, as we just went over. In the illustration in Figure 2.11, once again the three main time periods that we use are the monthly, the weekly, and the daily. When a congestion of pivot point numbers line up or congest at or near a specific price zone, this should heighten your awareness for possible reversals. It is important to note that if a market has been in a long uptrend, say more than two months, and if we are close to the end of the quarter, the market is ripe for a profit-taking correction. Generally speaking, portfolio managers trading managed funds receive payment by a performance fee (profits) at the end of a quarter. Since many of these large trading entities use pivot analysis or are aware that others use them, when a confluence of resistance develops especially near the end of a quarter, watch out below. It not only marks a prime opportunity for the market to react off that resistance level, but there is also a specific timing reason why a profit-taking correction can occur then. The same holds true for bottoms. After a long price decline, if the numbers line up and if it is near the end of a quarter, a profit-taking reversal could be in the works. That does not mean to say the original trend won't resume, but you could take a great countertrend reversal trade. Generally speaking, market sell-offs have more velocity than market rallies do. Therefore, spotting resistance confluences can be very lucrative opportunities, under the right circumstances.

I just explained the phrase "There is always strength in numbers." The concept can be explained further in that there is a strong analytical value

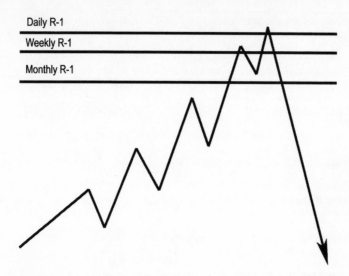

Daily R-1

Weekly R-1

Monthly R-1

FIGURE 2.11 Strength in Numbers: Confluence of Resistance Levels

found in the number three, not just in trading and technical analysis but also in our universe.

As you may be aware, the number three is found as a Fibonacci number. (If you are not familiar with Fibonacci analysis, it is fully described in Chapter 6.) When I look at confluences in the three different time periods, it represents the three different groups of traders. The daily numbers are used by day traders, the weekly numbers are used by swing traders, and the monthly numbers are used by longer-term position traders and institutions. The coincidental factor arrives from the fact that one set of numbers from one time frame generally has nothing to do with the others. The range of the past month had different values for the high, the low, and the close than the input values have for the weekly and the daily time frames.

Before I forge ahead and show you how to use the resistance numbers, I want to review one really important and helpful tactic. Recall that in Chapter 1, I stated that forex traders can borrow information from the futures industry. One such piece information is the Commodity Futures Trading Commission (CFTC) *Commitments of Traders (COT)* report. In essence, this report reveals whose hands "control" the market. If you look at Figure 2.12, you will see that the Commercials had built a sizable net short position of nearly 100,000 contracts, and it was the small speculators or the retail traders who were net long the market at the top!

The CFTC report showed that at the end of the trading session on May 30, 2006, the funds, or the Non-commercial category, were long 96,864 con-

```
EURO FX - CHICAGO MERCANTILE EXCHANGE                              Code-099741
FUTURES ONLY POSITIONS AS OF 05/30/06                           |
------------------------------------------------------------| NONREPORTABLE
        NON-COMMERCIAL     |   COMMERCIAL   |    TOTAL     | POSITIONS
------------------------|----------------|--------------|-----------------
  LONG  | SHORT |SPREADS| LONG  | SHORT  | LONG  | SHORT | LONG  | SHORT
-------------------------------------------------------------------------
(CONTRACTS OF 125,000 EUROS)                      OPEN INTEREST:   195,502
COMMITMENTS
 96,864  16,980   1,246  39,005 138,891 137,115 157,117  58,387  38,385

CHANGES FROM 05/23/06 (CHANGE IN OPEN INTEREST:    -2,304)
  9,503   1,695  -1,071 -11,074  -7,173  -2,642  -6,549     338   4,245

PERCENT OF OPEN INTEREST FOR EACH CATEGORY OF TRADERS
  49.5     8.7     0.6    20.0    71.0    70.1    80.4    29.9    19.6

NUMBER OF TRADERS IN EACH CATEGORY (TOTAL TRADERS:    126)
    70      16      14      25      28      99      54
```

FIGURE 2.12   CFTC *Commitments of Traders* Report—CME

tracts and short 16,980. That is a net short position of 79,884 contracts. Each futures contract is $125,000.00 worth of euro currency! The Commercials were long 39,005 contracts and short 138,891 positions. The Nonreportable positions category (small speculators) were long 58,387 contracts and short 38,502 positions. This means that the banks, or smart money, established a protective hedge position in the futures, betting that the spot euro would fall in value against the dollar. The Non-commercial category is considered professional speculators and smart money, too. The difference between these traders and the commercials are that they are speculating and will not generally take delivery of a futures contract. Keep in mind that this data is from the close on May 30, 2006, which was a Tuesday, and was not released until Friday June 2, 2006, at 3:30 P.M. (EST), well before the forex close. The next opening would be considered Sunday night. That leaves plenty of time to examine and digest the information. Now turn your attention to the chart in Figure 2.13 and see how the numbers in the spot forex euro currency line up. Keep in mind that the euro market made a tremendous upward price move from the low of 118.23 on February 27, 2006, until the high was made on June 4, 2006, at 129.79

Examine Figure 2.14 closely. You will see that the monthly R-1 was 130.07, the weekly R-1 was 129.92, the daily pivot R-1 was 129.66. The actual high price was 129.79, a very small margin of error as it relates to the proximity of the predicted pivot resistance level. Here we have a great example of how pivot point analysis pinpointed the exact day of the week in a specific month of the high from which a substantial price break occurred. The

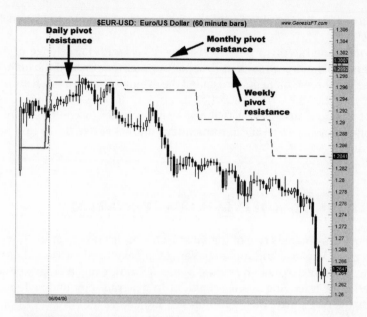

FIGURE 2.13 Pivots Predict a Top
Used with permission of GenesisFT.com.

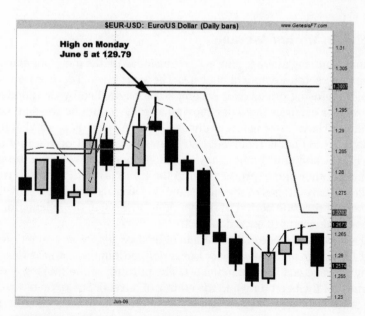

FIGURE 2.14 Market Crashed from Pivot Levels
Used with permission of GenesisFT.com.

euro proceeded to decline further in the month of June to 124.73 on June 23, 2006.

Combining the pivot point resistance levels with knowledge of a few bearish candle patterns such as the shooting star that formed the high, or if you see the three-candle pattern called the evening star formation and combine it with the CFTC *COT* report, you certainly have a strong case to enter a short position. Market tops that align with a cluster or confluence of various pivot points can result in tremendous market reversals, as this example shows.

PIVOT POINT MOVING AVERAGE SYSTEM

The moving average is one of the most widely utilized indicators in technical analysis because the moving average is easy to identify and easy to back-test. Many automated trading systems use moving averages or some derivation of a moving-average method to generate buy and sell signals. Moving averages are considered classic indicators and are very popular with traders today. Most technicians view the moving average as a way to signal a change in the direction of the trend, as well as a way to smooth out the volatility of the market.

The Simple Moving Average

The simple moving average (the arithmetic mean) is the most popular moving average used in technical analysis. The *simple moving average* is the sum of the closing prices over several sessions divided by the number of sessions. For example, a 20-day moving average would be the sum of the preceding 20 days' closing prices divided by 20. As new data is added to the calculation, old data is removed: Each new day would drop the first day's closing price and add the new day's closing price. By averaging the price data, a smoother line is produced, and the trend is much easier to recognize. The disadvantages of the simple moving average are that it only takes into account the time period of the sessions covered in the calculation and it gives equal weight to each day's price.

The moving average is the average of the *closing prices* (sometimes referred to as the *settlement price*) of a defined number of sessions. The moving average is a lagging indicator. The purpose of the moving average is to indicate the beginning and the ending of a trend. Since the moving average follows the market, the signals it generates occur after the trend has already changed.

It has been postulated that most traders lose their money in the markets. If most traders focus on moving-average values that are predetermined by default settings in their charting software packages or that use the media's favorite 200-day moving average, it's no wonder they lose. They are all following the same indicator, and a tremendously lagging indicator at that!

Be Smarter and Faster Than the Next Guy

If you want to make consistent profits, then you need to think and use a different set of values or understand how signals are generated. Also, you do not want to follow and base your trading strategies on what everyone else is looking at to enter or exit positions. So when it comes to moving averages, you want to look at different sets of conditions and time periods. Think for just a minute: If lots of traders are watching for trade signals on 20-, 50-, 100-, or 200-period moving averages, and if it is true that the majority of traders lose money, then why do I want to take trade signals based off those moving-average values? Some traders and technical analysts use various ways to calculate such moving averages as the simple, the weighted, and the exponential. I prefer the simple moving average and a different set of values for my moving average, namely the pivot point. As you will recall, the pivot point calculation provides the mean (average) for the session's trading range ($P = H + L + C/3$).

The moving-average section discusses how the moving average helps clarify the market's price flow by extending price analysis over a certain period of time. In this manner, moving averages can demonstrate when a market enters an extreme condition by how far it departs from the mean. Price action will move toward either the moving average in which it acts as a support or the resistance number. What I use is the combination of the price session information ($H + L + C/3$) known as the pivot point number over a specific period of time (moving average). This value utilizes cumulative data from the high, the low, and the close for a session; and, more important, the information provides a clear picture of the "average true price" for that time period. This moving average value I use is calculated by taking the pivot number from the past three periods. The time frames I use are daily, weekly, and monthly periods. It is important to note, however, that the longer the time frame, the more significance the number will hold. To calculate the market direction number, add three pivot points from the same session and divide by three. The purpose of using the pivot point as a moving-average calculation is that the pivot point gives me a truer sense of market value for a given period in time.

$$\frac{\text{Pivot} + \text{Pivot} + \text{Pivot}}{3}$$

The three-period pivot point moving average can act as a support number in bullish conditions and has a high degree of importance when one of the pivot point calculations for the current session coincides with the moving average or is close to it. This value holds true as a resistance number in a bear market condition. If other numbers coincide with the pivot point moving average, such as the actual pivot point or an R-1 number, then it would serve as the target high number for that specific time period. Another way of using the three-period pivot point moving average is as a point of reference or fair value. When the market price departs or deviates too far from the mean, then you can use the extreme support or resistance number, such as S-2 or R-2, or the farthest target number of that direction as a potential turning point.

When various time frames are incorporated into the analysis (daily, weekly, and monthly), there is more certainty that the target price level can generate the anticipated reaction. If the market gaps too far from the daily pivot point moving average, use the monthly and/or weekly target support and resistance numbers to help identify a targeted reversal support or resistance point.

Figure 2.15 shows a spot forex British pound daily chart with the three-period pivot point moving average overlaid on top of prices. Notice that as

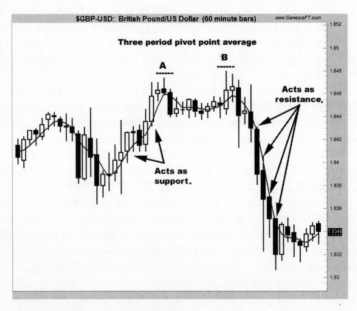

FIGURE 2.15 British Pound/U.S. Dollar (60-minute bars)
Used with permission of GenesisFT.com.

the market changes conditions from bullish (uptrend) to bearish (downtrend), prices tend to bounce off the moving average as a support line and trade off the moving average as a ceiling of resistance. You should also notice the topping price action. Now if we start with point A, you will see that point B is higher in price. Look at the corresponding points in the moving average values, and you will see that point B makes a higher high; but the moving average value is lower than when it is at point A. This is what I identify as a moving-average divergence. It serves as a strong clue that the market has peaked and that a significant reversal is due. Pivot point moving averages can help you filter out market noise (ranges) and can give you a truer picture of the market's value and direction.

The time period between point A and point B was a consolidation phase, as prices moved above and below the moving average. The moving average went virtually in a flat line with a bias to a downside slope. This was hinting that prices were getting ready to change direction. When you watch the moving average in relationship to the underlying price action, sometimes you can get clues as to the true market price direction using the pivot point average because it factors in the overall range and the relationship that the close of each time period has to that range. If the close is closer to the high, the average will be at a higher assigned value. As I just stated, using the three-period pivot point average will help you filter out much of the market noise and give you a truer sense of the market's fair value within the price range of the past three trading periods. This is very helpful information because forex markets do go in range-bound consolidation periods. These are called *sideways channels*, which we will discuss in the next few chapters.

At times, the slope (or the angle) of the moving average can give you a clue as to the market's true strength or weakness, especially when combined with candlestick charting. The slope helps filters out the noise and shows you whether the market's value is progressively appreciating or depreciating. When a market goes from the trending phase into the consolidation phase, it is the slope of the pivot point moving average that can help you identify the next potential price direction from the consolidating phase (e.g., a continuation or a trend reversal move). For added clarity, when you use a pivot point moving average combined with the ability to identify a high-probability bottom- or top-forming candle pattern, you have added confirmation of a potential reversal move. The graph in Figure 2.16 shows a representation of a pivot point moving average in a declining trend phase. Then as prices consolidate, the pivot point average measures the typical price rather than the close; and we can, therefore, determine what the true market value is and which way prices tend to be moving. Markets sometimes demonstrate extreme volatility at turning points. The moving average approach can help filter out the noise inflicted by wide price swings. These

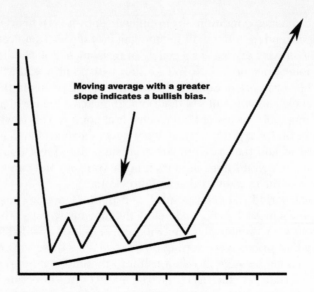

FIGURE 2.16   Slope and Bullish Bias

swings often lead to confusion; or, worse, traders get whipsawed or chewed up.

As the moving average slopes upward, it indicates that the market values are also tending to trade higher. Eventually, we see a trend reversal, which is what the direction of the moving average indicated. The three-period pivot point moving average works as a tool to confirm triggers and exits by showing price action closing above or below the moving average pivot line as well as indicating the potential trend direction by looking at the trend direction of the moving average itself. In Figure 2.17, I have a 30-minute chart on the spot forex British pound. Looking at the consolidation period as formed by an ascending triangle, we see that the market is starting to change from a bearish trend condition to a consolidation phase; and the upward slope of the moving average is giving a clue that the market may move into a reversal. This is the clue you are looking for to make money by watching for the reversal to occur, then entering in the market as it moves to ride the momentum so you can profit. Trading is not about being bullish or bearish, but just being in the market, on the right side, when it does move. That's how you will consistently make high-probability and profitable trades.

The British pound chart in Figure 2.18 provides a good example of the follow-through to the upside; and as prices continue higher, we see more bullish confirmation that the market will continue to the upside with a hammer candle pattern.

FIGURE 2.17 Profiting from Moving Averages
Used with permission of GenesisFT.com.

As the market starts to move upward by establishing higher highs and higher lows, you can see that it is also closing above prior highs and, most important, closing above the three-period pivot point moving average. The pivot point moving average will now start to act as a trend support.

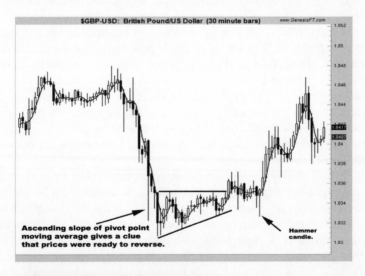

FIGURE 2.18 Moving Average Clues
Used with permission of GenesisFT.com.

PUTTING A PIVOT POINT TRADING STRATEGY TOGETHER

Buy Signals

Buy signals occur when a market is in a downtrend. Then as prices zoom down near a confluence of pivot point support levels, once prices close above the moving average, and as the market closes above the most recent or up to the prior three time periods' highs, look to enter a long position on the candle that establishes the higher closing high or on the open of the next time period. Place a stop initially below the lowest low point on the candle chart. Don't get cute and try to look for a significant pullback. Once a bottom forms, generally a violent breakout triggers reaction from the crowd to join in on the action.

Using a limit order significantly below the market may result in a missed opportunity. If the entry level at the current price level appears to be too much risk in comparison to where you feel your stop order should be placed, then scale back your lot size. Once the sequence of higher highs and higher lows develops, especially if the market is near a confluence of pivot support levels, other traders will see this and enter buy orders. This order flow can spark a highly profitable reversal. Once you are in this position, you should see quick results within one or two time periods. The forex market tends to attract more-savvy, technically oriented traders who use sophisticated trading software. These are the players who will come in once they see these conditional changes or buy signals. As the trade develops, monitor the relationship of prices to the moving average. Not only should the three-period pivot point average act as support, but the market should close above it. If you have multiple positions on, take into account these considerations; look at the pivot point resistance targets to scale out of partial positions and then "trail" your stops on the balance. *Trailing a stop* means to move it up as the market moves in your favor and to adjust it to account for changes in your lot sizes. Confluences on the various time frames of pivot point support levels can lead to massive moves that allow you at times to milk what was intended to be a simple day trade into a windfall-profit swing trade.

Figure 2.19 shows a euro/yen cross based on a 60-minute chart. This was a hot cross throughout 2006 and will likely continue to be so in the years to come. The euro was outpacing the value of the yen. In other words, either the yen was declining or not moving, and the euro was advancing in value; or at times, they were both declining, but the yen was losing more value than the euro. When trading the euro/yen, the bid/ask spreads are wider in these cross-currency transactions than they are in the major pairs

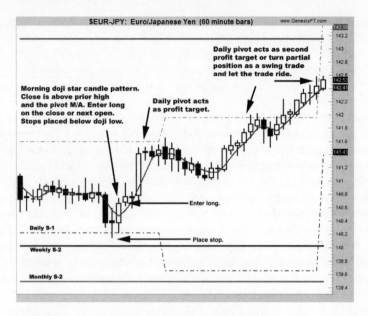

FIGURE 2.19 Textbook Trade Setup and Trigger
Used with permission of GenesisFT.com.

against the U.S. dollar. In any case, the market generated a great opportunity as it met the criteria for a long entry.

First, the market was in a downtrend; and as prices moved toward the daily, the weekly, and the monthly pivot point confluence value area, price action started to change. The market started to close above the three-period pivot point moving average, and a three-candle pattern called a morning doji star formed. In essence, we saw a shift in the condition of the downtrend. Prices closed above a prior high at the same time it closed above the moving average. It is at that time that you want to enter a market order on the close or on the next time frame's open. Your risk factor would be to place a stop below the low of the doji candle. If this price differential is too much risk, then consider cutting your lot size back. Your exit strategy can consist of several elements. You can use the end of the day; the low here was on May 17, 2006, at 11:00 A.M. (EST). This trade gave you plenty of time to trade profitably into the 5:00 P.M. (EST) close, which was near the daily pivot point resistance level. So you have a time and a price target for your exit strategy. If you do trade with multiple positions (which you should at these confluence opportunities) even if you scale back and trade mini-lots, you have the flexibility to liquidate a portion of your positions that will ensure a profit while moving your stops up from a loss, then breakeven, and so on. This is what we define as *trailing stop* orders. This book will disclose a trailing stop method as well in Chapter 10.

The big questions are how long should we let a trade ride and what do we look for to help us make decisions on when to sell the balance of the long positions? First, we integrate or introduce a different and higher time frame, such as a daily chart. For this technique, let's examine Figure 2.20. This is the daily chart for the euro/yen cross. The exact low that formed on a 60-minute chart was a doji candle; the daily chart actually formed a hammer bottom! As you can see, there is a very strong value level as identified by the confluence of the various time-frame pivot point support numbers. As prices moved higher, you can see the way the three-period pivot point moving average acted as support and the relationship of prices as the market closed above this moving average during the uptrend. The market went into a five-day rally mode as we see higher highs, higher lows, and higher closing highs right up to the following week's pivot resistance number. This resulted in a big move; and as time passed, this trend continued making new highs as I was finishing this book.

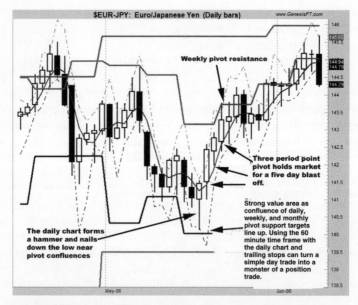

FIGURE 2.20   Pivot Point Analysis Helped Identify a Strong Trending Condition
Used with permission of GenesisFT.com.

Sell Signals

Sell signals are the opposite of the buy signal setups. The sell signal occurs after the market has been in a strong uptrend. Then as prices rocket up toward a confluence of pivot point resistance levels, traders need to wait for confirmation that the bullish momentum has died as not only do prices close below the moving average, but the price action will show the market starting to close below the most recent or up to the prior three time periods' lows. That is when you look to enter a short position once the candle establishes a lower closing low. Enter a market order to sell on the close of that time frame or on the open of the next time period. Place a stop initially above the highest high point on the candle chart. Think for a moment: If prices are in a bullish condition and trending higher, is this not a conditional change when prices close below the moving average (M/A) and below the prior time period's lows, with a sequence of lower highs and lower lows? Of course, it is; and that is what makes entering a short position with this information valid, since these conditions now confirm a downtrend reversal. Figures 2.21 and 2.22 illustrate a great case study on one more popular currency cross, which is the euro against the British pound.

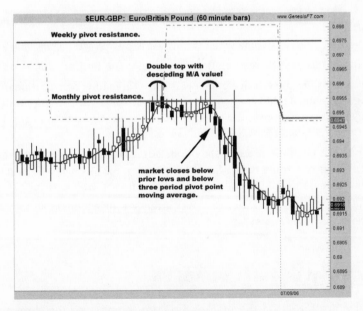

FIGURE 2.21 Points Confirm Double Top Selling Opportunities Used with permission of GenesisFT.com.

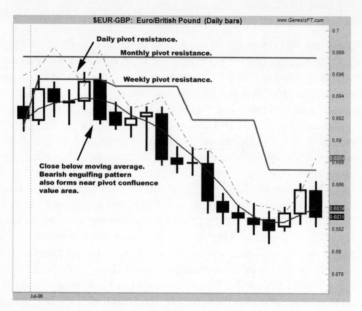

FIGURE 2.22 Profiting with Pivot Moving Average
Used with permission of GenesisFT.com.

IMPORTANT TRADING TIPS

- The best reversals come when the crowd is positioned heavily one way.
- Cut your lot size back when the entry level is too far from your stop level.
- Watch for the close above or below the last three time bars to trigger a buy or a sell signal. Market changes are often disguised and subtle. Watch the open/close relationships as well as the close as it relates to past price action, namely old highs, lows, and closes.
- Your exit or profit strategy should include a timing element. Don't expect more out of a trade than what the average move has been in the past for that time period. If the daily range is only 80 PIPs, why look for 120 PIPs?
- Bid/ask spreads are wider in cross-currency transactions than they are in the major pairs against the U.S. dollar.

MOVING AVERAGE VARIABLES

If trades are based on the market-direction number or the three-period pivot point moving average, there is no need to wait for the value of the moving average to start rising or falling to determine the trigger to enter the market. A close above the moving average will trigger a long position, and a close below the moving average will trigger a short position. However, we want to see the moving-average values follow the direction of the price move in the desired trade.

The conditional moving-average system incorporates the pivot point moving-average approach with another variable. This method combines two moving averages. The resulting system provides a powerful crossover trigger to enter the market as well as an indicator of the move's strength with the slope and the difference (or separation) of the moving-average lines.

A crossover provides both the entry and the exit signals, in addition to a set of rules or conditions. This system works on any time frame, five minutes and greater, in any high-volume market. It is an excellent short-term trading method for highly liquid markets such as forex, certain futures markets, and stocks that have ample trading volume.

There are other variations one can use, such as a five-period pivot point moving average with a two-period simple moving average of a close. I test various time periods and variables for my parameter settings because of the various trading conditions each market has. After all, bonds move differently than the Standard & Poor's index (S&P), or you may agree that forex currencies move differently than individual stocks. The bottom line is this: I use the two moving-average values to help me identify a shift in the market's momentum; and then as the conditions change, such as a close above or below the values of both moving averages, I use the pivot point filtering method to help me identify a potential profit target. Experiment with the individual pairs or cross currencies using different time varibles in your moving averages to see if one set of values "hugs," or traces better than, another.

For the purposes of this book, let me show you how to integrate the pivot point with the three-period moving average of the pivot point. In the previous section, I disclosed how to filter the pivot support and resistance levels by labeling the market condition as neutral, bullish, or bearish. We can also chart and track the conditional change of the market by plotting the directional change in the two moving-average settings.

Figure 2.23 shows both moving-average values declining; but as the pivot point crosses above the three-period moving averages, it alerts us that the internal market condition is changing to bullish.

Once both moving averages start to point up and the pivot point is above the three-period pivot point average, the market conditions confirm that we are in a bullish trend. As a general rule, a trader would look to buy from an area of support in a market that is trending upward (buy pullbacks).

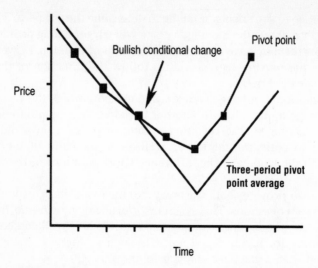

FIGURE 2.23   Pivot Point Moving Averages Indicate Market Turns

Note that prices traded above both moving average values and that the three-period pivot point moving average acted as support all the way up. The moving averages were moving in tandem with each other, and the slope of both averages was pointing in the direction of the trend.

This is an important point, so let me reiterate: What helps indicate the strength of a trend is using two or more sets of values for the moving averages and also these:

• The slope of both moving averages is pointing in the direction of the trend.
• The moving averages have a good degree of separation or are equidistant from each other, which indicates a steady trending condition.
• The moving averages are trending in tandem or are parallel with each other, rather than one outpacing the other.
• If the shorter-term moving average separates or moves too far away from the longer-term moving average, then you have a potential for an overbought condition, and you should start looking to liquidate half of your positions.
• When a crossover occurs, liquidate the entire position.

In Figure 2.24, let's go over what I have called my specialized conditional optimized moving average system (the COMAS™ method) using the one-period pivot point with the three-period pivot point moving average on a 15-minute chart for the spot forex British pound versus the dollar. The first noticeable benefit of a short-term time frame for the moving average

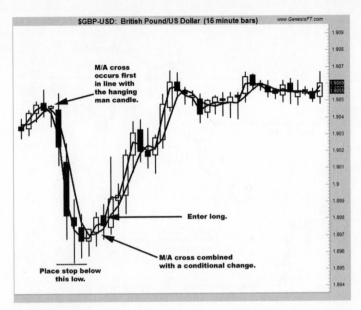

FIGURE 2.24   British Pound/U.S. Dollar (15-minute bars)
Used with permission of GenesisFT.com.

values is that they become more sensitive to price changes and can give a
trader an earlier warning of an impending market reversal. You can see
that at the top the crossover of the two moving averages occurs in line with
the hanging man candle pattern. Notice how, as the market descends in a
free fall, a hammer candle forms as the moving average values cross one
more time, indicating a potential directional price change. The confirmation of a reversal exists as a conditional change occurs as developed by a
higher closing high; prices are now closing above the open (white) candles,
and we have higher highs and higher lows and the market close above both
moving-average values. It is at this time that you can place a buy order at
the candle's close after the hammer forms or the next period's open; place
your stop below the lowest low of this series of lows.

This feature of using two pivot point moving averages allows you to
have an early warning system in place to help spot conditional price
changes. Figure 2.25 shows a daily chart with the spot forex British pound.
As you can see, the moving average crossover that occurs on July 19, 2006,
foretells the bullish trend reversal that carries the market from the 1.8420
level all the way up to the 1.8600 area. In that trend run, you will see how
the moving averages both lined up and acted as support. The market made
a short-term peak and corrected for two days before resuming its massive
rally. The candle chart formed an equal and opposite pattern (which forms
very frequently in the forex market). Notice how the moving average

FIGURE 2.25   British Pound/U.S. Dollar (daily bars)
Used with permission of GenesisFT.com.

crosses back down, giving you an early warning that the trend was in jeopardy. Then, sure enough, they crossed back up again, indicating the bullish trend might resume. In that trend run that occurred, the one- and three-period pivot point moving averages related quite closely with prices, indicating a support level all the way up to the peak on August 8 at 1.9144. Combining the candles with the pivot point moving averages is paramount in helping to stay long in a strong-trending market condition. I want you to study the sequence of events in respect to the candlestick charts: They have higher highs and higher lows, and the closes are above the opens. Prices close above past periods' or the prior time period's highs. Keep that in mind when you are trading. We are going to go over candle patterns in the coming section, and I will be reviewing these patterns in depth.

As illustrated in Figure 2.25, the COMAS™ method works in helping to determine changes in market conditions from a bearish downtrend phase to a bullish uptrend phase. Figure 2.26 illustrates a bearish conditional change in the market once the pivot point crosses beneath the three-period moving average pivot point. Once you have identified that a bearish condition exists, then you can trigger a short position. As a general rule, a trader would look to sell from an area of predetermined pivot point resistance levels, especially in a market that is in a longer-term downtrend. In other words, sell rallies in bear markets.

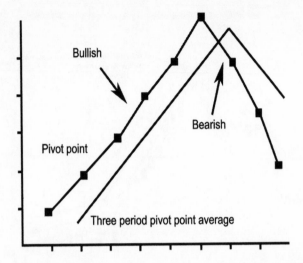

FIGURE 2.26   Pivot Point Moving Averages Improve Timing

In trading, as in life, timing is everything. There is nothing more frustrating to a trader than to correctly analyze the market, correctly predict the direction of the trend, get stopped out due to a premature entry, and watch the market launch in the predicted direction. As we all determine early in our trading careers, being correct about the direction of the trend is not enough. We must also be able to anticipate when the market is setting up to trigger an appropriate entry into the market. The pivot point combined with a moving average of the pivot point is one method worth utilizing in your trading approach; it can help you successfully identify when a conditional change may occur in the market.

Let's look at Figure 2.27, which is a 15-minute chart on the spot forex cross euro currency versus the Canadian dollar. Notice the three-period consolidation after the long white candle prices went in a sideways mode or consolidation phase. It is this period that pulls off the sidelines traders who are expecting a continuation of the trend and get long at the top. However, the pivot point moving averages made a negative cross, indicating a downward reversal. The crossover occurs followed by a low close doji sell signal, followed by a sequence of events with lower closing lows, lower highs, lower lows, and closes that are below the opens, as the dark candle represents. In addition, the sell signal was generated when the price closed beneath both moving-average values. As the market collapsed, you can see how the moving averages acted as resistance all the way down, until the market moved into a consolidation phase.

The concept of incorporating pivot point analysis with a moving-

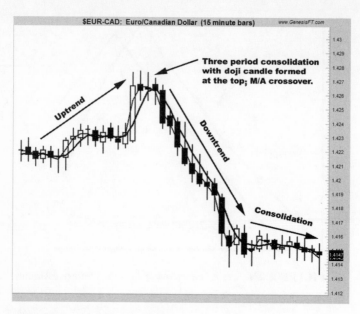

FIGURE 2.27   Euro/Canadian Dollar (15-minute bars)
Used with permission of GenesisFT.com.

average approach will give you a testable, mechanical, systematic approach to trading. In order to execute a trade, you need specific elements to occur. Knowledge of these elements will arm you with critical information that can help to prevent you from overtrading, as well as helping you avoid market and emotional pitfalls. For starters, in order to execute a trade, you need to see a change in market direction and commitment from the market to illustrate a change in market direction by closing above or below the moving averages. Next, you need to follow some simple rules, such as taking buy signals at support and taking sell signals at resistance. The importance of this trading method is that you must be able to apply the techniques on a consistent basis; this will allow you to make decisions in a mechanical and nonemotional way. A common mistake that traders make is that they do not test a strategy and make a logical determination if the strategy is viable for their trading style. Many traders adopt a new strategy, trade with it immediately, and start tweaking different components of the strategy. Then they decide that there is no merit to the strategy because they are not making a profit, and so they begin looking for a different strategy. A much better approach is to establish a defined set of trading rules and test those rules until a positive outcome is determined based on a reasonable number of trades. In order for you to be successful as a trader, you cannot anticipate an outcome; you must develop the patience to wait for your triggers, and you must also develop the discipline to follow through with that trigger. These character traits can be learned and developed by implementing this methodology. It is what I teach students and other highly successful professional traders. When the price target has been met and the trigger has presented itself, enter the trade without hesitation. Do not think about the entry; this should be a mechanical process. You have already done your homework, and you have satisfied your criteria. Your system is in place, and this is part of the system. If you do not place the trade when the trigger executes and confirms, you are not trading according to your plan. Successful traders have the courage to act and to act promptly. It is important to recognize the immediate environment or market condition. Is it up, down, or sideways? Let's say a bullish trend is established. It should consist of higher highs and higher lows; each period should close above the open, and we should see higher closing highs. The pivot point moving average should help verify this condition. In a bearish trend, we would want to see lower highs and lower lows; each period should close below the open, and we should see lower closing lows. Under these circumstances, the pivot point moving average should confirm this market condition as well. First and foremost, investors need to identify whether they are day, swing, or position traders; this will help them follow what time frame to follow a trending market and when to exit a trade or what to expect from a trade. Are you day trader? Are you a swing trader. who may be in a position that lasts two to five days? Or are you a position trader? Once you acknowledge what your time objective is, you can narrow down your goals and expectations for the trade. For example, when I am day trading, I will generally be able to identify what the average range for a day is and expect that if I miss 20 percent of the bottom and 20 percent of the top while waiting for a moving-average crossover signal, then I can expect to only capture 60 percent of the average daily range. Table 2.1 shows the breakdown of the

TABLE 2.1 Determining Daily Ranges

Date	High	Low	Range (PIPs)
8-09-06	1.2903	1.2760	143
8-08-06	1.2893	1.2803	90
8-07-06	1.2893	1.2810	83
8-04-06	1.2909	1.2773	136
8-03-06	1.2834	1.2738	96
8-02-06	1.2836	1.2773	63
8-01-06	1.2830	1.2716	114
7-31-06	1.2783	1.2737	46
7-28-06	1.2772	1.2654	118
7-27-06	1.2773	1.2676	97

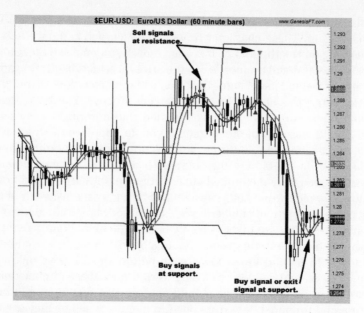

FIGURE 2.28 Buy Signals at Support and Sell Signals at Resistance
Used with permission of GenesisFT.com.

prior 10 sessions' ranges. It can be determined, on average, to expect at least a 98.6-PIP (percentage in points) range in the next few sessions with the highest range at 143 PIPs and the smallest at 46 PIPs.

If you can expect to capture at least 60 percent of the recent time period's average daily range, as this example shows, it would be 59 PIPs. So you can set your profit target goals based on recent historic price action for a realistic profit objective, or you can use the pivot point target levels as a guide. Figure 2.28 shows a 60-minute chart on the euro currency with the buy and the sell arrows with the predicted pivot point support and resistance levels. If you take the buy signals at support and take the sell signals at resistance, you can filter out better trades and allow yourself to have predetermined profit objectives based on historic data as well as on pivot point targets.

RIDE THE TIDE

Let's say you enter a trade based on the techniques covered so far. You enter a long position intending it to be a day trade. However, the market performs extremely well, closing sharply higher by the 5 P.M. (EST) close.

What do you do? If you are only in one lot position, stick to your plan, or place a hard stop beneath a reactionary low, or simply get out. If you have multiple lot positions on, take profits on a portion, and let the balance ride, placing stops at your break-even level or slightly higher, specifically if you have substantial profits built into the trade. This way, you can afford to ride the tide in case the market goes into a hyperbolic bullish trending mode. But if the market has been in a bullish trend, then you need to adjust your strategy and anticipate that the market might go into either a congestion phase or a trend reversal mode. This is where a trader really wants to apply the trading rules that state that you ignore buy signals at resistance and instead look to take sell signals at resistance. If you are day trading, as soon as a setup occurs and you enter a trade, using the methods discussed so far, you should be able to determine a loss strategy such as placing either a hard-stop or a mental-stop close only above a session's high (more on this later). My exit strategy for taking a profit can be figured in one of two ways: (1) I can use the predicted pivot point support target, or (2) if the trade does move in the desired direction, I can exit at the end of the trading session, which concludes at 5 P.M. (EST). If it is a Friday and you do not want to hold positions over the weekend, then your exit strategy would be to exit the trade before the close.

If the market has been trading on average in a wide range of 98 PIPs, as Table 2.1 showed, you can use that information to your advantage by expecting at least a 59-PIP profit target or more. Let me demonstrate as we review my theories as shown in the chart in Figure 2.29. This is a 15-minute chart from the trading session on August 10, 2006. As you can see, the market trades near to the predicted pivot resistance level, where if you practice patience and wait for a trigger to develop, which in this case we are looking for a sell signal at resistance, you would have been handsomely rewarded. Once the signal is generated, place a stop above the high. From the entry to sell at 1.2877 to the stop-loss placement at 1.2913, this translates to a 36-PIP risk factor. The first profit target would be 59 PIPs lower than your entry at 1.2877, that is, 1.2818; and the second profit target would be set at the predicted pivot point support target at 1.2779. That would give a trader a 98-PIP profit objective. As it turns out, this trade went profitable from the get-go. If you implemented a trailing stop from the initial 129.13 risk level down to your entry price at breakeven, you took absolutely no heat on this trade. This system of combining pivot points with the pivot point moving average will help keep you on the right side of the market and hopefully let you accrue consistent profits.

The methodology just discussed can be programmed in most software. The method is extremely robust and can be improved with just a few simple discretionary inputs, such as take sell signals at resistance, ignore the buy signals when they are generated near resistance, only take buy signals

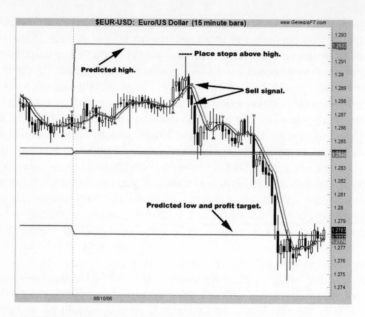

FIGURE 2.29 Entry Triggers and Profit Target Methods
Used with permission of GenesisFT.com.

at or near support, and ignore sell signals. Use the predicted support and resistance levels as profit-setting targets; and, most important of all, wait for
the signal to trigger—do not anticipate a signal. This system works across
various time periods and under different conditions, such as bullish, bearish, or neutral. This gives it a high rating for being a very robust methodology. As I stated earlier, the parameters I use in this book are a variation of
what is programmed in my proprietary library with Genesis software. This
is a system that generates buy and sell signals based on the principles we
have gone over so far. The greatest feature with this software is that it highlights a sell signal with a red triangle pointing down, and it signals when the
trigger occurs to buy with a green triangle pointing up. These signals coincide against resistance levels to sell and support levels to buy. As you will
see in many of the charts in this book, when the arrow indicators line up
against pivot point support and resistance numbers, it offers a fantastic visual trade confirmation, based on solid technical analysis theory using predefined strategies. It is a system like this that can definitely help traders
stay focused and can help reduce the destructive emotional element of fear
that forces traders out of winning trades too soon and the greed that generally gets traders to buy the top of rallies. These indicators help traders develop patience by waiting for the actual signals to generate, rather than
acting on anticipation. These signals and methods covered in this book can

be applied with most charting packages. In fact, 26 years ago, I was calculating the pivot point support and resistance numbers with a hand-held calculator; and I was not using candle patterns, which show depth and breadth of the current market condition in a colorful manner versus one-dimensional single-colored bar charts that we used in those days.

One of the neat things about this book is that it comes complete with your own pivot point and Fibonacci calculators. All that needs to be done is to input the data for the high, the low, and the close; and you will have R-3 down to the S-3 numbers calculated for you. It is very easy to use; all you need are the prices for the forex market for the time frame you wish to research, such as the daily, the weekly, the monthly, or even a quarterly time period.

CHAPTER 3

Candlestick Charting

The first recorded futures transactions occurred in the 1700s in the Japanese rice markets, where Munehisa Homma amassed a fortune trading the market. His system included the study of price action, the psychology of the market, and the seasonality of the weather. Candlestick charts evolved from Homma's system and are the subject of this chapter. This section covers the fundamentals of candlestick charting and explains how to utilize candle charts to analyze, enter, and exit trades.

The main advantage that candlestick charting provides over bar charting is that the candlestick provides immediate visual recognition of the open, the high, the low, and the close. Many traders who employ candlestick charting techniques set their charting software so that the candlesticks are one color for a lower close than the open (such as red or black as shown in Figure 3.1) and another color for a higher close than the open (such as green or white as shown in Figure 3.2). For the purpose of this book, a candle with a higher close than the open will be referred to as a white candle. A candle with a lower close than the open will be referred to as a black candle. A single candle does not tell you if the close is higher or lower than in the previous time period. The single candle only shows whether the close is higher or lower than the open for each candle.

Each candle has different characteristics that provide insight into price movement by the distance between the open, the high, the low, and the close. The candlesticks formed for each time session also indicate if the price movement shows a level of increasing or decreasing pressure by the size of the candle, or its "real body." Each candle pictured has a differ-

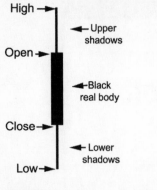

FIGURE 3.1   Selling, or Short

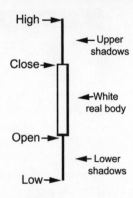

FIGURE 3.2   Buying, or Long

ent characteristic that represents the difference or the distance between the open, the high, the low, and the close. Candlestick charting techniques can be used from data for whatever time period you are looking at from as little as one minute to one hour, one day, one week, or one month. The candle still allows for use of traditional Western philosophy of technical analysis of pattern recognition, trend-line support and resistance, and other helpful tools as we will go into in detail in Chapter 5.

COMPONENTS OF A CANDLESTICK

The components of a candlestick are derived from the open, the high, the low, and the close. The main components that we need to identify are:

- Relationship between open and close (the candle bodies).
- Real-body colors.
- Shadows and correlations to the candle body.
- Size of shadows.
- Range or length of the candle.

In uptrends or bullish market conditions, buying comes in on the open; and the market should settle closer to the highs and should close above the open. That is why in bullish market conditions, we see hollow or white candles.

And I assign a higher close than the open. This helps me to identify that buyers are supporting prices. I can tell if the bulls are dominating the market by the distance between the open and the close. If the market opens on the low and has a large range where it closes at the high of the session, that signifies that the bulls are firmly in control. However, if we have a wide-range session and the market price closes back near where it opened, let's say in the middle of the range, that is not a good sign that bulls dominate the market for that particular time period.

In a bearish market condition or in a strong downtrend, we would see black or red real-body candles as shown in the accompanying CD. This represents sellers entering the market on the open and dominating the session right into the close of that time period. If the market opens on the high and prices decline where the close is at or near the low, this shows that the bears are firmly in control. This is why I assign these candles a negative (–) reading. The distance factor between the open and the close is illustrated in a much more defined way in candle charts than in bar charts due to the shape and color coordinates.

Shadows and Correlations to Candle Body

The shadows or wicks are what are made from the distance of a low and/or a high in relationship to the real body as created by the open and the close. They can really illustrate the market's denial of a support or resistance level. Long shadows or tails or wicks that form after a long downtrend indicate a potential that the trend has exhausted itself and that demand is increasing or supply is dwindling. Shadows formed at the tops of real bodies, especially after a long price advance, indicate that demand is drying up and supply is increasing. The overall size of shadows is important to watch in relationship to a real body and they can be easily identified.

Size or Length of the Overall Candle

A long real-body candle is hard to miss using the color-coded method of candle charts. An extraordinarily long-ranged candle that opens at the bottom and closes at the high would be an abnormal occurrence and has significant meaning. After a long downtrend, seeing this formation indicates that a major trend reversal is taking place. After a long uptrend, seeing an unusually long candle that closes above the open or a positive value would indicate that an exhaustion, or a blow-off-top condition, may exist. The reverse is true in downtrends; after a long price decline, a tall red or dark candle represents the market closing below the open or a negative assigned value and may indicate that a capitulation or exhaustion bottom has formed. After a long uptrend or price advance, if that same candle was formed, it might indicate that a major trend reversal is occurring.

The candle development will give us immediate identification of the current market's environment and the market participants' acceptance or rejection of a support or resistance level in a clearly visual manner. Pay special attention to the shadows and closes of ranges in relationship to past highs or lows and to where the market closes.

The Doji

The secret weapon of candlestick charting is the doji. Dojis indicate indecision; the market close ends where it began, on the opening of the time session. Figure 3.3 shows a full-range high and low with the cross mark across the line, representing that the market has no real body as prices closed exactly where they opened. This goes to show that confidence is lost from buyers or sellers on the open because the market made a lot of intraday noise as the range was established. In a bullish or bearish trending market, indecision is the last thing you want to see.

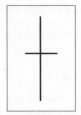

FIGURE 3.3   Doji

Strong rejection or failure from the high and/or the low is a significant telltale sign that changes are coming. In a strong uptrending market, usually the prices will close near a high since larger capitalized traders will hold positions overnight. If the large money traders are not confident that the market will move higher in price, then usually the market closes back near the open.

Traders use the phrasing of Newton's law in the markets an awful lot because it really applies to market moves. "A body in motion tends to stay in motion until a force or obstacle stops or changes that motion." I believe and teach that the doji represents that force; it generally stops or changes the motion or momentum due to the uncertainty or indecision that is created at peak and troughs.

Doji formations help confirm reversals. There are different names and nuances associated with certain dojis, such as the *gravestone* shown in Figure 3.4, the *dragonfly* shown in Figure 3.5, and the *long-legged* or *rickshaw doji* shown in Figure 3.6. All have the same qualities—they close where the session began. After a major trend has occurred, when one of these candles forms, it signals that the trend is near an end or that there is a change in market conditions. What distinguishes the doji from all other

FIGURE 3.4   Gravestone

FIGURE 3.5   Dragonfly

FIGURE 3.6   Long-Legged (Rickshaw) Doji

candle formations is that the close of this candle is nearly exactly at the same price as the open. I am generally a little more lenient with this formation. If after a long-range trading session the close is less than 8 percent of the overall high and low, I consider it a doji. In spot forex markets, if, for example, the British pound had a 150-point range and the market closed within 12 points of the open, I would consider that a doji formation.

Candle patterns can be subjective, and there are many variations to each pattern. The key element to this system is identifying where a market closes in relationship to the prior highs or lows. Certain candles have significant meaning besides the doji. Bearish reversal patterns include dark clouds; engulfing, harami, and harami doji crosses; falling three methods; and evening doji stars. These are all indeed powerful setup chart patterns. The reverse of these are the bullish bottom pattern formations, such as bullish piercing, bullish harami, morning doji star, and even the hammer candle. The candle hammer is what I call the "stop," or "seek and destroy" action. The bearish version is a shooting star candle.

The Hammer

The *hammer* shown in Figure 3.7 indicates that a reversal or a bottom is near in a downtrend. When this pattern appears at the top of an uptrend, the name becomes hanging man, and it indicates that a top is near. You

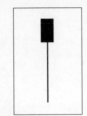

FIGURE 3.7   Hammer

need to know that there are three main characteristics necessary in order for a candle to qualify as a hammer:

1. The real body is at the upper end of the trading range; the color (white or black) is not important.
2. The lower part or the "shadow" should be at least twice the length of the real body.
3. It should have little or no upper shadow, otherwise known as a *shaved head* candle.

The Shooting Star

One of the single most important bearish candle formations that I wish to share with you is the *star*, sometimes referred to as the *shooting star* candle. It is the inverted formation of the hammer and forms at tops.

The shooting star in Figure 3.8 is the reverse of the hammer, but it forms at the top of an uptrend. It usually signals a major reversal. Here again, the color does not matter, but the body should be at the lower end of the trading range with a long shadow. Its significance is that it shows the market opening near the low of the day, followed by an explosive rally that failed and then closed back down near the low of the day.

FIGURE 3.8   Shooting Star

Usually there is little or no lower shadow, like a shaven bottom. When it is at the bottom of a downtrend, it is known as an inverted hammer.

The Morning Doji Star

The *morning doji star* is a major bottom reversal pattern that is a three-candle formation. The first candle has a long black real body; the second candle has a small real body or doji, as shown in Figure 3.9, and gaps lower than the first candle's body. The third candle's body sometimes gaps higher than the second one, but this does not happen often. It is important that it is a white candle and closes well above the midpoint of the first candle's real body.

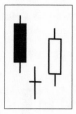

FIGURE 3.9   Morning Doji Star

The Evening Doji Star

The *evening doji star* shown in Figure 3.10 is the exact opposite of the morning doji star. This is the second-most-bearish top pattern next to the abandoned baby or island top formation.

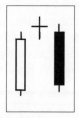

FIGURE 3.10   Evening Doji Star

 HOT TIP

Gaps are not too prevalent in forex trading. Therefore, it is very rare to see a textbook morning or evening doji star formation. In candlestick terminology, a *gap* is called a "window." It is said, generally speaking, that if a gap forms or a window opens, the market will most times trade back to fill the gap or close the window. The trick is knowing when gaps are sometimes "filled" right away and when prices do not return to fill the gap or close the window for quite a while. Gap levels can and do act as support and resistance. So pay attention to the price behavior at these loctions.

The Harami

The *harami* is a small real body within the body of the prior body's candle. This is known as a reversal pattern or a warning of a trend change, especially at tops of markets. It is not important that the colors be opposite, but I notice that the more reliable signals are generated when they are. After a long uptrend, if there is a tall white candle, it can indicate an exhaustion especially followed by a small-real-body candle, as shown in Figure 3.11.

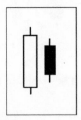

FIGURE 3.11   Harami

Bearish Harami Doji Cross

The *bearish harami doji cross* shown in Figure 3.12 is a formation that appears when a long white candle occurs, signifying that the market has closed above the open with little or no shadows at both ends of the candle; this candle is then followed in the next time period by a doji within the middle of the white candle's real body. This tells me bulls no longer dominate.

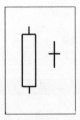

FIGURE 3.12   Bearish Harami Doji Cross

Bullish Harami Doji Cross

The *bullish harami doji cross* in Figure 3.13 is the opposite of the bearish harami. This pattern will form in a downtrending market. The first candle is usually a long dark candle, signifying that the market has closed below the open with little or no real shadows at both ends; a doji then forms during the next trading session.

FIGURE 3.13   Bullish Harami Doji Cross

The Dark Cloud Cover

The *dark cloud cover* is a bearish reversal signal. Usually it appears after an uptrend. The first white candle is followed by a black candle. The important features here are that the dark candle should open higher than the white candle's high and that the close should pierce well below the midpoint of the white candle's real body, as shown in Figure 3.14.

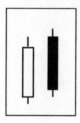

FIGURE 3.14   Dark Cloud Cover

The Bullish Piercing Pattern

The *bullish piercing pattern* is the opposite of the dark cloud cover, as you can see in Figure 3.15. It requires that the first candle be a long dark candle and that the second candle gap open lower than the first candle. The other important characteristic is that it closes well above the midpoint of the long dark first candle. Look for 50 percent penetration of the long dark candle.

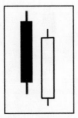

FIGURE 3.15   Bullish Piercing Pattern

The Bullish Engulfing Pattern

The *bullish engulfing pattern* is a powerful setup. Study the pattern as shown in Figure 3.16. It forms when a white candle's real body completely covers the previous black candle's real body. It is also relevant to note that the more "wraps," or past candles, that are engulfed, the stronger the signal.

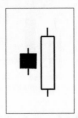

FIGURE 3.16   Bullish Engulfing Pattern

The Bearish Engulfing Pattern

The *bearish engulfing pattern* shown in Figure 3.17 is the opposite of the bullish engulfing pattern. When a black candle's real body completely covers the previous white candle's real body and even closes below the prior candle's low, it is a more potent signal. It is also relevant to note that the more "wraps," or past candles, that are engulfed, the stronger the signal.

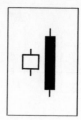

FIGURE 3.17   Bearish Engulfing Pattern

Falling Three Methods

The bearish *falling three methods* is a continuation pattern often used like a bear flag formation. The three little candles usually remain within the range of the first black candle that includes both the real body and the shadow. Some argue that it works with from two up to five candles in the middle. The last dark candle closes below the first candle's close, as Figure 3.18 shows.

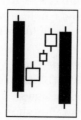

FIGURE 3.18   Bearish Falling Three Methods

Rising Three Methods

Rising three methods is a bullish continuation pattern with the same characteristics as in the bearish falling three methods but just the opposite. During the beginning stages of an advancing price trend, an unusually long white candle is preceded by three smaller dark or black candles. The three bullish methods pattern needs to stay within the range of the first long white candle. Again, it can have from two up to five candles; but the textbook version is three smaller candles, as Figure 3.19 shows. The last white candle shows a powerful advancing white candle that should open above the previous session's close and should close above the first long white candle's close.

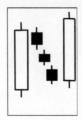

FIGURE 3.19   Bullish Rising Three Methods

Tweezers Tops and Bottoms

The *tweezer* is a double-top or double-bottom formation that can be disguised by a few variations. The *tweezer top* forms after an uptrend followed by two consecutive time periods making an equal high. This signals that there is strong resistance and a short-term top is in place. One variation is that the first day usually consists of a long body candle with a higher close than open (+).

The second day is usually an equal-and-opposite-color real-body candle that has a high equal to the prior day's high. A strong signal exists that a reversal is forming when the second candle's color is the opposite of the first candle's color. A *tweezer bottom* would be the exact opposite of this formation.

Other variations are called *equal-and-opposite* or *chopstick* patterns. In Chinese, it would be called the yin (black or negative close candle) and the yang (white or hollow positive close candle). At times, these real bodies are not perfectly opposite in size, but they should be close.

In Figure 3.20 the tweezer bottom looks more like a pair of thin chopsticks. In Figure 3.21, the tweezer top resembles a pair of fat chopsticks; but notice that the dark candle engulfs the first candle's real body. That is evidence that a top or a peak price has been established. The equal-and-opposite formations occur with false breakouts and key reversals; they are powerful signals that should be respected.

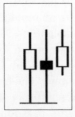

FIGURE 3.20   Tweezer Bottom

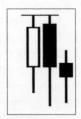

FIGURE 3.21   Tweezer Top

YIN AND YANG: THE EQUAL-AND-OPPOSITE TRADE STRATEGY

Forex traders take note: These *equal-and-opposite* patterns show up frequently in the currency pairs as well as in cross-currency markets. We see periods of low volatility between the European and the U.S. sessions; and, as a result, sideways channels form, otherwise known as a *longer-term intraday consolidation period*.

Oftentimes, we see false breakdowns and breakouts that create the equal-and-opposite (yin and yang) formations. We, therefore, have a trigger to enter a position if the market price is near an important pivot point support level. We would buy on the close of the second candle's time period or the immediate opening of the next time frame. Place a stop at least 10 PIPs (percentage in points) beneath the lowest low point. You should see immediate results as the markets move higher. Adjust your stop accordingly.

Figure 3.22 is a 60-minute chart on the euro currency versus the U.S. dollar on July 19, 2006. The exact low occurred at 9:00 A.M. (EST) and was not prompted by any special report. That morning the German Producer Price Index (PPI) came out, but at 2:00 A.M. (EST). Two U.S. economic numbers—housing starts and real earnings—were released; but those re-

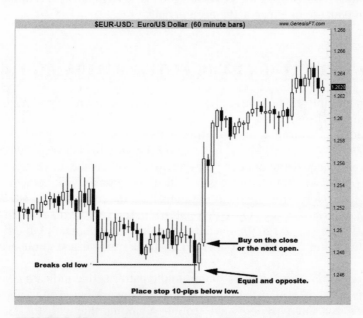

FIGURE 3.22   Equal-and-Opposite Candle Revelations
Used with permission of GenesisFT.com.

ports were released at 8:30 A.M. (EST), one and a half hours earlier. The dollar got pummeled as U.S. traders started to digest the news. It seems to happen at times that there is a delayed reaction to the economic reports. But looking at the false breakdown of the low of the range that was created in the prior 22 hours of trading shows that an equal-and-opposite candle formed, and it was at that time that the buy programs kicked in as a very powerful reversal took place. In fact, the majority of the move on this 60-minute chart took place in 10 minutes. The market ruthlessly exploded and increased in value over 90 PIPs in just 10 minutes. The 60-minute chart showed an equal-and-opposite pattern.

Basically the market went hunting for stops as it broke the low, and shorts covered as the market reversed like a rocket. You need to look for these opportunities because the price action in the forex market behaves like this on a frequent basis. This is a classic failed-pattern breakdown. Traders saw the market making newer lows as prices broke below the low; and when there was absolutely no follow-through, it had a slingshot effect in the opposite direction. This was an ironclad bear trap. By following the rules on equal-and-opposite patterns, especially when a setup fails to materialize, such as a breakdown of support, this is a powerful signal to take a long position. We exercise prudent risk-management techniques placing a stop 10 PIPs below the lowest low point; and as the trade progresses, you can adjust your stop or look to exit if the market gives you a windfall profit that is equal to or exceeds the normal daily range.

MULTIPLE TIME-FRAME CONFIRMATION TACTICS

Using multiple time-frame analysis will help you confirm a great trading opportunity. Through various time dimensions, if a buy signal is evident, you should see confirming patterns throughout these various time periods. If the 60-minute chart is showing a high-probability bullish reversal pattern, such as the equal-and-opposite candle, then if we break it down to a smaller time frame, we should see signs or bullish patterns as well. Look at Figure 3.23; this is a five-minute chart detailing how the low was formed. We are going to cover the high close doji pattern in the very next section; but for now, I want you to see the magnitude of this strong breakout and the fact that the lower time frame confirmed the higher time frame's bullish signal.

To summarize, there are many candle patterns that indicate reversals. Some are more potent than others, and some work better in various time frames. But many traders have trouble adapting; they get stuck in a rut looking for the same results and fail to exploit highly recognizable pattern failures, such as false breakouts. If you learn to understand the sequence

FIGURE 3.23 Candles Light the Path to Profits
Used with permission of GenesisFT.com.

and the value of the open close relationship, then you will have a better-than-average chance of making serious money. The best trades usually come in the form of blindsiding traders who are heavily positioned the wrong way or who have overstayed their welcome in a position. It is this rush for traders to get to the exit door in a panic that accelerates market moves. The equal-and-opposite pattern is a major sign of a false breakout. Think about this: If a market does not do what is expected, such as when it breaks a long-term support and there is no follow-through, who wants to hold a short position in the hole? Not many people. Watch for the yin and the yang, especially at extenuated trend extremes or at congestion points.

HIGH CLOSE DOJI SETUP

Out of all the candlestick reversal patterns, the *high close doji* (HCD) is the best and most reliable setup that I have encountered. Figure 3.23 showed a classic pattern on a five-minute chart period. It is based off a simplified morning doji star formation. Instead of looking for the traditional three-candle pattern, this setup merely focuses on the doji and the event that follows the formation of the doji.

Figure 3.24 shows the exact sequence we need: the next one to three time periods after a doji forms to close above the high of that doji candle. That is the key; the close is the confirmation that a bullish transition took place. All that is left is for a trader to act when there is a shift in momentum. In this pattern, we are looking for a specific conditional change to take place in the market, namely, a higher closing high above a doji's high, especially when it occurs near a pivot point support level. This is the pattern I call the high close doji, or the HCD, method. It has dimensions of specific criteria that need to fall in place, which will help to eliminate and filter out false signals. It is a simple and basic approach that is a high-probability winning strategy.

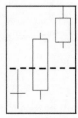

FIGURE 3.24   High Close Doji

Here are the rules to act on when this pattern develops:

- Buy on the close or on the next time period's open once a new *closing* high is made from the previous time period's bullish candle reversal pattern or if a doji forms against a pivot number.
- Initially, use a hard stop or a mental stop close only (SCO) below the low of the doji. Once the market begins to produce a profit and moves in the desired direction, then you can change to a hard stop and continually trail the stop. Whatever time you are trading, the SCO is specific for that time frame wherever the signal might occur. For example, if it is an intraday signal, then you need to use a mental stop that requires you to wait until the end of the time period, whether that is based on a 5-, 15-, 30-, or 60-minute time frame. Most trading platforms do not have intraday SCO features, rather just the end-of-day SCOs.
- Sell or exit the trade on the close or on the first open of a candle that makes a lower low at or near a pivot point resistance calculation.
- Use a "filter" or backup process to confirm the buy signal, such as a bullish convergence pattern on stochastic or moving average convergence/divergence (MACD).

The term *extreme range expansion*, or what I call overoverstretched and unsustainable valuations, is valuable information when it occurs near pivot point calculations. Especially in a runaway bull market, when I start to see a sudden loss of momentum and halting or reversing price action at a resistance level, I certainly consider that I have sufficient cause to begin taking profits from a long position or establishing a new short position.

If I see evidence that the move is getting drained by smaller ranges or subsequent closes closer to each low, or if I see a climax with a larger-than-normal-size real body or other evidence that supply is returning to the market, thus turning back price, I start to take several forms of action. I reduce my position by at least one-half to two-thirds and tighten stops.

Now, let's put these rules into practice by examining active trading markets, such as the foreign currency market. The first example, Figure 3.25, is a 15-minute time period candle chart on the spot British pound. Taking the data from September 29 and using the close from the 5 P.M. (EST) New York bank settlement, we have a high of 177.04, a low of 175.92, and a close of 176.13. Once we calculate our pivot points, we have our first support (S-1) figured as 175.68. Our first resistance (R-1) is figured as 176.80. As you can see, the market trades for almost two hours at the pivot support; but at 4:30, a doji forms. Two time periods later, a close above the

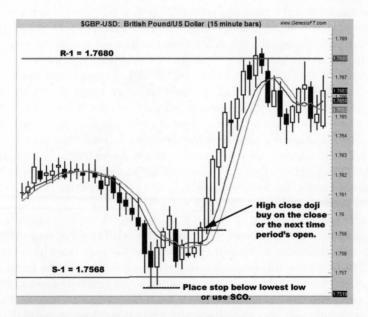

FIGURE 3.25 HCD Triggers Action to Buy
Used with permission of GenesisFT.com.

doji's high occurs. Also note that the market closes above both moving-average values. In addition, the COMAS™ method shows the shorter-term moving average crossing above the longer-term average, confirming a trigger to go long.

The trigger to enter a long position would be on the time period's close or on the very next session's open; the entry price would be 175.95. As the market blasts off into trend mode, you can see the money-making sequence of events transpire: higher highs, higher lows, and higher closing highs. As the trade matures, watch the reaction at the pivot resistance R-1 of 176.80. Observe the bullish momentum dry up; and for the first time, we have a lower closing low and price closes below both moving average values. The moving averages also form a negative cross, confirming a trigger to exit the long position. As a day trader, you have completed your mission to capture money from the market.

This example would have had you exit the position at 176.57. For each full-lot-size contract, that would be a 62-PIP profit, or $620 gain. Granted, we did not buy the low or sell the high, but we certainly did what you always want to do: capture a nice chunk of the middle of a price move. If you understand that markets move from trend mode to consolidation or congestion phase, then you will realize that at this time it is best to walk away, as you are now vulnerable for getting whipsawed in the market. That is why most successful traders make their money and walk away.

As you look at the chart in Figure 3.26, notice how the pattern seems to look identical to the pattern in Figure 3.25. The market bases out in a consolidating sideways pattern, a doji forms, the moving averages cross over, and a high close doji triggers a buy signal. Almost instantly, we see positive results as the market makes higher highs, higher closes than opens, and prices are maintaining values above the moving averages. One thing about this particular chart is that the market did not trade down to the S-1 or quite make it to the midpoint between the pivot point and S-1. That is why I use pivot levels as a guide rather than the signal itself. I am interested in what the price action does at the pivot support levels. As we learned earlier, if the market is truly bullish, the pivot point will act as a support level on its own. That is the case in this example; and this is a very important point, so take note. In bullish conditions, the pivot will act as support.

Once again, as shown in Figure 3.27, we have a similar pattern as the doji forms at or near the pivot point support level. The pivot support helps target a potential low and a spot where the market may react by reversing direction. We have a few considerations in order to make a trade. For starters, we look for the doji pattern; but it is not until the market closes back above the doji's high that the trigger to go long is generated. As you see, the moving averages also cross over, and prices close above both moving average values. That is the true trigger to go long; once prices close

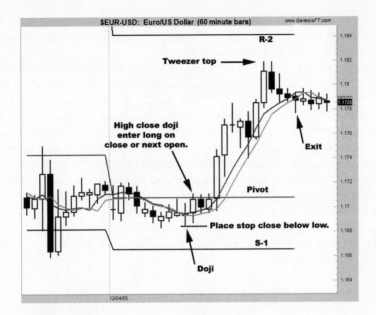

FIGURE 3.26 The Power of the Doji Signal
Used with permission of GenesisFT.com.

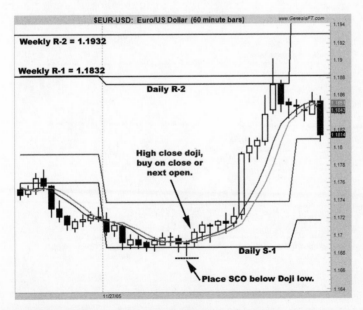

FIGURE 3.27 The Doji Setup Provides Consistent Results
Used with permission of GenesisFT.com.

above the doji high, a higher assigned value has taken place, and the market takes off for almost a 200-PIP move. This market moves immediately with no pressure on the trade whatsoever.

I want to now show you how the signals work using the Genesis Software with my formulas plugged in, which identify the momentum shifts with the buy and sell signals indicated by the arrows as shown in Figure 3.28. The system gives buy and sell signals based on the moving averages and on the proximity of the pivot support and resistance levels. In addition, there is an algorithm designated for depicting when a high close doji occurs. As you can see, the buy signal triggers perfectly off the pivot support level; and the market trades right up to the pivot point resistance where a doji forms, alerting you to scale out of partial positions to lock in your gains and to tighten stops accordingly. This is a 15-minute chart; so you can see the system kept you in the trend the entire length of the trade, which was initiated by the high close doji. This trade worked out for $630 per lot or position.

To summarize, when you identify a doji at or near the pivot support target level, wait for confirmation of the next candle up to the next three candles to close above the doji's high. This event of the higher closing high

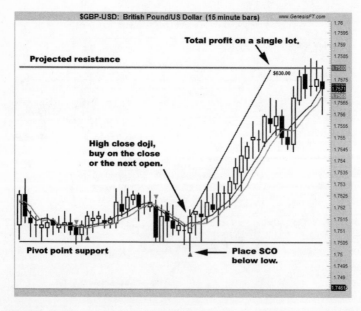

FIGURE 3.28 Pivots, COMAS, and Candles Generate Consistent Signals
Used with permission of GenesisFT.com.

constitutes a higher assigned value, and you should see immediate results to follow.

BEARISH TRADING PLAN FORMULA: LOW CLOSE DOJI

The next trading signal, the *low close doji* (LCD), is the opposite of the high close doji. It is a setup developed on the premise that once the market has rallied and established a high, if a doji forms, it is indicating that there is indecision. Then once we establish a lower closing low below the doji's low, this establishes that there is a loss in bullish momentum and we can initiate a short position. Figure 3.29 shows that the black candle closes below the low of the doji.

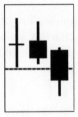

FIGURE 3.29   Low Close Doji

Watch for this setup after the market has had an extended advance to the upside; and if it is near a predetermined pivot point resistance level, generally speaking, the market will reach an overbought condition as well. Once the doji appears, it is indicating indecision and weakness of buyers to maintain an upward trend. Those conditions make it ripe for a sharp reversal, allowing for a juicy high-probability, low-risk trade.

Here are the rules to act on when this pattern develops:

- When prices are at or near a pivot point resistance number, sell on the close or the next time period's open when a new closing low is made from the previous time period's (or past three candles) doji. One can use a filter-confirming signal, such as a bearish divergence stochastic pattern or an MACD zero-line cross.
- Initially use an SCO above the high of the doji. Once the market begins to produce a profit and moves in the desired direction, then you can change to a hard stop and continually trail the stop. Whatever time you

are trading, the SCO is specific for that time frame, wherever the signal might occur. For example, if it is an intraday signal, then you need to initially use a mental stop that requires you to wait until the end of the time period, whether that is based on a 5-, 15-, 30-, or 60-minute time frame. Most trading platforms do not have intraday SCO features; rather, they have just the end-of-day orders.

- Buy or exit on the open of the first candle after the previous candle makes a higher closing high than the previous candle.

Let's examine market price action and how to execute this signal. You have your predetermined pivot point resistance levels already mapped out for you. Once you have the predetermined support and resistance numbers, it is the second variable that is just as important, which is looking for a signal that triggers a call to action. Figure 3.30 is a spot forex euro currency that shows once again why it is important to wait for sell signals at resistance rather than buying breakouts.

The euro chart shows the market breaking out above the R-1 level. As a standard rule, I do not like to take buy signals at resistance. I would rather wait for a sell signal to develop and then go with the declining momentum.

I believe one reason why this signal works so well is that many traders

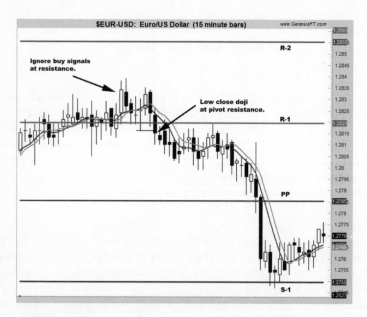

FIGURE 3.30   The LCD Pattern Is a High Quality Setup
Used with permission of GenesisFT.com.

are trying to trade breakouts of pivot point resistance levels by going long once they see the breakout above the R-1 level. Once there is little follow-through and prices start to retreat, then they are scrambling to sell to get out of their losing trade. In this chart example, notice, too, where we have a moving average crossover and not only do prices close below the doji, but they also close below both moving-average values. The trigger to sell short was executed at 1.2815, and an immediate reaction occurred as prices plunged. The sequence of events that we want to see, as we do in this example, is lower close than the openings; lower highs; lower lows; and, most important, lower closing lows. Now we can make a decision. Instead of keeping the mental SCO above the initial doji high, we could decide that since the move was a decent distance away from our initial entry, we can place a hard stop on the position.

As the market enters in a consolidation phase, we see that prices never close above the high of the first reactionary low's high. That keeps prices contained in a sideways channel or similar to a bear flag formation. As we follow the flow of the market, notice how the market declines by the end of the day to the S-1 of 1.2750. As a day trader, there is no question as to where you need to exit the position. It is the end of the day, and you have managed a trade all day and ridden a very nice trending market condition. This is a great example of how to use the pivot levels for a profit target.

Figure 3.31 shows a textbook setup in the Japanese yen. This is a five-minute chart without the pivot point moving averages overlaid to help you see the progression of the trade and the sequence of the open/close relationship that candlestick charts display.

As the market advances toward the projected pivot point daily R-2, traders may assume the market conditions are in a bullish mode. When you get in that mindset, you tend to forget to look at the current market conditions.

The top pattern is not a traditional or classic morning doji star formation because the third candle does not close below the midpoint of the tall white candle. However, it does close below the doji's low. That is the conditional change that takes place, giving us the clue that the bullish momentum has dried up. First, we have a lower closing low; then the market closes below the open, and prices reverse direction once we tapped the pivot point resistance level. Therefore, we want to sell on the close or the very next time period's open, placing our stop (*initially*) as a mental SCO above the high of the doji, which is 118.18. That is just three PIPs above the daily pivot point resistance level, too. Again, what we want to see is almost instant follow-through for the price to decline.

As you can see, with this trade, there was immediate follow-through. Notice the progression of the market as it declines from the entry price at 118.07 straight down to 117.87, for a quick 20-PIP gain. The market then

FIGURE 3.31   The LCD Pattern Provides Consistent Results
Used with permission of GenesisFT.com.

trades back and forth, creating small-range candles, which form a sideways channel. If you look closely at each candle's close, notice how it does not close back above the high of the candle that established the first reactionary low. As a trader, you may want to hold all positions or, at this time, cover half of your position. One reason we do that is because, as powerful and reliable as these triggers are, we still do not know the outcome of how far prices can or will actually move. The markets could easily reverse back and challenge the highs. By taking money out of the market, you immediately have profits on half of your positions; and then you also reduce your risk exposure in the market.

Examine this chart further and see how the candles show the true direction of the market: The dark candles reflect closes below the open, and there are more of those and they are bigger than the white candles. For the most part, there are more of the dark or negative assigned candles, which are establishing lower closing lows, than there are white or positive assigned candles; but notice that these candles have smaller ranges and hardly ever make higher closing highs. This shows that every time the market rallies just a little bit, sellers are present. Long negative assigned candles represent bears, or sellers, dominating this market. Therefore, staying short on the balance of the position is warranted. Now as the market price disintegrates, demonstrating the conviction of sellers, we can place a hard stop at breakeven on the balance of the position and start to adjust the stop to protect profits accordingly. As a short-term trader, it is imperative to trade with the current flow or momentum of the market. Since there are so many variables that can influence your trading decisions, using the methods described here will help you keep focused and alleviate the problems of trading on emotional impulses. When you are focused on what the potential resistance levels are, have learned what to look for (such as a low close doji signal), and then applied trade management techniques, you can capture profits. It is literally up to you to pull the money out of the markets. This method cannot tell you how much money you will make on each trade; every outcome will be different. However, there is a strong possibility that based on historic reference, you will see a decline in prices.

In Figure 3.31, we see an immediate reaction as a sequence of lower highs, lower lows, and lower closing lows occurs. In fact, by using the moving averages, you will notice the confirmation of a negative crossover and prices closing below the moving averages as well. This short-term downtrend ends when we see a change in conditions once the moving averages cross back up and prices start to close above both moving-average values. This is a sign that the negative forces or selling pressure are fading and it is time to exit our position. The key is in being able to identify true conditional changes that will make you act on facts, triggering a call to action by a set of rules rather than on emotional impulses. If you have the discipline to trade by a set of rules and follow those rules, you will increase your trading profits.

Here are guidelines for trade and risk management:

- Get out of half of your positions on the first shift in momentum by a higher closing high, and move your stops. There will be times that you have to make a judgment on whether the risk is too excessive by the distance of the proposed entry and the SCO.
- The SCO is for whatever time period you are trading in. For example, if it is an intraday signal, then you need to use a mental stop that requires that you wait until the end of the time period, whether that is based on a 5-, 15-, 30-, or 60-minute time frame. Most trading platforms do not have intraday SCO features, rather just end-of-day SCO.

CHAPTER 4

Traditional Chart Patterns

FLAG PATTERNS

A *flag formation* or pattern generally develops after significant or abrupt price moves. It is a pausing formation before the trend continues. You want to remember that the body of the flag is generally angled or sloped against the initial trend, as Figure 4.1 shows, but can be found with a sideways pattern. The base of the flag is the starting point for a substantial price advance (or decline, in the case of a bear flag formation). It is then followed by erratic and choppy downward or sideways price action that lasts for several time periods, like a consolidation time or a "time out" before prices continue on. Analysts measure the distance from the bottom of the "flagpole" to the top of the pole (the distance between point A and point B). They then take that distance and measure from the bottom of the flag (point C) and extend it up to the resistance line drawn from the top of the flag pattern (point D), or down to the support line in a bear flag formation, to get an idea of how far prices will move. The length of time that the flag portion of this pattern takes to evolve varies, depending on the time frame in which you are trading. As far as on a daily chart, we should see the breakout occur within two weeks. In daytrading, we should see this pattern evolve within 10 bars, candles, or time periods. Figures 4.2 and 4.3 depict a more common setup, with flags as they occur in the forex market.

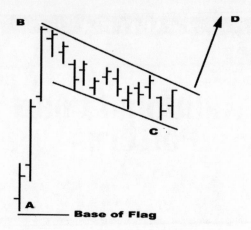

FIGURE 4.1   Flags as a Measuring Tool

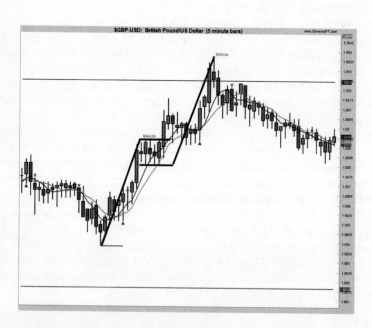

FIGURE 4.2   The Flag Measures out the Price Objective
Used with permission of GenesisFT.com.

FIGURE 4.3 Bull and Bear Flags Meet Price Objectives
Used with permission of GenesisFT.com.

HOT TIP

If a pattern fails to move in accordance with its predisposed tendency, it is generally a great reversal opportunity. For example, if a bull flag does not have the follow-through momentum or upward thrust that is typically associated with the breakout, then it is a failed pattern and can be traded from the short side.

TRIANGLE CHART PATTERNS

There are three main types of triangle patterns, as shown in Figures 4.4, 4.7, and 4.8 which are symmetrical, ascending, and descending, respectively. A fourth type, known as a pennant formation, resembles the symmetrical triangle—it has two equal sides—as shown in Figure 4.5. The ascending triangles indicate an upward bias, and the descending triangles indicate a downward bias. They are used as a measuring guide for continuation price moves. The length of time, being the distance the "triangle" or congestion area takes to form, is believed to be the distance the market will move once the market "breaks out" of the triangle pattern.

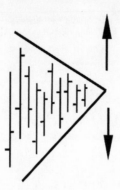

FIGURE 4.4   Symmetrical Triangle

1. *Symmetrical triangles* are considered consolidation patterns that occur within a trending phase. The symmetrical triangle develops when prices consolidate as the trading range narrows; the shape forms as prices compress in a coiling pattern. The highs are lower and the lows are higher, as shown in Figure 4.5. As with any time you draw a trend, you need two points of interest, such as two consecutive highs or lows. When drawing out the trend for the triangle, we look for at least four to six points of interest. The true test on determining whether a triangle

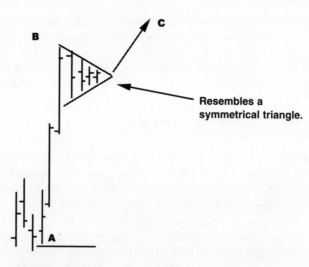

FIGURE 4.5   Pennant Formation

has formed is that prices do not come to test the apex of the triangle. In fact, the reliability of this pattern depends on the fact that the consolidation period in price only reaches three-quarters of the distance to the apex. This pattern is considered a neutral indication, which requires one to watch and wait for a breakout. In order to determine the direction of the breakout, I like to look for a two-period close above the upper resistance trend line. The opposite is true for a breakdown.

2. *Pennant formations* have the same characteristics as the flag in the sense that they represent a price consolidation after a sharp rally. As Figures 4.5 and 4.6 show, the shape resembles a symmetrical triangle, and the measuring technique is similar to that used with the flag. The difference in the shape of the pennant's consolidation is obvious compared to the flag. The difference is that pennants take less time to form—generally one week or 10 periods—and lean toward the direction of the price move. In order to use this formation as a measuring tool, we take the distance from the base of where prices started (point A) to the peak or top of the extended move (point B), as shown in Figure 4.6. Consider this consolidation as the midpoint of the overall move, which would give a targeted price projection that would mark point C as the objective for the price move.

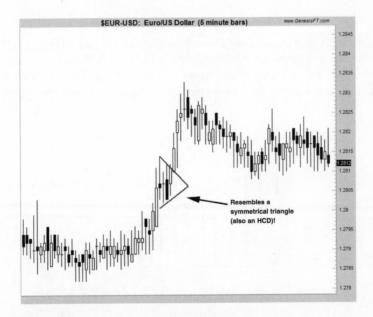

FIGURE 4.6 Pennants Act Similar in Nature to Flags
Used with permission of GenesisFT.com.

3. *Ascending triangles* are similar in nature to symmetrical triangles but have a slight twist in how to use them for price measurement techniques. The bottom trend line slopes up, as shown in Figure 4.7, giving us the clue that the breakout will be to the upside. We can take the widest part of the difference between the upper trend line and the lower trend line and use that amount to gauge how far prices may extend once we see a definitive move.

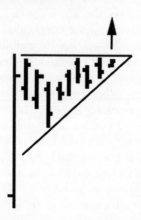

FIGURE 4.7   Ascending Triangle

4. *Descending triangles* are the opposite of ascending triangles. The resistance line slopes down, as shown in Figure 4.8. What I do to help determine the true breakout is to watch for a two-period close below the horizontal support line. If you use this pattern to enter a trade, you can

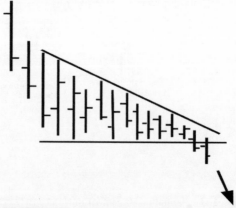

FIGURE 4.8   Descending Triangle

use a stop above the resistance line that slopes downward. Measuring the greatest distance from the beginning point of the descending trend line to the bottom of the support line will give you the price measurement; we should see a breakdown in price occur to help determine a profit objective.

HOT TIP

- Many technicians feel that triangles will have no less than six and no more than eight bounces between the support and resistance lines that determine the triangle formation. We like to see the number three as the "hit" number as that represents triple bottoms and triple tops.
- Watch for the false breakout by avoiding trading the pattern until there is a two-period close outside the trend lines.
- Watch for pattern failure traps as well. This is when the market moves in the desired direction but suddenly reverses and closes back into the body of the congestion pattern.

Let's examine the euro currency chart in Figure 4.9. The symmetrical triangle is a neutral pattern, meaning it does not give a solid clue as to

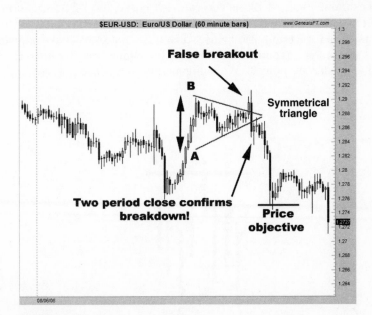

FIGURE 4.9   Single-Close Trap
Used with permission of GenesisFT.com.

the direction of the breakout. We want to watch for what I call the single-close trap, which is what occurs when we see a false breakout on one side for a single period and then an immediate reversal. What you want to focus in on is a sustained price move as prices close at least twice outside the trend lines.

Here is how the measuring technique can help you: Take the widest distance between point A and point B, and then extend that down from the break at the apex of the triangle. That measurement will give you your initial price objective.

1-2-3 PATTERNS

One of the more reliable 1-2-3 patterns is a *"W" bottom*. It is also known as a double bottom with a higher right side breakout; and, of course, it is similarly dubbed a 1-2-3 swing bottom formation, as shown in Figure 4.10. The opposite is what we call an *"M" top*, or double-top pattern, as illustrated in Figure 4.11.

You want to be sensitive to these chart patterns due to the higher frequency of occurrences. Not all "W" bottoms have the same type of reaction and come disguised as rounding bottoms or the cup-and-handle pattern. Let's examine Figure 4.12. As you can clearly see, the 1-2-3 formation was confirmed once the market closed above the first high, or point 2. Once that occurs, look for a two-period close to confirm that prices have adjusted to test a new range expansion. Fibonacci techniques can be introduced in helping to identify point 3. We will generally see a 0.50 percent but more

FIGURE 4.10   1-2-3 Bottom

FIGURE 4.11 1-2-3 Top

than likely a 0.618 percent retracement from the low of point 1 to the high of point 2. The Canadian dollar chart shown in Figure 4.12 is a five-minute chart. We see that prices did trade back as point 3 formed, but never did the price violate or close below the 0.618 percent retracement level. This market broke out once confirmed by the two-period close, which it added on a 48-PIP (percentage in points) gain in less than 50 minutes.

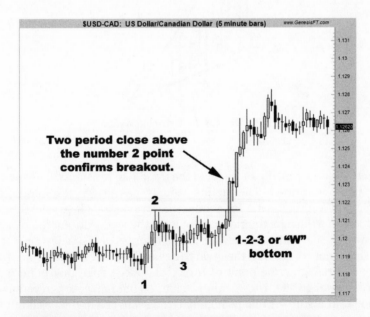

FIGURE 4.12 U.S. Dollar/Canadian Dollar (5-minute bars)
Used with permission of GenesisFT.com.

HOT TIP

The 1-2-3 bottom formations are the beginnings of an Elliott wave pattern. These are generally some of the most powerful buy signals. Watch for point 3 to hold a 0.50 percent or 0.618 percent Fibonacci retracement.

MODIFIED PATTERNS

Falling Wedge Patterns

A *falling wedge pattern* is simply a long-term price pattern that resembles a downward sloping triangle formation, as Figure 4.13 shows. The measurement from the distance of the wedge "opening" to the point of the breakout that occurs near the apex gives the extension or measuring distance used to determine a price objective.

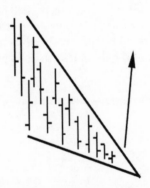

FIGURE 4.13   Declining Wedge

Watch for the first dip or retest of the trend-line resistance line once the breakout is confirmed. This action usually has prices responding like bouncing off a springboard. Remember the two-period close rule: If prices start accepting the new trading zone outside the wedge formation by more than two periods, odds increase for prices to press or test a new high territory. That's not to say that they want to wash you out of the game by retracing and retesting the point of breakout. Once again, that point is the upward resistance line. The 30-minute chart on the Japanese yen versus the U.S. dollar in Figure 4.14 helps highlight the sequence of the breakout and retracement job right before the violent and explosive short covering move takes place.

FIGURE 4.14 Declining Wedges Warn of Sharp Reversals
Used with permission of GenesisFT.com.

Rising Wedge Patterns

Rising wedge patterns are narrowing peaks, as Figure 4.15 illustrates. We can generally see these show up on our radar screens when using moving average convergence/divergence (MACD) or stochastics as they form bearish divergence patterns. We see this formation at the fifth extension wave, which is the end of an Elliott wave cycle. The markets hardly ever reward the masses; and when we see this pattern form, the natural tendency is for traders to overlook the negative implications and only see that prices are making new highs.

Be warned, because after a prolonged uptrend, the narrowing effect of each price range that completes the rising wedge gives a clue that prices are ready to reverse. Keep in mind that after a prolonged uptrend, bulls may be overextending their welcome in the trade. A classic example is shown in Figure 4.16, as descending triangle patterns form as prices plummet. You should watch for these narrowing patterns, and keep in mind that the markets can retest the breakdown support line before resuming the descent, as shown in the Canadian dollar chart.

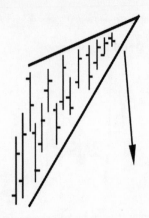

FIGURE 4.15   Rising Wedge

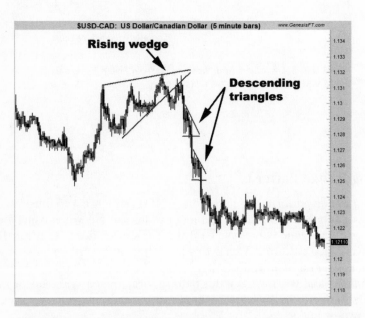

FIGURE 4.16   Rising Wedges Warn of Impending Tops
Used with permission of GenesisFT.com.

FIGURE 4.17   Narrow Sideways Channels

Sideways Trend Channels

A *sideways trend channel* is a type of flag formation. There is not much to explain on how to identify a channel; the market bounces between two parallel trend lines between highs and lows, namely, the support and the resistance trend lines. Figure 4.17 shows it best.

There is a trick, and that is to successfully identify the support or resistance lines early in the channel's development. Once they are established, traders can go long or buy near the support line or sell short or liquidate longs near resistance lines. The element of risk exists when the market finally breaks out from this channel, or band. Chartists can trade another method of these so-called bands by buying once the market breaks out above the resistance line, as confirmed by two consecutive closes above the resistance line, or by taking a short position once the market breaks below the support line, as confirmed by two consecutive lower closes below the support level. Forex traders will see countless opportunities to trade these patterns because they form frequently. One rule of thumb is that the longer the channel, the bigger the breakout. Also watch out for the false breaks. There are many instances where an equal-and-opposite candle pattern will form, thus tricking traders into losing positions. Since sideways channels indicate indecision or a pause, it is only natural for dojis to appear with these ranges. Therefore, I like to watch for shifts in the momentum by trying to spot a high close or a low close doji. Figure 4.18 shows a great example of a low close doji signal within the sideways channel. Treat this setup as you would an LCD pattern. That involves selling on the close of the candle that closes below the doji low or the next time frame's open.

FIGURE 4.18   LCD Setups in Sideways Channels
Used with permission of GenesisFT.com.

Head and Shoulders

Head and shoulders patterns are types of "M" tops. The head and shoulders top or inverted head and shoulders bottom can be used not only as a directional price-indicating pattern but also as a measuring or price-projecting indicator.

A textbook topping pattern is illustrated in Figure 4.19 as the head and shoulders top formation. Head and shoulders tops or bottoms are considered to be strong indicators of major trend reversals. There are four components involved with the head and shoulders pattern: (1) The left shoulder is formed. (2) A higher high occurs forming the head. (3) The development of the right shoulder is formed. (4) The so-called neckline is formed. The symmetry or distance is important. The distance from the left shoulder to the head should be about the same as the distance from the right shoulder to the head. If you measure the distance from the bottom of the head to the neckline, that will give you the next price target level. In other words, by measuring from the bottom of the head to the bottom of the neckline in a head and shoulders top formation, you will be able to project approximately where prices may go. Figure 4.20 shows a perfectly conceived head and shoulders top pattern. If you are looking for a trade based off this formation, keep in mind that this type of pattern is easily recognized by the

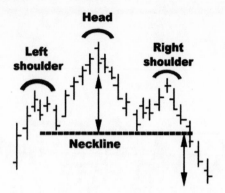

FIGURE 4.19   Head and Shoulders Formation

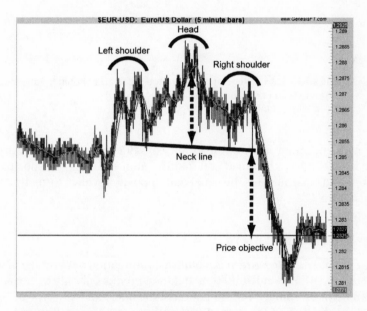

FIGURE 4.20   Euro/U.S. Dollar (5-minute bars)
Used with permission of GenesisFT.com.

masses and, therefore, sometimes does not work. If you sell short, look for a two-period close below the neckline, and make sure the price action does not rally back and take out the high of the right shoulder.

The opposite is true for an inverted head and shoulders bottom formation. If this pattern works, it is great; but you need to be aware of the traps associated with certain patterns, and the failed neckline breakout is a common one. I again stress that you would like to see a two-period close above

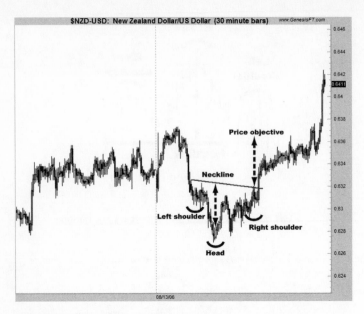

FIGURE 4.21   Regular and Inverted Head and Shoulder Patterns
often Exceed Price Objectives
Used with permission of GenesisFT.com.

the neckline in an inverted head and shoulders bottom to confirm that
prices indeed have reversed and that the momentum is now positive. The
two-period close negates the equal-and-opposite reversal formation as well
(see Figure 4.21).

Cup and Handle Pattern

The *cup and handle pattern* is a bullish continuation pattern that is formed
with a saucer or rounded bottom and then breaks out only to correct back
down before resuming a continuation of the uptrend. It is a type of "W" bottom. William O'Neil is credited with introducing this pattern in his book,
How to Make Money in Stocks (McGraw-Hill, 1988). Figure 4.22 shows the
making of this pattern; there is a high frequency of this variation that occurs
in the forex market since the concept is based on the premise that it forms
in a bullish accumulation period. As its name implies, there are two parts to
the pattern: the cup and the handle. The cup forms after a decline; and as
prices consolidate, the market forms the rounded bottom. As the cup formation completes, a small trading range develops on the right-hand side,
and the handle is formed. A breakout from the handle's trading range signals a continuation of the prior advance.

FIGURE 4.22 Cup and Handle Pattern

Ideally, the depth of the cup should retrace 0.38 percent or less of the previous advance. The handle forms after the high is established from the first rally made on the right side of the cup. Many times the handle resembles a flag or a pennant formation. The handle represents the final consolidation phase before prices go into hyperrally mode. The correction can retrace by 0.38 percent of the cup's advance, but usually not more. The smaller the retracement is, the more bullish the formation and the more significant the breakout.

As with most chart patterns, it is more important to capture the concept of the pattern than every detail; and the one concept with which you should familiarize yourself is a consolidating rounded double bottom. The

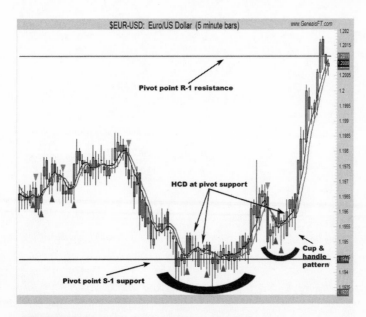

FIGURE 4.23 The Classic Cup and Handle Pattern
Used with permission of GenesisFT.com.

cup is a saucer-shape consolidation, and the handle is a short pullback followed by a breakout. The measuring technique to determine the minimum upside price objective for a cup and handle pattern is figured by adding the height of the cup or saucer bottom to the breakout point from the handle.

Figure 4.23 shows a classic cup and handle pattern as it forms at the pivot point support target in the euro currency based on a five-minute time period. This is the essence of an accumulation period. It tires and bores traders; and as the handle forms, it scare traders into exiting longs or, even worse, going short at support. It is this period of consolidation that creates indecision. Once prices take off, it causes shorts to run like mad for cover.

SUMMARY

The chart patterns covered here integrate with candle charts and all aspects of technical analysis that we will be covering in the next few chapters. As a discretionary trader, once you understand how these patterns form, the psychology behind the consolidation phases will give you the confidence needed to conquer the forex market.

CHAPTER 5

Indicators and Oscillators: Stochastics and MACD

S tochastics is a range-based indicator with the readings set between 0 percent and 100 percent. It is otherwise referred to as a momentum oscillator indicator. George C. Lane is credited with creating the formula. His indicator is a popular technical tool used to help determine whether a market is *overbought,* meaning prices have advanced too far, too soon, and are due for a downside correction, or *oversold,* meaning prices have declined too far, too soon, and are due for an upside correction. It is based on a mathematical formula that is computed to compare the settlement price of a specific time period to the price range of a specific number of past periods.

The theory is based only on the assumption that in a bull, or uptrending, market, prices tend to make higher highs and the settlement price usually tends to be in the upper end of that time period's trading range. When the momentum starts to slow, the settlement price will start to fade from the upper boundaries of the range, and the stochastics indicator will show that the bullish momentum is starting to change. The exact opposite is true for bear, or downtrending, markets.

There are two lines that are referred to as %K and %D. These are plotted on a horizontal axis for a given time period on a vertical axis from 0 percent to 100 percent. This is what the stochastics formula measures on a percentage basis where the closing price is in relationship to the total price range for a predetermined number of days. There is a fast stochastics and a slow stochastics category for most trading software programs. The difference is in how the parameters are set to measure the change in price, which is referred to as a *gauge in sensitivity*. A higher rate of sensitivity will require the number of periods in the calculation to be decreased. This is what "fast" stochastics does—it enables one to generate faster and higher frequency trading signals in a short time period. The fast stochastics setting is best for short-term forex traders. The formula to calculate the first component of fast stochastics using a 14-period setting for %K is as follows:

$$\%K = c - Ln/Hn - Ln * 100$$

where c = closing price of current period
Ln = lowest low during n periods of time
Hn = highest high during n periods of time
n = number of periods

The second calculation is the %D (3-period). It is the moving average of %K.

$$\%D = 100(Hn/Ln)$$

where Hn = the n period sum of $(c - Ln)$.

What is important when using stochastics as a trading tool is understanding the rules of how to interpret buy or sell signals. When the readings are above 80 percent, when %K crosses over the %D line, and when both lines are pointing down, a "hook" sell signal is generated. A confirmed sell signal is triggered once both %K and %D close back beneath the 80 percent line. The exact opposite is true to generate a buy signal: When %K crosses above %D, when the reading is below 20 percent, and when both lines are both pointing up, a "hook" buy signal is generated. A confirmed buy signal is triggered once both %K and %D are crossed over each other and then close back above the 20 percent line.

Markets need volatility in order to move, and we need markets to move in order to trade. We also need to base our trading plans on reliable signals. Setups that trigger an entry don't always work perfectly; therefore, if we have a better understanding of the markets' overall condition or trend direction, then we can apply and use the tools more effectively. I like to exploit the strengths of each trading tool to the best advantage. In order to do so, I need to understand what constitutes their makeup and what strengths or weaknesses these trading tools have. I also use them with more than one confirmation factor, such as pattern recognition, location of prices in relationship to pivot support and resistance levels, and also the phase or condition that the market is in.

Stochastics can be integrated with several techniques, from the Elliott

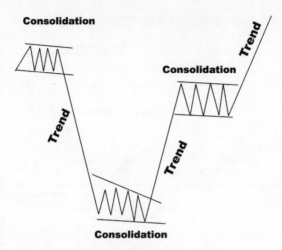

FIGURE 5.1   Market Cycles

wave to simple trend-following tactics, to help you identify opportunities and to help filter better setups and triggers. Understanding that market gyrations move in cycles or phases is another form of pattern observation. Prices move from trend to consolidation and back to trend. Figure 5.1 shows that prices tend to consolidate then trend but also can cycle from highs to lows to highs again within certain periods. I believe that traders get caught in bull and bear traps because they are constantly forming bullish and bearish opinions and fail to realize that while they could be correct in their market predictions in the long term, it is the timing of their entries within these cycle highs and lows that chops them up.

These cycles can often gyrate between support and resistance levels, otherwise referred to as *sideways channels,* or bounce intraday between the predicted pivot support and resistance levels. Using what we have covered already to capture clues for shifts in momentum with the stochastics oscillator, we have the aid of using candle patterns, especially the high close dojis (HCDs) and low close dojis (LCDs), moving average crossovers, and pivot point analysis. These are confirming signals that may corroborate where a turning point might be in the market and help better time an entry or exit for a trade. The stochastics oscillator might help you see what condition the market is in from a perspective of a cycle high period or cycle low period.

Figure 5.2 shows other confirming signals to corroborate the stochastics trading signals. It might benefit you to see if the methodology works in a diverse group of noncorrelated markets. When you test to see how robust or how well a signal responds in different markets, if there is a higher per-

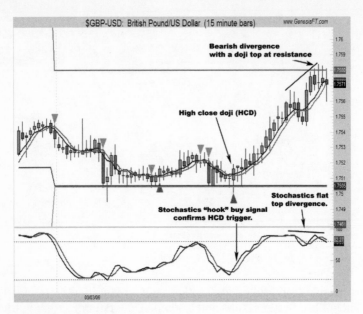

FIGURE 5.2   Stochastics Helps Identify Cycle Highs and Lows
Used with permission of GenesisFT.com.

centage of positive outcomes in various markets in different time periods, then this should help validate the reliability of that signal, which in turn will help you be more confident and give you an edge in your trading. Notice that the high close doji and the moving average crossover corresponded to the stochastics hook buy signal; then as the market reached the projected pivot resistance and as a doji candle formed, the stochastics warned of a bearish divergence. This would give a trader ample warning or confirmation to either tighten stops or exit the trade.

Figure 5.3 is a spot forex euro currency that demonstrates the same setup and trigger that would enter a long position with the %K and %D crossover above the 20 percent line with a confirming higher closing high candle pattern. The sell signal also works well as confirmed when %K and %D both cross over and close back below the 80 percent line. Stochastics helps traders find when the market makes cycles from highs to lows and back again.

The beauty of stochastics is that the formula measures the rate of price change or the momentum of the price movement; when prices are in an uptrend or bullish mode, the close tends to manifest toward the highs. Once this variable starts to fade and prices close closer to the lows, it will warn you that there is a change in the market condition. Prices will cycle from low to high and then back to low. The exception to this is when the market

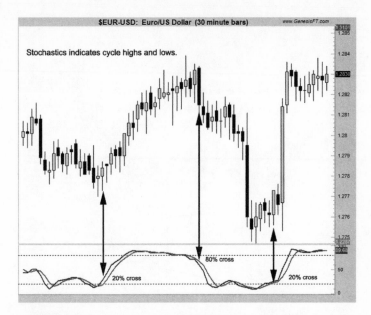

FIGURE 5.3 Stochastics Triggers Buy and Sell Signals
Used with permission of GenesisFT.com.

is in a strong trending condition, leading the stochastics indicator as an in-effective tool.

One other method in which to use the stochastics indicator is trading with a pattern called bullish convergence, as shown in Figure 5. 4. It is used in identifying market bottoms. This is where the market price itself makes a lower low from a previous low, but the underlying stochastics pattern makes a higher low. This indicates that the low is a "false bottom" and can resort to a turnaround for a price reversal. Market prices can and usually do vacillate around the actual pivot point number before making a decision on a directional price move. It is at these points, or market conditions, that you want to use an indicator to help measure the true strength or weakness of the price action. That is what the stochastics indicator does. In Figure 5.4, we see how a secondary low is marked with a higher indicator low. Once we draw the corresponding lines, it appears as if prices and the indicator are actually converging. This is hinting that the secondary low is *not* as bearish as it seems and that a market rally can occur. In essence, this is exactly what happens; and as prices trade above both moving average values, we have a nice trigger to go long for a quick profitable scalp.

Another signal is a trading pattern called bearish divergence, shown in Figure 5.5. It is used in identifying *market tops*: where the market price makes a higher high from a previous high, but the underlying stochastics

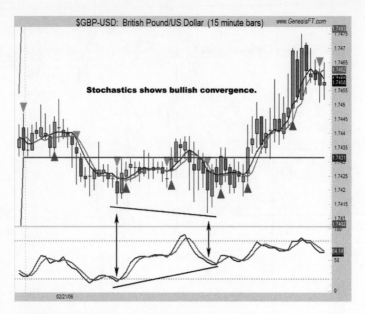

FIGURE 5.4   Bullish Convergence Buy Signal Setup
Used with permission of GenesisFT.com.

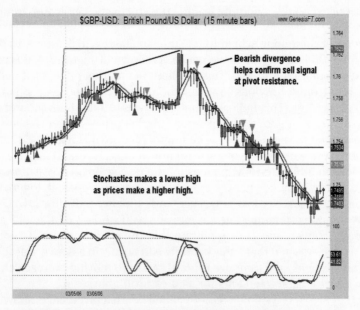

FIGURE 5.5   Bearish Divergence Sell Signal Setup
Used with permission of GenesisFT.com.

pattern makes a lower high. This indicates that the second high is a weak high and can resort to a turnaround for a lower price reversal. The chart shows how the market makes a secondary high, but the corresponding high in the stochastics is at a lower level than the primary high point. This pattern can alert you that if the market appears to be ready for a new bull trend, the stochastics readings should be equal to or higher than the primary peak level. Likewise, a higher high that is accompanied with a lower stochastics reading indicates a potential trend reversal, especially when prices are near a pivot resistance level. Notice the lower closing low off the secondary peak and that %K and %D both cross over and are beneath the 80 percent line. This helps confirm the sell signal that was triggered with the moving average crossovers and the lower closing lows. Bearish divergence signals warn you that there is an impending downtrend of a substantial amount. Therefore, it is important to monitor for divergence patterns.

The bearish divergence pattern signals or forecasts that there is an impending reversal in prices and that one is ready to occur. As I mentioned previously, you can get ready to place an order to act on the signal; but you should not act until the confirmation of a lower closing low triggers the entry, which is on the close or the next open. Here are four rules to guide you to trading a stochastics bearish divergence pattern:

1. The first peak in prices should correspond with a peak in the %K and %D readings above the 80 percent level.
2. The second peak should correspond to a significant higher secondary price high point.
3. If the secondary stochastics peak is less than or under the 80 percent level, this signals a stronger sell signal.
4. Prices should make a lower closing low to confirm a trigger to enter a short position. Enter on the close of the first lower closing low or the next open. The protective stop should be initially placed as a stop close only above the high of the secondary high.

MOVING AVERAGE CONVERGENCE/DIVERGENCE

In simplest terms, *moving average convergence/divergence* (MACD) is an indicator that shows when a short-term moving average crosses over a longer-term moving average. Gerald Appel developed this indicator as we know it today, and he developed it for the purpose of stock trading. It is now widely used for short-term trading signals in stocks, futures, and forex markets, as well as for swing and position traders. It is composed of using three exponential moving averages. The initial inputs for the calculations were the difference between a 12-day and a 26-day exponential smoothed average. The signal line used is a 9-day smoothing of today's MACD value, subtracted from the last time period's MACD value. Most charting packages give the 12-period and 26-period averages and use the smoothed average of a 9-period average for the signal line.

There are many variations, and most charting software packages allow you to change the parameters. Just remember that the fewer time periods you input, the more sensitive the indicator will be to price changes. Therefore, with fewer time periods, an indicator will generate more signals. Longer time periods help smooth out the false crossover signals. Some variations to consider are using 10-period and 24-period averages and an 8-period input for the smoothed average signal line.

The concept behind this indicator is to calculate a value that is the difference between the two exponential moving averages, which then compares that to the 9-period exponential moving average. What we get is a moving average crossover feature and a zero-line oscillator, and that helps us to identify overbought and oversold market conditions. These moving average crossovers also show us shifts in momentum that help identify buy and sell signals, as Figure 5.6 illustrates.

I might add that since traders are now more computer savvy than ever before, many charting software packages allow changing or optimizing the

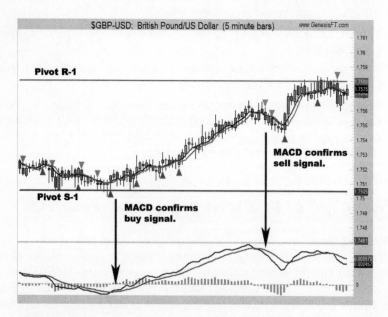

FIGURE 5.6   MACD Triggers Buy and Sell Signals
Used with permission of GenesisFT.com.

settings or parameters. In other words, it is easy to change, or tweak, the variables in original calculations. Traders can increase the time periods in the moving average calculations to generate fewer trade signals and can shorten the time periods to generate more trade signals. Just as is the case for most indicators, the higher the number of time periods used, the less sensitive the indicator will be to changes in price movements.

MACD signals react quickly to changes in the market, and that is why a lot of analysts, including myself, use it. It helps clear the picture when moving average crossovers occur. Figure 5.7 shows that where the moving averages cross over at corresponding low points on the chart, a bullish convergence develops as prices make a lower low but the moving average component makes a higher low. Since MACD measures the relative strength between current prices as compared to past time frames, giving a short-term perspective relative to a longer-term perspective, we are able to detect internal changes in the market, such as a bullish reversal.

Here are a few general points to help you understand how to use this indicator: When the fast line crosses above the slow line, a buy signal is generated; the opposite is true for sell signals. The MACD also has a zero-baseline component called the *histogram* that is created by subtracting the slower signal line from the MACD line. If the MACD line is above the zero line, prices are usually trending higher. The opposite is true if the

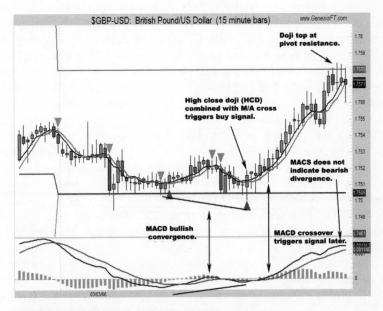

FIGURE 5.7 MACD Bullish Convergence Signals
Used with permission of GenesisFT.com.

MACD is declining below the zero line. The MACD is a lagging indicator because it is based off moving averages. We want to look for the zero-line crossovers to identify market changes and to help confirm trade entries or to trigger action to exit a position. Watching for clues that identify shifts in momentum as the market moves from one extreme to another or from overbought to oversold to trigger a trading opportunity can be identified with the aid of MACD readings in both the moving average and the histogram component. While it is more profitable in buying the absolute bottom, that is a haphazard guessing game to play.

Trading based on a set of rules and being able to use a confirming indicator to identify a change in price direction and then following that price movement is the essence of how to make money in the markets. The guidelines for taking buy and sell signals using bullish and bearish divergence as described at the beginning of the chapter can also be applied using MACD. However, with the MACD, we can see the convergence and divergence in the moving average lines. These convergence bottoms and divergence top patterns form more often in the histogram bars. But you absolutely need to pay attention to the moving average component, which can act as an excellent guide in detecting shifts in momentum. The key to effectively trading bullish convergence or bearish divergence patterns is that they must occur within a relatively short period of time. For example, on a daily chart, you would want to see a pattern form within 30 days.

Take, for example, the daily chart in Figure 5.8 of the spot Swiss franc. The MACD histogram helped identify a bullish divergence pattern, but the moving average component rally stood out as identifying the reversal. See how the secondary low on the price chart was significantly lower than the first low, while the corresponding lows of the moving average component of the MACD made higher highs. The pattern in the MACD was a higher right-side double bottom, while the actual price made a lower low. When a convergence like this develops on a daily chart pattern, day traders should be using a shorter time period to take buy signals within a newly formed uptrend. Signals like these will keep you on the right side of the market. Using convergence and divergence signals from higher time frames is a very powerful methodology for finding high-probability trading opportunities for short-term traders. If there is a bullish trend reversal signal that is clearly identified using stochastics or an MACD indicator on a daily chart, then you want to look for corresponding buy signals on the 60- or 15-minute time frames.

Looking at Figure 5.9 in the Canadian dollar, you should notice that the top pattern peaks with a corresponding lower double-top pattern within the MACD moving average component. The process took less than one month to form and, as such, met the criteria that a bearish divergence pattern formed. Now traders can seek out shorter-term sell signals.

Markets spend a majority of the time in consolidation phases and have

FIGURE 5.8   MACD Bullish Convergence Shows in Moving
Average Component
Used with permission of GenesisFT.com.

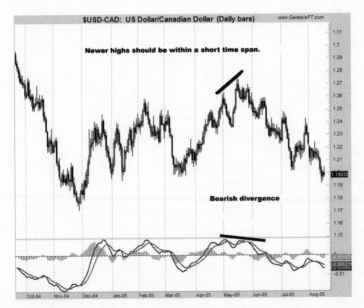

FIGURE 5.9   MACD Bearish Divergence Shows in Moving
Average Component
Used with permission of GenesisFT.com.

a tendency to explode in a breakout trend in relatively short order. This price behavior occurs while the majority of traders are either on the sidelines or on the wrong side. That is why I prefer stochastics over the MACD study. The fast stochastics indicator generally gives confirmation on triggers earlier than the MACD studies do. In the chart in Figure 5.10, notice that the high close doji triggers a buy that is confirmed and is in sync with the stochastics signal. The MACD triggers substantially later.

Let's examine this relationship more closely by studying the euro currency chart in Figure 5.11. The pivot point system signals are more in line with the cycles of the stochastics as the MACD confirms price reactions much later. This is not bad; it is just that the pivot point moving average component and stochastics are better. As I have previously stated, markets move in cycles, from trend to consolidation; as such, the aid of these two indicators will give you a better read on market conditions. It is reasonable to believe that as prices move, using both indicators will allow you to identify whether you are in the beginning of a trend or closer to the end. That is what will help you to be more selective in your trades. Add to this mix of studies the ability to understand the psychology behind candle patterns, and your reaction to market behavior should improve greatly. See how the tweezer top formation on this 30-minute chart corresponded with a stochastics bearish divergence and how, as the trade system gave a sell signal,

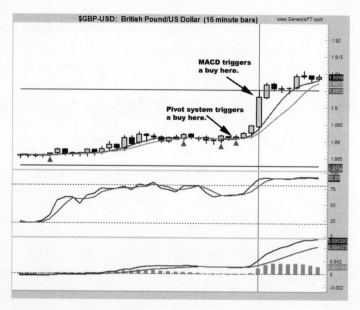

FIGURE 5.10   Stochastics Triggers Signal before MACD
Used with permission of GenesisFT.com.

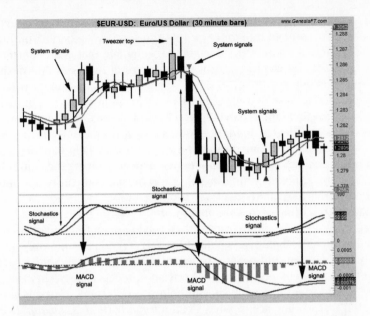

FIGURE 5.11 Tweezer Top Candles and Stochastics Triggers before MACD
Used with permission of GenesisFT.com.

the stochastics %K and %D both closed back under the 80 percent line. The MACD gives a valid confirmation. but unfortunately it gives a signal nearly 40 PIPs (percentage in points) late. That difference alone can define what makes a profitable day trade versus an unprofitable one.

ANTICIPATING TRADE SIGNALS

Many traders inappropriately anticipate trading signals. Under certain conditions or circumstances, you need to do this in order to gain an edge in the market. Scanning for convergence and divergence patterns is one of the few times you can and should anticipate. However, it is important to act on a confirmation of a trigger. These triggers come at the close of each time period.

TREND LINE CONFIRMATIONS

Up to now, we have covered basic as well as advanced techniques using the stochastics and MACD indicators and have demonstrated how they integrate with each other, how candle patterns can help confirm trade signals generated by these indicators, and how to use them in conjunction with pivot points. (We will go into more on this subject as we examine building a trading system in Chapter 8.) One simple technique that is an enormous help that you should use to confirm potential trend reversals and trading opportunities is using simple trend line analysis. When combined with either stochastics or MACD trade signals, as we have just learned, applying simple trend line techniques can help you not only identify but also confirm entry as well as exit levels. Pivot points will give you a heads-up on a target level to watch in a given time period; the indicators can help you identify if a trend is weakening, especially in a convergence or divergence situation arises. Then, by applying simple trend line analysis, you can really determine your entries and build on a trading opportunity.

Drawing trend lines is extremely important for the hands-on trader. If you need to look at the charts rather than relying on automatically generated trading signals, then this is a must for you. Trend lines not only serve as identifying support and resistance levels but also quickly identify reversal points and shifts in momentum, otherwise stated as changes in price direction. Simple trend line analysis can help you determine if prices move too far, too fast, if they are in what I call a *hyperbolic unsustainable extreme price move*, which we see with very steep trend lines drawn. If the market moves sideways or tries to trend higher, we see a low-angle or flat trend line. The best trend to follow is when prices move along a 45-degree angle. This is a healthy development and indicates a sustainable move. In an uptrend, prices should move up and bounce against the support trend line for a good period of time.

With this angle, you should expect a nice price advance. Therefore, it will help you demonstrate patience in order to allow the trade to mature to maximize profits. Figure 5.12 shows the three categories of trend conditions in a bullish mode; the opposite would be true for downtrends. Always remember that the 45-degree angle is the ideal trend formation. This is how you want prices to trend when you want to stay with a trade. As the old saying goes, the trend is your friend; any trend that is too steep can also be your friend, as long as you do not over stay your welcome.

In order to determine when a bullish market officially makes a trend line break, I like to use the lower closing low and the two-period close rule, as we went over earlier, to confirm that prices have indeed signaled an imminent price change or an early warning of a trend reversal. Here is how I use trend line breaks combined with stochastics or MACD indicators to help identify trading opportunities:

- I want to see lower closing lows from one or two prior time periods.
- I want to see confirmation of a price change with two consecutive closes below a support line.

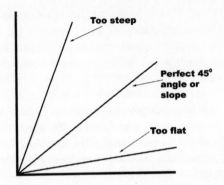

FIGURE 5.12 Trend Line Angles in Bullish Mode

Let's examine Figure 5.13. Focus on point A along the chart. The price graph in the top section of the chart shows the peak in prices as formed by a shooting star candle. See how that peak is higher than the past 10 sessions' high. The corresponding points as referred to in the middle section of the chart is the fast stochastic indicator, where we see prices making a higher high but the indicator has a lower low (bearish divergence). The

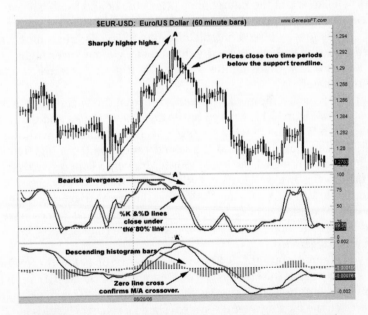

FIGURE 5.13 Stochastics and MACD Confirm Trendline Break
Used with permission of GenesisFT.com.

bottom section is the MACD indicator that does not show the moving average component illustrating a divergence pattern. However, the histogram component shows declining bars; and as the market breaks and closes not one but two time periods below the trend line, see how a zero-line cross is confirmed in the MACD histogram? Here is how you would trade this setup. You identify the market moving higher and draw a support line under the series of lows. You have ample clues that the bullish condition is weakening as the momentum indicators signal the bearish divergence pattern. What really highlights this sell signal is the fact that the %K and the %D components of the stochastics have met our criteria, as they have now crossed and closed back below the 80 percent level. Once prices close for the second period below the trend line, you would sell at the market. Your stop-loss order can be one of several choices:

1. Place a hard stop above the high formed by the shooting star candle.
2. Place a mental stop-close-only order above the high, and use a trailing stop method once the market moves in the desired price direction.
3. Use a time condition set so that if you do not see performance of the trade as desired within two to three time periods, you will exit the position at the market.

As you can see in the figure, once prices break and establish two consecutive closes below the upward support line, a sell signal would be triggered. At this time, we see immediate results follow as prices move in the desired direction and condition. By this, I mean we see lower highs, lower lows, and new lower closing lows. The trade is seeing positive results almost immediately.

Let's step back a moment now and start from the beginning. Compare Figure 5.13 to Figure 5.14, where I have added pivot points and the Defcon III indicators. With the moving averages overlaid, combined with the predicted pivot support levels and the added candle patterns highlighting a high close doji buy signal, we could look at drawing a supportive trend line from the lows as prices advance. Let's say you took the buy signal in the euro and followed the move up. Notice that the arrow triggering the exit or a new short position occurs at point A. Notice also that prices have not closed below the support line by two consecutive time periods, but a sell signal was triggered.

If you entered a buy at 128.40 and used a hard stop below the low of the doji, using the aid of the stochastics oscillator and/or the MACD, both indicators were confirming to stay long until the signal to sell occurs at point A. Once we see the moving average system signal a sell, stochastics confirms

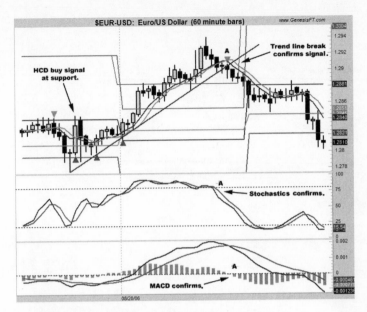

FIGURE 5.14 Euro/U.S. Dollar (60-minute bars)
Used with permission of GenesisFT.com.

with an 80 percent line cross by the %K and %D lines. The MACD follows one bar later. The moving average component of MACD and the zero-line cross coincide with the second close below the trend line as well. If you can learn to spot these triggers and act on these specific patterns and sequence of events, especially as the divergence warns, you will see significant improvement in your bottom line.

MAKING GOOD USE OF TREND LINES

Let's make good use of learning the importance of trend line analysis as it corroborates other techniques in technical analysis. We previously looked at when the market peaked. Then we took a step back and studied the pattern and trade signal from buy to sell. Now let's follow the progress of the last sell signal. Figure 5.15 shows how we drew the resistance trend line from the peak, or the highest point made from the shooting star at 129.40, and extended it out to the first reactionary high at 128.80 and then shifted the line all the way to the right of the chart.

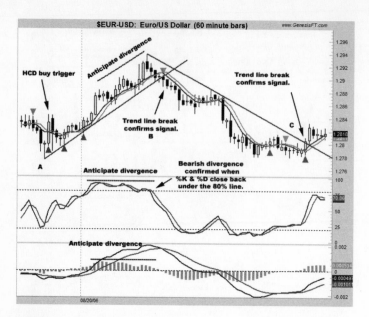

FIGURE 5.15 Bearish Divergence Confirms Trendline Breaks
Used with permission of GenesisFT.com.

SUMMARY

Stochastics is used to identify that a trend has reversed or that a new cycle
phase has developed. MACD signals are given after a market has moved in
a new trend; therefore, this indicator is mostly used as a confirmation tool,
rather than as a trigger tool. Finding a setup pattern that meets your trade
objectives from your entry, the loss or risk factor as well as the exit plan
can all be achieved using the steps we have disclosed in the book up to this
point. The most important factor is that you trade based on a defined set of
rules, mostly using the guidelines and theories presented so far. Following
trend and mean reversion techniques can be rewarding when you stick to a
game plan. However, no matter how well you execute a trading decision,
you need to manage and monitor the trade and base your exit strategy
within the time frame or price objectives dictated by the market. Indicators,
trend lines, and pivot points, as great as they are, only go so far.

CHAPTER 6

Fibonacci Combined with Pivot Points

This chapter highlights the many benefits that leading price indicators like Fibonacci price extensions, projections, and retracement analysis can offer you. Fibonacci analysis is popular; yet some believe it is a complex study. Most traders are familiar with the common correction numbers—38 percent, 50 percent, and 0.618 percent levels. However, there is a lot more to Fibonacci than just these ratios and how to use them. This chapter is designed to give you a good understanding of how to use this technical tool as it applies with other measuring techniques, such as Elliott wave theory, which we will cover shortly, and how to incorporate Fibonacci price levels using pivot point analysis. In addition, the CD (compact disk) that comes with this book includes a Fibonacci calculator and a pivot point calculator so that you can develop your own trading plan based on these studies without having to purchase extra software. Or perhaps these calculators will help support the software you currently use. Best of all, these calculators may give you an edge in determining longer-term price objectives, such as quarterly or annual price outlooks, which most software cannot do.

WHO AND WHAT IS FIBONACCI?

Leonardo Fibonacci (1170–1240) of Pisa, Italy, was a thirteenth-century mathematician who discovered that there was a relationship with adding numbers together; from that, the dividing relationship resulted in repetitive percentage figures. Simply put, a *Fibonacci series* is an infinite series of numbers such that the sum of any two consecutive numbers is the next number in the series. An example is 1, 2, 3, 5, 8, 13, 21, 34, 55, 89, 144, 233, 377, 610, 987, and so on. If you take 1 + 2, you get 3; then if you take 2+ 3, you get 5; and if you take 3 + 5, you get 8; and so on. Incidentally, the Chinese practice of feng shui gives a high value to the number eight. It is regarded as a wealth symbol. Even though feng shui is not related to Fibonacci numbers, the number 8 itself is; and 8 is a figure some technicians use to determine the amount of time periods a market might move in a consecutive trend. After a market moves up 8 bars, or time periods, many will exit the trade as the number 8 was the period of times a move occurred. This is just one of the coincidences with the number 8 in various cultures.

Fibonacci ratios are numbers derived from the calculations within the Fibonacci series numbers. The most common numbers are 0.382 percent, 0.50 percent, 0.618 percent, 0.786 percent, 1.00 percent, 1.272 percent, and 1.618 percent. The *Golden ratio* is often referred to for the number 0.618 due to the many coincidences that reoccur with that number; for example, 89 = 0.618 of 144, 144 divided by 233 = 0.618, 0.382 + 0.618 = 1.00, 0.786 = square root of 0.618.

HOT TIP

The 50 percent correction level is widely followed by the masses. Therefore, it is important to identify a correction at that percentage level on several different time frames, such as the yearly range, the monthly range, the weekly range, the daily range, and, of course, the current wave or price move in which you are trading.

FIBONACCI CORRECTION

This section is going to discuss how to use these ratios to determine predicting price corrections as well as extending out in time a potential price objective based on waves or prior moves. I have an observation that when a market is in sync or respects a Fibonacci ratio price level, it can and generally does stay in sync with the Fibonacci ratio correction or extension price projections. With that said, let's go over what the difference is between the terms *correction projection* and *extensions* and how I use and define them.

Also referred to as a retracement, when a market makes a move from

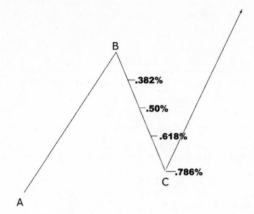

FIGURE 6.1   Fibonacci Retracement Percentages

a low to a high, prices will have a tendency to pull back, retrace, or correct. The percentage of the pullback can be 0.382 percent, 0.50 percent, 0.618 percent, 0.786 percent, and, at times, even 1.00 percent. When looking for bullish setups, it makes sense that we want to target buying opportunities especially on pullbacks when the market is in an uptrend. This is when we will use a Fibonacci tool to identify the percentage figure and look for that as a potential support to enter a long position.

Figure 6.1 shows the correction point C can be the percentage of the distance from point A to point B. Once that retracement is completed, then we look for the market to reverse and to continue in the direction of the initial trend.

FIBONACCI EXTENSIONS

There are times when a pullback can retrace beyond the original starting point and exceed 100 percent of the initial wave or trend. So a *Fibonacci extension* is essentially a correction that exceeds the low of the initial trend. Technicians will use the 100 percent, 1.272 percent, and 1.618 percent ratios to target a pullback level. This state of correction can be considered a double bottom at the 100 percent pullback level; and when we see that correction exceed the low of point A, we see raids on stops. By using the extension tool, you may have a great spot to place your stop orders and keep stop-loss orders out of harm's way by using the hidden, or invisible, support and resistance levels, as determined by the Fibonacci extension technique. As you can see in Figure 6.2, prices penetrate below the low as indicated at point A. Let's say you went long; you could determine a dollar

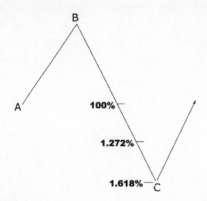

FIGURE 6.2   Fibonacci Extension Percentages

amount risk factor based on these Fibonacci extension levels or use them as add-on points of entry.

FIBONACCI PROJECTIONS

A *Fibonacci projection* is simply the determining of a potential price objective and is a vital component in Elliott wave theory. It is an excellent confirmation tool to identify potential trend-exhaustion turning points. Figure 6.3 shows how to determine a bullish upside objective by measuring the range of the wave, or the swing, as it is also called. Multiply that sum by

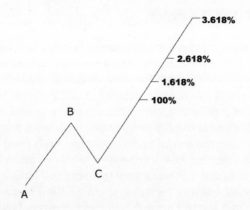

FIGURE 6.3   Fibonacci Bullish Projection Ratios

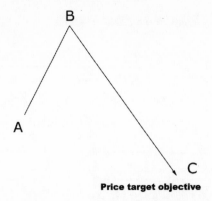

FIGURE 6.4 Fibonacci Corrections

the corresponding ratios, which are 0.618 percent; 1.00 percent; 1.618 percent; 2.618 percent; and, for extreme moves, 3.618 percent. In a bullish trend, add that figure to the low, or point C, which is the correction low; this will give you the projected extension price objective.

Figure 6.4 shows how to use the Fibonacci ratios to determine bearish price projections. If point C is a correction, take the measurement of A – B, multiply that amount by the corresponding Fibonacci ratio, and subtract that figure from point B, which will give you a downside price objective, or the targeted support level of point C.

As you examine Figure 6.5, which is a spot euro FX, you will see how to effectively use the Fibonacci tool. If in a given time period that the pivot point analysis or pivot support or resistance numbers have hit you are looking for further clues as to price direction or support or resistance levels within the pivot numbers, Fibonacci will be your greatest tool. Once we indicate what the established low is at point A, as the market rallies, we see a top, which is formed by a doji. All that is needed is to figure what the possible support or targeted low will be on the correction. Point C is the exact 50 percent retracement on the pullback. One of the most important elements to watch here is this: If the support holds and is a valid spot to buy the retracement, then you want the market to continue to close above the support numbers. That is exactly what happens here.

Let's see how we would use the Fibonacci extension method to establish an upside price objective. Take a look at Figure 6.6: The first step is to establish the low, shown on the euro currency chart as point A. Then as the peak, or top, is determined at point B, we would extend that distance by 1.618 percent or 2.00 percent. If the market respects a 50 percent pullback and begins to resume the uptrend, using a Fibonacci extension tool will help alert you to a profit target. As I stated before, I like to think that a mar-

FIGURE 6.5 Market Respects 50 Percent Correction Levels
Used with permission of GenesisFT.com.

ket that is in sync with the Fibonacci ratio numbers stays in sync with Fibonacci price objections. In this chart, the pullback was 50 percent of A – B move, and the market held the Fibonacci extension resistance targets.

Fibonacci works with day trading to determine support and resistance levels within the pivot point areas as well as to help forecast the projected ranges. Figure 6.7 is a euro currency chart that shows the daily pivot lines with the 0.38 percent retracement level. The Fibonacci correction tool can be used as a way to identify whether the trend will reverse or continue. Let's study the chart in Figure 6.7. The market is already on a downtrend; if you missed the sell signal at the very top, when do you join the trend and sell or look for a buying opportunity? As the market establishes a bottom, as indicated at point B, using the Fibonacci tool, we see the correction levels indicating resistance at the 38 percent, 50 percent, and 618 percent retracement areas. Point C stops dead on a dime at the 38 percent level.

In fact, that reversal triggers a sell signal using the pivot point moving average method; and as you can see, the market resumes the downtrend. The arrows illustrate a sell signal as the market closes below a prior low and below the moving averages. It was the rejection of the Fibonacci 38 percent resistance that helped confirm a trading opportunity. If you take a short position at the 0.38 percent rejection level, you should use an initial stop-close-only above the high at point C and then adjust the stop-loss ac-

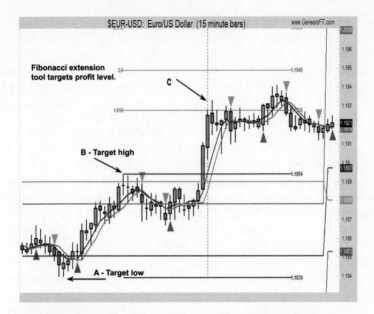

FIGURE 6.6 Prices Move in Sync from Fibonacci Corrections to Extension Objectives
Used with permission of GenesisFT.com.

FIGURE 6.7 Rejection at Fibonacci Resistance Triggers a Sell
Used with permission of GenesisFT.com.

cordingly. This means we change from a mental stop-close-only to a hard stop; then, depending on whether you scale out of a portion of your position, you adjust your stop according to how many lots you have left on.

Here is how you can put Fibonacci correction levels to good use while integrating them with pivot point support and resistance numbers. This is a technique that is more in line with what day traders will encounter on a more frequent basis. Figure 6.8 shows a 15-minute chart on the Aussie dollar. As you can see, the market moved into a bullish trend mode early, only to stall at the projected pivot resistance level. The high of the session is formed by a doji, which indicates indecision. No call to action is made just yet; as a system or rule-based trader, you need to wait until there is confirmation of a breakdown of either support or a conditional change in prices by a series of lower highs, lower closes than opens, lower lows, and closes below prior lows. Most important, you want confirmation of a sell signal when the market closes below the low of the doji.

The trigger to sell would be on that candle's close or the next time period's open. The stop would be placed initially as a stop-close-only above the high of the doji. Immediately, we see instant gratification as prices plunge. But as what can normally occur is an upside correction that takes

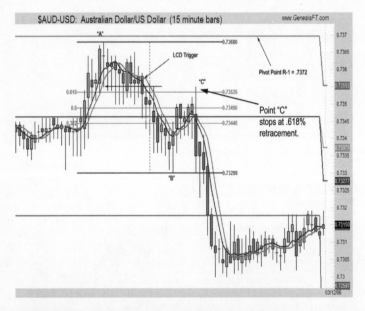

FIGURE 6.8   Doji Top Forms at Pivot Resistance Where Fibonacci Analysis Takes Over to Help Traders
Used with permission of GenesisFT.com.

place, in this example, the correction takes the form of a consolidation period that lasts nearly one hour and forty-five minutes. This period of indecision can create havoc, doubt, and uncertainty; and your mind can start to play tricks on you.

This is the consolidation period that generates indecision. At this point, you have a good setup, prices have violated support, resistance has held, and there is a high-probability pattern that you recognize that generates reliable price action, namely the low close doji sell signal. But you are faced with these internal forces that may cause you to exit a well-defined trade. After all, you have a risk factor and a potential reward objective already mapped out. However, this consolidation period is creating more and more doubt about whether you should stay in the trade. Here is when you need to take advantage of the time the market is in the pause period and go to work. You now have a distinguishable high and a low made. Using the Fibonacci ratios, you determine the correction levels. As such, you have identified that the 50 percent and the 0.618 percent Fibonacci retracement levels are holding the market down.

Armed with this information, you will not be surprised or forced to react emotionally when prices rebound but do not penetrate above these levels. As Figure 6.8 shows, the correction hits the 0.618 percent retracement level as defined by point C and almost immediately prices collapse. The market rewards the disciplined and patient trader, as such Fibonacci correction levels will help you to identify what I consider pattern traps. What generally occurs in order for the market to finally fall out of bed, like it does as shown in Figure 6.8, is a period of time to consolidate and attract buyers. It is within this congestion period, when it fails to support and prices breach below the lows, that traders are forced to sell like mad. This setup was a textbook sell signal as this book has taught you from the beginning. There was little to no heat to take on the trade. It did require patience and discipline to see the trade through. But this is how the Fibonacci tool can work in your favor. Use the Fibonacci tool to help you uncover the hidden resistance levels within a newly defined trend and stay on the right side of the market longer.

I prefer pivot points, but the fact is that no single tool is the holy grail. There are many instances where Fibonacci studies outperform pivot point analysis to help target price-measurement objectives. There will be times when the daily pivot numbers will not come into play as they will be too far away from the current market price or the market will blow right past them, for example, if a prior trading session has an unusually small-range day and then, during the following session, a major report or event wreaks havoc on the market. With an increase in volatility, we can assume that there might be an expanded range and that the pivot support or resistance numbers may not be as effective. This is where you can harness the predictive power of the Fibonacci correction or extension technique to help uncover hidden value areas.

In Figure 6.9, using the Fibonacci extension tool, once we have the high identified, as shown at point A, we need to look for a low point, or a reactionary low, as it is called. As the chart shows, the price action blows right past the daily predicted pivot point support level and forms point B. The market now goes into another consolidation phase, in which we can see the pivot support level now acting as a resistance level as prices hold at point C. By using the Fibonacci extension tool, we can determine how far the market can decline. The first objective is the 1.618 percent extension and the next level is the 2.00 percent objective—point D on the chart. This technique really does help you determine a good profit target objective when all else fails.

The reason why this is a valuable tool is fairly obvious: If you are scale trading and peeling off positions and milking the trade by trailing stops on portions of your positions, the Fibonacci tool gives you profit target levels so you let the trade run. All that is needed is to manage the trade set orders to cover shorts at these hidden target levels. This book comes with a Fibonacci calculator that includes the correction and extension tool. I believe that if you are new to trading and do not have a charting software package

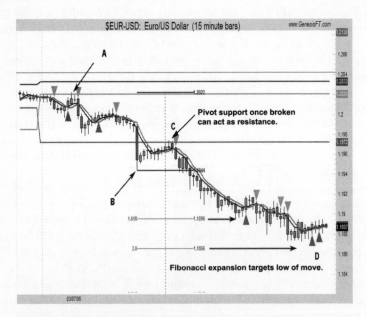

FIGURE 6.9 Fibonacci Extensions Target Profit Objectives
Used with permission of GenesisFT.com.

that includes this feature, you will find the CD extremely helpful. Once you determine the calculations, you can simply use a drawing tool on your charts with the figures. I have included a simulated demonstration on the CD as well.

SUMMARY

Fibonacci analysis is not complicated when using the numbers as a tool to determine retracement levels for intraday trading. I find that pivot points on the various time frames, such as daily, weekly, and monthly, work more effectively more times than not; so for me, Fibonacci is doing double the work for longer-term analysis. However, with the software like Genesis, it certainly does not hurt to use Fibonacci analysis; and it works extremely effectively for day trading corrections on strong-trending days. The narrow-range days, where pivot analysis will be ineffective for the most part, will occur but not that frequently; but when these narrow-range days occur, I believe you will be glad you know how to use and apply Fibonacci calculations.

CHAPTER 7

Elliott Wave Theory

R alph Nelson Elliott (1871–1948) studied the stock market exten-
sively. Back in the 1920s, he observed that both bullish and bearish
market moves occur in three distinct phases. He began to develop
theories and views that the overall prices in stock market averages move in
waves. This was presumed to fall in line with the understanding of the work
of Charles Dow as defined in the Dow Theory. Elliott was able to see patterns reoccur and reflected this in his work titled *Nature's Law—The Se-
crets of the Universe* (1946), in which he states, "Even though we may not
understand the cause underlying a particular phenomenon, we can, by observation, predict that phenomenon's recurrence" (p. 4).

The purpose of this chapter is to give you an introduction to what Elliott wave theory is and how you can apply this method in the forex market
in combination with what we have already covered—incorporating such
traditional chart patterns as triangles and wedges alongside Fibonacci
analysis. I believe it is important that traders have a complete understanding of not only chart patterns, cycles, and trends but also phases or waves.
Elliott wave principles can help you uncover just that and, more specifically, what phase, or wave, the market trend is in. As you may have already
discovered, the forex market trades in phases, from periods of consolida-
tions to trending modes. With the knowledge of Elliott wave principles, this
information may give you a better understanding of which side the market
to be on and how to capture profitable moves with surgical precision.
Hopefully, more times than not, you will be trading from the winning side.

THE WAVE CYCLE

Since many of the concepts explained already are great tools in themselves, combining them with Elliott wave is something that has been achieved and practiced even by Mr. Elliott himself. His discoveries were simply a compelling phenomenon in the art of forecasting price moves. I will cover the basis for his discoveries and the overall strengths and weaknesses of his work. Keep in mind that Elliott wave is a fractal concept in which it works in multiple time frames; so it can truly benefit all styles of trading for day, swing, and position traders. *Fractal concept* is defined as cycles or patterns that repeat in shorter-term and develop in longer-term time periods, meaning there are waves within waves.

A completed Elliott wave cycle from bullish to bearish or bearish to bullish consists of eight waves. There are two distinct wave definitions: (1) *Impulse waves* are the ones moving with the main trend. Impulse waves have five primary price movements. (2) *Corrective waves* move against the main trend. Corrective waves are seen as having three primary price movements, which are lettered and run opposite to the direction of the main trend. A healthy long-term trend follows the indication of heavier volume during the impulse waves (1, 3, and 5). In forex, we do not have access to volume studies or data; however, we can borrow this information once again from the futures markets or the stock market with the exchange traded funds, such as the Euro Currency Trust (FXE) as discussed in Chapter 1.

It is assumed that Elliott used some of Fibonacci work because a complete wave cycle is composed of eight price moves, five up and three down (remember that 3, 5, and 8 are coincidentally Fibonacci numbers). The fundamental concept behind Elliott's theory is that bull markets have a tendency to follow a basic five-wave advance, followed by a three-wave decline. Figure 7.1 best defines a bullish cycle. The exact opposite is true for bear markets. More experienced chartists would recognize that the end of a bullish-move fifth point could possibly be considered the number-one point of a 1-2-3 formation, or the top of a head and shoulders formation.

The one thing Elliott most wanted chartists to recognize is that his wave theory worked on long-term charts as well as on intraday charts. It does not matter what time frame you trade in; a wave is a wave. The idea here is that each wave is simply a subset of another wave, just to a lesser degree. Each wave is itself part of the higher-degree wave. We can define this by saying that waves of one time frame can be expanded to relate to a higher time period and that one time frame can be subdivided into a shorter-term time frame.

Figure 7.2 might help define that description. Another way of explaining this concept is that you might see a five-wave count on a 60-minute

Uptrend contains five numbered waves.

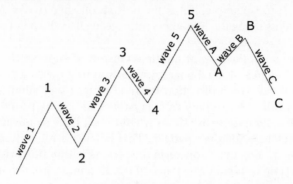

Correction contains three lettered waves.

FIGURE 7.1 Elliott Wave Cycle

chart that, when converted to a weekly chart, would be one full wave count for the weekly time period. Also we can see a five-wave count on a five-minute chart that composes just one wave on a daily chart.

Elliott wave theory combines the best of traditional charting techniques and price pattern formations, such as triangles and wedges. These are simply consolidation patterns within trends. These trend phases are considered waves. Price objectives from predicting possible highs or lows can be determined through the use of Fibonacci ratios and the corresponding rules associated with each wave description. I have had

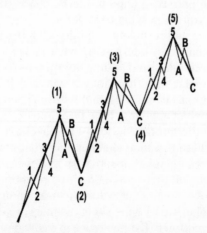

FIGURE 7.2 Elliott Wave Fractal Concept

tremendous success identifying turning points as indicated by the maturity of a price move; for example, if it is the bottom of wave two or four, look for support targets using the Fibonacci ratios as well as the pivot point support targets.

When I see a confluence, or multiple cluster, of support targets from using both techniques, it heightens my assertion to go with a position because I understand which direction to trade from. I will admit there are times when an Elliott wave pattern is crystal clear and helps me trade on the winning side; then there are times when I don't have a clue and cannot make out any clear or distinct pattern. That is when I rely on other techniques, such as trading in a short-term time frame within the direction of a higher-degree time frame. For instance, if the 15-minute trend is up, classified by the market trading above a set of moving averages (namely, pivot point averages), then I look for buy signals as defined by a series of higher highs, higher lows, and higher closing highs as prices trade above a set of moving averages on the five-minute time period.

Elliott wave relates well with the forex market and is a valuable technical tool. Trading is not about being rigid and sticking with just one method. Market conditions change, which requires using an assortment of tools to improve your market forecasting abilities. I believe studying and using Elliott wave will improve your chances for success. The fact that it is comprised of wave forms, Fibonacci correction, and projection ratios and has a time element as waves' magnitudes are concerned makes it a complete and comprehensive analytical tool. The Elliott wave principle was originally applied for the stock market, but the core foundation of its decipherable use was based on the premise of mass human psychology. Due to the exorbitant extent of trading on a global scale in foreign currency, I find it works well; when the patterns jump out on the charts, they really are a major asset, as long as you know what to look for.

In a world of chaotic and turbulent volatility, Elliott wave attempts to give a trader a better chance of interpreting what phase a market is in, a price objective, and, more important, a time duration as to when to expect a specific move to take place and how long it will last. It is considered a very subjective form of market analysis, and I strongly suggest sticking to the rules I will outline when applying these principles in your trading. Besides wave counts and the interaction with Fibonacci extension and correction relationships, there is a time element and what is referred to as a proportionate and alternate relationship with the measurement of the waves. Elliott concluded that there was a "key" to predicting the variable or alternation in price move, such as, if wave two was complex, then wave four would be simple. This theory runs along the lines of not expecting the same magnitude of correction to happen twice in a row. Forex traders take heed to this observation because individuals tend to get complacent, expecting repeat or similar results with any given method. Trading requires a trader to be cognizant of historic moves but not to expect similar results each time. The alternate rule of not expecting the same magnitude is an important concept.

Remember that each wave has its own set of characteristics and rules. Here is a summary of these rules that you can apply in your trading approach.

Wave One

The first wave is the base or starting point derived from a consolidation trading phase after a prolonged price decline. It usually appears to be simply a small corrective bounce from a previous trend. It is the smallest in price moves as compared to the three impulse waves. This stage or wave is what technicians have discovered to be an accumulation phase. Using what we have learned with Fibonacci calculations so far, we can apply the ratio numbers to develop a technique to give price projections for a typical five-wave pattern. In order to help determine the peak of a five-wave move, we can use several techniques. Using software that includes a Fibonacci correction and expansion tool, such as Genesis provides, we can easily determine a price objective with fairly good accuracy. If your charting software program does not have this feature, then the Fibonacci calculator that is included with this book will come in handy. Here are the methods to employ. Figure 7.3 shows that once we have determined the overall measurement or amplitude of wave one, we extend that amount by 3.236 and add that sum to the bottom of wave one. I have seen a higher frequency of the 2.618 percent ratio work as well.

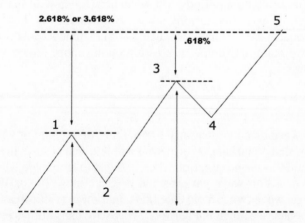

FIGURE 7.3 Fibonacci with Elliott Wave

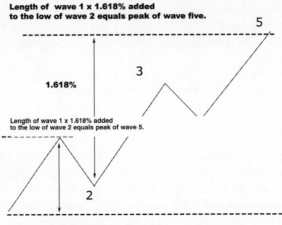

Length of wave 1 x 1.618% added
to the low of wave 2 equals peak of wave five.

1.618%

Length of wave 1 x 1.618% added
to the low of wave 2 equals peak of wave 5.

FIGURE 7.4 Fibonacci with Elliott Wave

Another method to predict the peak in wave five for a specific time period is to take the measurement from the bottom of wave one to the top of wave three and multiply out by 1.618 percent. Figure 7.4 shows the variation that you should employ. The one drawback in using this method is the consideration of how long it takes for a swing measurement to reach its objective.

Using Fibonacci extensions just gives us an idea of a potential move; it does not give us a time frame in which the move will occur. The move could take days, weeks, or months to meet the objective. That is why I have included examples of integrating longer-term pivot point analysis, such as weekly and monthly time periods. These seem to be more effective in predicting both time and price turning points. Besides, they do help corroborate the Fibonacci extensions. Also, using both technical tools can help us nail down the potential timing of a turning point more effectively in the forex market.

Wave Two

The second wave usually retraces 0.618 percent of the sum of wave one. I stated earlier that a market that is in sync with Fibonacci stays in sync with Fibonacci, and this is one situation where it helps to anticipate when a market will follow Elliott wave patterns and predictability. The 0.618 percent retracement in wave two is a big clue that a market may stay in a five-wave pattern sequence, as shown in Figure 7.5. Wave two can at times retrace 100 percent of the entire previous trend, or wave one, but not beyond the be-

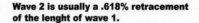

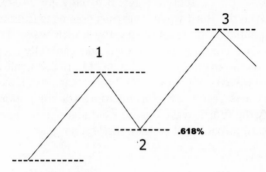

FIGURE 7.5   Fibonacci with Elliott Wave

ginning of that wave—if it is a bullish cycle, wave two will not make a lower low; and if it is a bearish cycle, it will not make a higher high. This is what technicians generally consider the makings of "W" patterns (or double bottoms) or "M" patterns (or double tops). These are commonly referred to as 1-2-3 patterns and resemble a head and shoulders chart pattern. Traders have also been able to use the number-two point to predict the top of wave five by taking the sum of the price move in wave one, multiplying that amount out by 1.618 percent and then adding that figure to the price point of the bottom of wave two.

Wave Three

The third wave is one of the most important. This is where you will see your trend confirmation occur. This wave is the largest of the three impulse waves. It is accompanied with heavy volume. From a fundamental aspect, this is where you will start to hear more and more bullish news, which in turn will support the move upward. Generally speaking, the top of wave three equals a measurement of the length of wave one multiplied out by a factor of 1.618 percent. Another way to predict the top of wave three is to take the overall length of wave one, multiply that amount by 2.168, and then take that sum and add it to the price point of the low of wave two. Technicians jump on the trend and place market orders to enter a position from the breakout above wave one. You usually see a large increase in volume and open interest at that point. This is where breakaway gaps will occur. Here is one rule that needs to be followed and watched: For the third wave to be a true wave, it cannot be the shortest of the five waves.

Wave Four

The fourth wave is the corrective wave. It usually gives back some of the advancement from the third wave. One may see measuring chart patterns like triangles, pennants, or flags during the fourth wave. Triangles, pennants, and flags are continuation patterns and generally break out in the same direction as the overall trend. The most important rule to remember about the fourth wave is: The low of the fourth wave can never overlap the top of the first wave. You will find tremendous trading opportunities once you can identify the fourth wave because old highs (resistance), once broken, will later turn into a new low (support) on a retest.

Wave Five

The fifth wave is usually the strongest for some commodities, such as gold, crude oil, and currencies. This is where the longest leg of the waves will be formed. It is also during this final phase that the price advance begins to slow. From the rule of using multiple analysis techniques, other indicators and oscillators, such as stochastics and MACD (moving average convergence/divergence), will begin to show signs of being overbought in a bullish trend or oversold in a bearish trend. We notice during this period that the market is beginning to lose momentum and that the trend may be exhausting itself. One classic chart pattern that is associated with giving clues that the peak in prices has occurred in wave five is the formation of a wedge pattern, as Figure 7.6 shows.

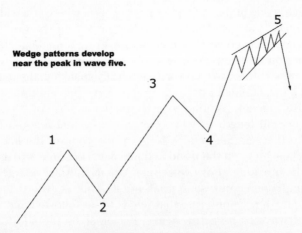

FIGURE 7.6 Fifth Wave Wedges

Lettered Waves

The lettered waves (A, B, and C) are shown in Figure 7.1.

- Wave A is usually mistaken for a regular pullback in the trend; but this is where you could possibly start seeing the makings of W or M (1-2-3) patterns, double tops or bottoms, or a head and shoulders chart pattern.
- Wave B is a small retracement back toward the high of wave five, but it does not quite reach that point. This is where traders will exit their position and/or begin their position for a move in the opposite direction.
- Wave C confirms the end of the uptrend; and when confirmation is made by going beyond wave A, then another cycle begins in the opposite direction.

There are more observations to understand, and they are quite subjective rather than absolute rules regarding Elliott wave theory. One is the concept of alternation. Such is the case that, when we have a five-wave pattern, usually the corrective waves two and four will alternate in their complexities. As I stated earlier, this means no two waves may have the same amplitude and/or time duration of a move.

PRACTICE THE PRINCIPLES OF ELLIOTT WAVE IN FOREX

Having the ability to look at a chart and see the corresponding trends or waves in the market will help you determine which side of the market to trade on. One such setup is identifying a higher right-side double bottom form as wave two forms. Remember that it will look like a double bottom or will correct near the 0.618 percent retracement level. Wave two can also retrace 100 percent of wave one; so this information will give you a better idea of how much to risk on a trade. For example, as you see a fourth wave develop, it will be better to wait for a buy signal, rather than chasing the market as it declines and selling short just as it starts building an upside reversal that forms into wave five. Better yet, knowing what the characteristics of a fifth wave might look like, you can:

- Set profit objectives.
- Use it as a filtering method in order to look for better triggers to sell short as the maturity of a long-term trend starts dissipating.
- Use Elliott wave analysis to help you learn to time entries and exits better.

- Identify a potential trend exhaustion level so you learn not to stick around in a trade too long.

Another aspect is to be able to manage risk by helping determine sell and buy stop-loss points as figured by the Fibonacci retracement relationships and pivot support and resistance calculations. Let's examine a longer-term price movement of the Japanese yen, as shown in Figure 7.7, to see how we may have applied Elliott wave theory when combined with Fibonacci relationships. If the price swings or waves interact and respect the rules as described, then learning more on this subject could help you in future trading decisions. I will demonstrate pivot point analysis integrated with these prices swings and see if this technical analysis method would have been effective. To start, we need to establish a low point, or bottom; and as this chart shows, the low at 101.67 was made on January 21, 2005.

As prices move up, we see a breakout to newer highs to 108.92. This is what establishes the first wave, labeled point 1. The R-2 pivot point resistance target number for April was 108.69. Using the longer-term pivot point analysis is instrumental in the building-block process of nailing down the tops and the bottoms of price moves in Elliott wave cycles.

Then, as a correction occurs, we see the market make a significant decline back down to 104.20. This is what makes up the second wave, labeled

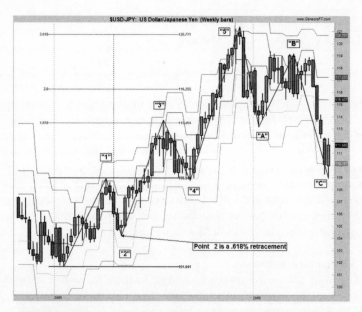

FIGURE 7.7 Combining Elliott Wave, Fibonacci, and Pivot Analysis Helps Identify Entries, Exits, and Stop-Loss Objectives
Used with permission of GenesisFT.com.

point 2. This price correction reaches, within a small margin of error, the Fibonacci 0.618 percent retracement value of 104.41. As prices start advancing again, it validates that point 2 is an Elliott wave; and we now have wave one confirmed. At this point, we can apply our Fibonacci extension calculations of 2.618 percent and 3.618 percent to help identify where this trend may end up. Using the 2.618 percent Fibonacci extension of the distance of wave one gives us an objective of 120.77. The actual high of the entire move made in the fifth wave was 121.39. This was established on December 9, 2005, 11 months from the low at 101.67!

Once again, using the monthly pivot point analysis from the November data, we have the targeted R-1 calculated at 121.04. While the Fibonacci extension tool gave an 11-month warning of what the overall price objective would be, it was the monthly pivot point analysis that came closer in determining both the actual target numbers and the specific time period. From the fifth wave peak in price of 121.30, the sell-off down to the low, marked point A, was 113.38; and as you can tell on the chart, the majority of that downdraft occurred in just one month. If you were found chasing the market and buying at the top of wave five, you may have found it to be a very painful experience, at least from a financial perspective. In fact, throughout the creation of this Elliott wave pattern, the monthly pivot analysis was extremely useful. The high at point 3 the week of July 22, 2005, was 113.73; the monthly pivot R-2 target was 113.96. The bottom of the fourth wave, at point 4, was 108.74 the week of September 9; the monthly S-1 calculation was 108.83, less than 9 PIPs (percentage in points)! Pivot point analysis in this example certainly proved to be a useful and highly accurate tool. And I believe that it not only integrates well with many trading tools, but it is highly effective in helping discover peaks and troughs in Elliott waves.

Let's look at a short-term time frame on a different currency and see if Elliott wave theory has merits on shorter-term time frames, as we covered in regard to factual time dimensions. The chart in Figure 7.8 is a 60-minute time period with the British pound. The low on July 17 at 181.72, extended up to form point 1, was established as the beginning of a potential Elliott wave when the low of the second wave was confirmed when the 0.618 percent Fibonacci correction number held. The distance between the low at 181.72 and the high of 183.29 multiplied by 0.618 percent equaled 182.32. The exact low was 182.25! Again, we see a small margin of error when prices slightly penetrated the support by seven PIPs. The point is that the support targets held. As you look at the chart, see how the market made a rounded bottom and then rallied to form wave one; then as the pullback was made in wave two, it respects the Fibonacci ratios. Also notice that the chart pattern resembles the cup and handle formation as we discussed in Chapter 4.

Once again, here is a perfect example of when you will see multiple in-

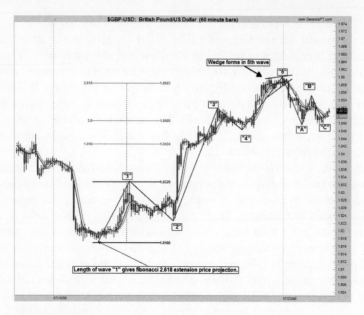

FIGURE 7.8 Elliott Wave Combined with Fibonacci Analysis
Used with permission of GenesisFT.com.

dications of a particular move that lines up with various technical analysis methods. I believe the market's job is to move with the least amount of people on the right side of the market. Here is a great example. The market formed a bottom; rallied; and, without warning, sold off in a sharp price break. It is obvious that some traders got burned on the pullback before the market launched into a very defined uptrend. From the low at point 2 to the high at point 3, the majority or the price advance was made in short order. Using the techniques covered in this book can help you stay on the right side of the market. Imagine seeing the 0.618 percent retracement level hold if you were long. You would most likely have had a higher degree of confidence to stay in a long position and would not have been stopped out with a loss right before a major move occurred. Once the first wave was confirmed when wave two held per the Elliott wave theory rules, you could apply the Fibonacci extension rules and determine what the overall price objective might be. The 2.618 percent extension measures up to 1.8583, the actual high on this completed Elliott wave cycle was 1.8601 on July 21.

Again, there was a small margin of error of only 16 PIPs from the actual high and the high predicted using the Fibonacci tool; but it was a small enough margin of error to manage to either exit a trade or look to establish a new short position. Furthermore, the daily pivot point resistance was targeting the high for July 21 at 1.8579. Once again, this is where integrating Fibonacci and pivot point analysis with Elliott wave can truly be instrumental by confirming each other and resulting in helping you make the right decision on entering a trade; but combining these techniques can be just as important in helping you with the thought process of when not to take a trade.

POP QUIZ

The chart in Figure 7.9 shows the Fibonacci extension tool highlighting a 2.618 percent expansion of the amplitude of wave one. The chart also outlines the five waves. You will see a wedge pattern that has formed as outlined by the trend lines. If you use what we have learned so far, would this pattern call to action to enter a long position on a pullback or to look for a potential short position?

As you can see in Figure 7.10, the answer should have been to start looking for a selling opportunity. At the very least, you should not be looking at buying at the top of this fifth wave, which was near the Fibonacci 2.618 percent extension. Elliott wave analysis is a very subjective technical

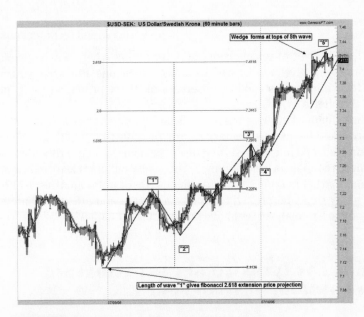

FIGURE 7.9 Wedge Patterns in Fifth Wave Indicate Tops
Used with permission of GenesisFT.com.

FIGURE 7.10   U.S. Dollar/Swedish Krona (60-minute bars)
Used with permission of GenesisFT.com.

tool. There is a lot of wiggle room in determining where wave one starts
and where wave five ends or when a new cycle begins. But when you combine a few simple rules and key observations, these principles really jump
out on the charts.

When the market price respects these Fibonacci ratios on the corrective waves and the extensions target a top of wave five, and then when you
apply simple trend line analysis and discover rising wedge formations, once
all of these techniques are combined, you really will increase your productivity and market-making trading decisions. Pivot point analysis, as I have
stated many times before, will be more accurate and effective than most
forms of market analysis, as I have shown in this chapter so far.

IS THERE AN INTERMARKET RELATIONSHIP WITH COMMODITIES AND FOREX?

You can bet your bottom dollar there is one such market, and that one is
crude oil! There is a small correlation with the relationship with certain

currencies: When crude oil prices rise in value, so does the British pound and the Canadian dollar, as both countries are producers to a degree. Even the euro benefits as the Middle East Organization of Petroleum Exporting Countries (OPEC) sell oil, receive dollars, and convert to euros. Japan is a net importer of oil; so when we see periods of high prices, the yen tends to be depressed against the dollar. Let's look at a long-term chart on crude oil to see first how Elliott wave theory can be applied to identify each wave and then the Fibonacci relationships on the corresponding correction and extensions as the rules apply that we disclosed. As we study the chart in Figure 7.11, we can easily identify wave one; the wave two correction is almost exactly equal to the Fibonacci 0.618 percent ratio. Wave four does not exceed the top of wave one. Now notice the Fibonacci 3.618 percent extension calculated by the amplitude of wave one that identifies a potential top in the market followed by a wedge formation.

This is the chart I presented to a group of investors on August 4 when prices were headed to rechallenge the highs. I was warning people that we were in a fifth wave price advance and that the long-term upside price objectives had been fulfilled. The market in this chart was based on the September contract; at the time, prices were at 76.16 a barrel. Here are some facts to consider: The 2.618 percent extension was projecting resistance at

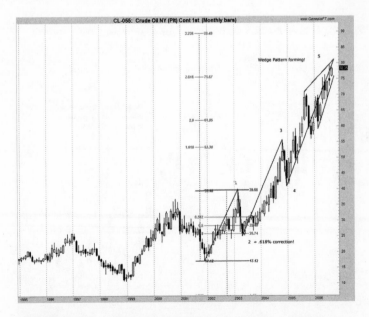

FIGURE 7.11   Elliott Wave Combined with Fibonacci and Pivot
Analysis Predicted the Top in Crude Oil
Used with permission of GenesisFT.com.

75.67 per barrel. As this monthly chart shows, there was a defined wedge pattern; and as we have covered, this is consistent in developing in fifth waves. The monthly pivot R-1 for August was projected at 78.60. Less than one week after I made this presentation, the actual high was made at 78.80. Now that is one shocking coincidence.

If you look at Figure 7.12, I have a closeup of the price action on a daily chart. Several items come up here: We see that the candle pattern the prior month that made the all-time high was formed by a shooting star. Notice that in August, before the market plunged back below 69.00 per barrel, the top was formed by a dark cloud cover pattern; and as prices retreat, we see a bear flag formation, which projects a measurement to the 67.00 level.

As I was trying to finish this manuscript, the price in crude oil had declined to a low nearly touching 67.00 on September 7. Since oil has a major influence on global economies, using these techniques may help you uncover opportunities in these correlated currencies, such as the yen, the Canadian dollar, and the British pound. If crude oil prices did, in fact, continue to decline, it might put pressure on the U.S. dollar because the Federal Reserve might feel less inclined to continue to raise interest rates in a move to combat inflationary pressures as a result of higher energy costs. One more consideration is that if OPEC countries are selling oil, receiving

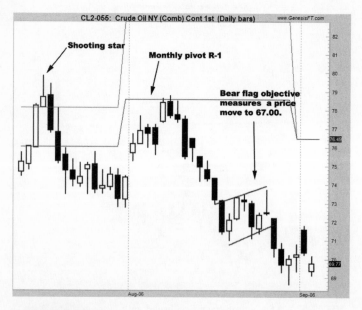

FIGURE 7.12
Used with permission of GenesisFT.com.

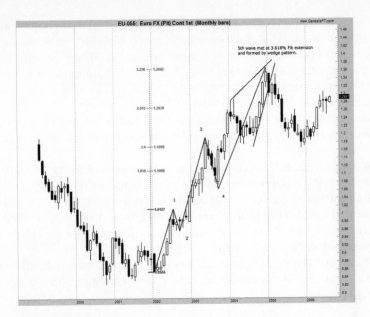

FIGURE 7.13   Elliott Wave and Wedge Patterns Identify Tops
Used with permission of GenesisFT.com.

dollars, and converting to euros, then, as the price of oil moves lower, this could put pressure on the euro; also, as with cheaper oil, there is less conversion action.

Let's take a look at the euro currency chart in Figure 7.13. Notice that the chart shows the various waves and the corresponding Fibonacci relationships. Wave two is a small correction, less than the typical 0.50 percent or 0.618 percent Fibonacci ratio; but as we examine wave four, notice that it does not penetrate below the peak of wave one. Also, see how the Fibonacci 3.618 percent extension, as calculated by the amplitude of wave one, identifies that the top in the market followed, which was formed with a wedge pattern.

SUMMARY

Elliott wave theory works in most markets that are influenced by mass psychology. The theory combines the best of traditional charting techniques. When you apply the Fibonacci ratios, you can better determine not only entry points but also levels at which to place your protective stop-loss orders. If you master identifying a fifth wave bullish trend, you might save a tremendous amount of money by not falling into the trap of buying a false breakout at the peak of a major upside move. The fifth wave phase normally is during times of extreme bullish sentiment. When the euro hit the peak near 134.68, it seemed that every hour on CNBC, analysts were calling for the euro to reach 145 and even to go as high as 150. This is a perfect example of a classic fifth wave extension. The general masses were buying at the top and expecting a market to move even higher, especially after a prolonged market advance. Keep in mind these specific technical points:

- Wave five can be determined by using extension Fibonacci 2.618 percent and 3.618 percent extensions of the length of wave one.
- The bottom of wave two can be identified by using the Fibonacci 0.50 percent or the 0.618 percent ratio correction of the length of wave one.
- Look to buy a 0.618 percent retracement of wave three, and place your stops below the peak level of wave one.
- Wave four should not penetrate below the top of wave one; otherwise, the dynamics of the market structure have changed, and a bear trend may develop.

CHAPTER 8

Trading Systems: Combining Pivots with Indicators

In this chapter, my goal is to explain the importance not only of what it takes to develop a trading system but also of how to evaluate it from a hypothetical standpoint and then apply it with real money. I am going to draw together what we have learned so far and help you learn how to develop a trading program and what to look for so that you can expand your creative drive to expand into other systems. This chapter will reveal how we integrate pivot point analysis with three popular trading indicators: stochastics, moving average convergence/divergence (MACD), and a pivot point moving average method. There are many factors to consider in a mechanical trading system; but when you get right down to it, there are really only three main elements you want to focus on:

1. Clear-cut rules for entries and exits.
2. Rules for exiting at profit targets.
3. Rules for exiting at loss targets.

First, we need to define the terms that are important for understanding the dynamics of a trading system and how to extrapolate the information. The best way to benefit from this information is to uncover not whether the overall system or trading idea is profitable but whether it is profitable with limited equity swings: Does the method have excessive drawdown periods? Do losses exceed gains more than what is tolerable to equity traders? When a string of multiple winners and substantial profits accrue, does the trading method experience periods of time that result in significant losses that give back the majority of those gains? That is what we refer to as *drawdowns*. The best part of using this information is not only to help you determine what benefits or validity your trading ideas hold but also to help you understand and identify the negative side of the system or to spot the weaknesses, such as the drawdown factor. One of what I would consider the top-10 destructive traits traders possess is that they overtrade—not just in-and-out style, but abusing the power of leverage and trading too many positions at once.

MONEY MANAGEMENT TOOLS

Most traders do not know when to correctly add on trading positions. In 1989, Ralph Vince wrote *Portfolio Management Formulas: Mathematical Trading Methods for Futures, Options, and Stock Markets* (John Wiley & Sons, 1990). This book set the standard for money managers by using a formula that set the optimal transaction size as a function derived from the ratio of a given transaction's expected return to its associated likely worst-case single-trade loss. This concept gives a trader a more precise way to determine when to add on to positions as the portfolio increases in value. In other words, as a trading account increases in profits, a trader will know when the time is right to increase lot size.

Kelly Formula

Another money management tool used by system traders is the Kelly formula. John Kelly, an employee for AT&T's Bell Laboratory, originally developed the Kelly criterion formula to assist AT&T with its long distance telephone signal–noise issues. After his method and formula were published as "A New Interpretation of Information Rate" (1956), believe it or not, the gamblers and oddsmakers realized its potential as an optimal betting system in horse racing. It enabled gamblers to maximize the size of their bets on consecutive races and was used to help in determining how much to parlay winnings into the next bet. The system is, as you can guess, used by many traders as a money management tool with the same goals in mind: to try to determine how much money to place on the next trade.

There are two basic components to the Kelly formula:

1. Win probability—The probability that any given trade you make will return a positive amount.
2. Win/loss ratio—The total positive trade amounts divided by the total negative trade amounts.

These two factors are then put into Kelly's formula:

$$K = W - [(1 - W)/R]$$

where K = Kelly ratio percent value
          W = Winning probability
          R = Win/loss ratio

The theory behind this ratio as it applies to trading can not only help to determine what percent of your total account you could ideally be willing to risk on each trade to maximize your total returns (e.g., if a system shows a Kelly ratio of 0.25 (K), then you could supposedly risk 25 percent of your account on each trade). In reality, most people would agree that the Kelly ratio provides too high a number for this purpose; so possibly cutting it in half might get you closer to a more reasonable risk level. Another variation of how you can apply the ratio is to effectively compare different trading systems. For example, assume "System 1" wins a lot of the time; but when it loses, it loses big, such as it has a high winning percentage (number of wins versus number of trades) but a low payout ratio (average wins versus average losses). Say "System 2" doesn't win very often; but when it wins, it makes big money. System 2 demonstrates a low winning percentage but a high payout ratio. In order to determine which system is better, the Kelly ratio algorithmically combines both the winning percentages and the payout ratio to come up with a single number that may be used to "compare" the effectiveness of two very different systems. In order to make that determination, look for the system that has the highest Kelly ratio. Since the Kelly ratio works from a purely statistical perspective and does not take into account some other factors that someone might deem important, such as the historical max drawdown, it is often just one of a number of things a person will want to look at when comparing systems and criteria in a trading method.

The essence of back-testing is to evaluate your methods and to show the strengths and the weaknesses of your system; moreover, it will help you define your goals and expectations for performance. Therefore, back-testing can help you achieve the highest trading profits with the lowest risks in most trading market conditions.

Sharpe Ratio

The next top classification you need to know, especially if you plan on forming a forex fund, is the term at which all money brokers, banks, and private placement managers look: the *Sharpe ratio*. This formula was developed by Nobel laureate Bill Sharpe in order to measure risk-adjusted performance. It is calculated by subtracting the risk-free rate from the rate of return for a portfolio and dividing the result by the standard deviation of the portfolio returns. This is the standard factor used to evaluate the risk-to-reward efficiency of investments in order to create efficient portfolios by which almost all registered and professionally managed funds are judged. The formula to calculate the Sharpe ratio [$S(I)$] is:

$$S(I) = (r_r - R_S) / \text{StdDev}(i)$$

where
$$i = \text{Investment}$$
$$r_r = \text{Expected annual rate of return of investment}$$
$$R_s = \text{Risk-free rate (Treasury bill rate)}$$
$$\text{StdDev}(i) = \text{Standard deviation of } r_r$$

Mr. Sharpe is now a professor at Stanford University; he was one of three economists who received the Nobel Prize in Economics in 1990 for their contributions to what is now called "Modern Portfolio Theory." If you want to learn more on the theory, visit his web site at http://www.sharpe.stanford.edu.

How Can a Forex Trader Use the Sharpe Ratio?

Simply stated, the calculation helps investors determine the best place to put money. Before you place money in some investment, you calculate the value of your investment account (including the initial investment plus the profit versus loss) periodically, say, every month. You then calculate the percentage return each month. It doesn't matter what kind of investment you choose. It could be simply buying and holding a single stock, or it could be trading several different commodities or trading various currency pairs with several different trading systems. All that matters is that you want to take into consideration the account value at the end of each month. You will divide the average of the excess returns (the returns generated by the strategy minus the risk-free return) by the standard deviation of the returns and then calculate the average monthly return over some number of months, say, 12 months, by averaging the returns for the 12 months. You also calculate the standard deviation of the monthly returns over the same period. Then you annualize the numbers by multiplying the average monthly return by 12 and then multiplying the standard deviation of the monthly returns by the square root of 12. It seems slightly complicated; but with the help of computers or an Excel spreadsheet, it becomes clear. To further calculate, you need an input value for the risk-free return (Treasury bill rate), which is the annualized return. You now calculate what we consider the excess return, which is the annualized return achieved by your investment in excess of the risk-free rate of return available. This is the extra return you receive by assuming some risk.

It's a way to level the playing field. The Sharpe ratio lets you compare the risk-to-reward profiles of different types of strategies. Instead of trying to figure out if an expected annual return of 40 percent and a standard deviation of 30 percent is better than an expected return of 50 percent with a standard deviation of 40 percent, you just pick the one with the highest Sharpe ratio. The Sharpe ratio will tell you if the returns of one strategy or methodology are due to a better trading ideal or to just getting lucky in a winning streak that has excess risk over a period of time. This measurement is very useful because although one strategy can make bigger returns than other traders or systems, it is only a good investment if those higher returns are not associated with excessive risk or potential risk exposure in the future based on the performance record of the past. Just keep in mind that the greater a portfolio's Sharpe ratio, the better its risk-adjusted performance has been.

When trading a forex account that introduces leverage, remember that the Sharpe ratio, which is a tool designed to measure the risk-to-reward ratio, is independent of the leverage. Increasing the leverage increases the risk-and-reward potential on a proportionate scale. In fact, at some point, increasing leverage can potentially decrease the return over time because the amount lost in periods of drawdowns, which could be days, weeks, and even months, may not be made up for several months. So before developing, enhancing, or creating your own system, it will help you to understand and run the Sharpe ratio in order to understand the potential risks involved in trading it. As we say in the business, if the risks are not worth the rewards, then don't take the trade.

Trade System Terms to Know

Review Table 8.1. These are the basic terms to refer to when determining whether a trading system has merits to test with real money, especially when it's your own. Most software companies with back-testing capabilities use these terms. These are considered standard industry terms. The table shows the important ones you want to follow.

Now that we have covered the importance of how and why to analyze a system, I want to disclose a building block or foundation of a system or a concept behind three systems that integrate three popular technical tools with pivot point support and resistance analysis:

1. Stochastics.
2. MACD.
3. Moving averages (M/A).

TABLE 8.1   Definitions and Classifications Traders Should Know

Total net profit	How much the system made after slippage, commissions, and fees and losses.
Payout ratio	On a profit/loss (P/L) basis, the percent by which winners outpace losers.
Average number of bars for winners	The average time period before a trade was offset in order to establish a profit.
Win percent	Figure that shows how many winners versus losers were generated by a trade.
Kelly ratio	A math calculation used to derive the number of contracts to trade in relationship to the ratio of winning trades to losing trades.
Largest win	Figure that shows the largest single winning trade. This number shows whether profits on a single trade are larger than 20 percent of the overall net profit; if so, it indicates the trade signals may be invalid.
Largest loss	Figure that helps traders identify whether single losses are bigger than winners so they implement a better risk management approach.
Average winning trade	Figure that shows what to expect on the average-size winning trade.
Average losing trade	Figure that shows what the average-size loss is.
Return %	Percent of profit on the initial-size starting account.

Let's start with one of my favorite technical tools combined with pivot points—the *stochastics oscillator*. This tool measures the strength and the weakness of the momentum in prices. The math formula measures where the close is in relationship to the high, the low, and past closing prices in a given time period. It is very important for you to understand what makes this tool tick, so to speak. The concept is based on the premise that if market prices are bullish, they will tend to close at or near the top of their given range; and if market prices are bearish, prices will close at or near the lows of their respective ranges. This concept is important because as prices near a critical pivot resistance level, we want confirmation of a price reversal to trigger a short. That is what the stochastics does. It will give us a clue as to whether a rally or an uptrend is exhausting itself. If this is true, then the close will not be at the high end of the trading range. For this system, I use the fast stochastic with the 14-period setting for %K and the 3-period averages for %D. This is the normal default setting for most charting software packages. Keep in mind that the results are based on an entirely mechanical trading method. There are no discretionary decisions or inputs, such as selecting which trades to take based on economic report release times or, removing or trailing the stop-loss orders. This system is considered a countertrend trading method; but we are keeping with the golden trading rules for short-term traders, which is to sell resistance and buy support. All these systems were run on 15-minute time periods and during all trading sessions, meaning a 24-hour period from a 5:05 P.M. (EST) open to a 5 P.M. (EST) close.

The pivot points were calculated at the 5 P.M. (EST) Bank of New York settlement time. Here are the parameters for the stochastics system sell signals, which are programmed to trigger within 10 PIPs (percentage in points) above or below the pivot point resistance 1 (R-1), resistance 2 (R-2), and resistance 3 (R-3) levels; once the stochastics indicator is above 80 percent, it then scans for a cross-over of %K and %D to occur as these lines close back below the 70 percent level. The testing signals are included at the R-1 level; but the parameters do not define a wide enough price extreme or departure from the means as defined by the typical price or the actual pivot point. When prices have had an extreme price move from the prior session, R-1 would be calculated at a significant enough distance that I would consider a move as being in a short-term overbought state. Once the sell signals are generated and trigger a short position, we use a 100-PIP initial stop from entry price with a 40-point profit target. Granted, that is not the optimal risk/reward ratio that is in everyday trading books; however, I selected that risk amount for three reasons: (1) It is approximately 1.20 percent more than the average daily range; (2) in order for prices to reach a daily R-1, R-2, or, for the extreme, R-3 number, prices would tend to be in an overbought market condition and ripe for a price correction; (3) looking at the back-test results shows that the system without risk parameters has an average loss of $884. Therefore, if an unexpected extreme price move occurred against the initial entry, we might escape harm from prematurely being stopped out of the market 100 PIPs further away.

Once prices have expanded and reached an extreme level, such as a pivot R-1 or R-2 price zone and because this is a countertrend trade, I am only looking for a short-term move. Statistically speaking, the average gross win is $808 and the average net profit is $255. If you find the average of these two components, we are roughly at $531.50, which works out to 53 PIPs. I might have a margin of error of 10 percent on entry and exit, which then brings us to a 43-PIP objective; and if there is a 3-PIP spread, we have a 40-point profit target opportunity. As such, the average daily range is near 86 PIPs in the euro. If I capture half of that range on a systematic trading program, the odds favor the market "regressing to the mean," or returning to a fair value level. So determining a 40-PIP profit target seemed reasonable.

Check if your charting service has the Average True Range indicator (ATR). You can utilize that to show you what the average price range of an individual currency is per day over the default period, which is usually calculated over a 14-day period. If a specific currency ATR is 86 PIPs, if you are in a trade closer to the 5 p.m. New York close, and if prices have risen on the day by 80 PIPs, at this point you have a pretty good idea the market has reached its full potential, thus giving you an edge to cut the trade on a discretionary basis.

Genesis Code

The 100-PIP risk level is mainly used as an emergency stop, which can be programmed to be trailed or moved as prices move in the desired direction. For this case study, we did not program this feature in the system. Using Trade Navigator by Genesisft.com, the trade sense language programming code is written as follows:

Trading System Code
IF Near (High, NumPips, JP R1 Daily) Or Near (High, NumPips, JP R2 Daily) Or Near (High, NumPips, JP R3 Daily) And Crosses Below (StochD (14, 3, 3), StochSellPercent) if true, then sell at market.

Default Values for Rule Inputs
numpips = 10
Stoch Sell Percent = 72
IF Near (Low, NumPips, JP S1 Daily) Or Near (Low, NumPips, JP S2 Daily) Or Near (Low, NumPips, JP S3 Daily) And Crosses Above (StochD (14, 3, 3), StochBuyPercent) if true, then buy at market.

TradeStation Code

For those who have used TradeStation, another popular charting software package with programming and back-testing capabilities, the codes for TradeStation in EasyLanguage are the following:

Strategy: JP Piv FastStoch

Inputs: NumPIPs(10), StpPIPs(100), PrftPIPs(40), StochBuyPercent(22), StochSellPercent(72), StochLength(14), SmoothingLength1(3), SmoothingLength2(3);

```
Variables: S1( 0 ), S2( 0 ), S3( 0 ), R1( 0 ), R2( 0 ), R3( 0 ), PP( 0 ), TodaysHigh(
0 ), YestHigh( 0 ), TodaysLow( 0 ), YestLow( 0 ), TodaysClose( 0 ), YestClose(
0 ),oFastK( 0 ), oFastD( 0 ), oSlowK( 0 ), oSlowD( 0 ) ;

If Time = SessionFirstBarTime(1, 1) then begin
        YestHigh = TodaysHigh ;
        YestLow = TodaysLow ;
        YestClose = Close[1] ;
        TodaysHigh = High ;
        TodaysLow = Low ;
        PP = ( YestHigh + YestLow + YestClose ) / 3 ;
        R1 = PP * 2 – YestLow ;
        R2 = PP + YestHigh – YestLow ;
        R3 = R2 + YestHigh – YestLow ;
        S1 = PP * 2 – YestHigh ;
        S2 = PP – YestHigh + YestLow ;
        S3 = S2 – YestHigh + YestLow ;
end
else begin
        if High > TodaysHigh then
                TodaysHigh = High ;
        if Low < TodaysLow then
                TodaysLow = Low ;
end ;

Value1 = Stochastic( High, Low, Close, StochLength, SmoothingLength1,
SmoothingLength2, 1, oFastK, oFastD, oSlowK, oSlowD ) ;

If MRO(oFastK crosses over StochBuyPercent, 5, 1) > –1 and MRO(oFastD
crosses over StochBuyPercent, 5, 1) > –1 and
        oFastK > StochBuyPercent and oFastD > StochBuyPercent and
        (Low > S1 – NumPIPs points and Low < S1 + NumPIPs points) or
        (Low > S2 – NumPIPs points and Low < S2 + NumPIPs points) or
        (Low > S3 – NumPIPs points and Low < S3 + NumPIPs points) then
                Buy next bar at market;

If MRO(oFastK crosses under StochSellPercent, 5, 1) > –1 and MRO(oFastD
crosses under StochSellPercent, 5, 1) > –1 and
        oFastK < StochSellPercent and oFastD < StochSellPercent and
        (High > R1 – NumPIPs points and High < R1 + NumPIPs points) or
        (High > R2 – NumPIPs points and High < R2 + NumPIPs points) or
```

      (High > R3 – NumPIPs points and High < R3 + NumPIPs points) then
              Sellshort next bar at market;

SetStopLoss(StpPIPs points * BigPointValue);
SetProfitTarget(PrftPIPs points * BigPointValue);

Default Values for Rule Inputs
numPIPs = 10
StochBuyPercent = 22

    The buy signals are programmed in a similar fashion, with prices having to be within 10 PIPs above or below the pivot S-1, S-2, or S-3. The exception here is that we need the stochastics to be below the 22 percent level, %D to cross above %K, and both values to cross and close back above the 22 percent level. The chart in Figure 8.1 shows you the exact pattern and sequence of events that this system scans for. A sell signal was generated as prices were within 10 PIPs of the R-2 level for the day. Stochastics was above the 80 percent level, and it was not until %K and %D crossed and closed back below the 70 percent level that a trigger to sell short was made. The entry was at 128.08 using the emergency 100-PIP stop-loss; and as

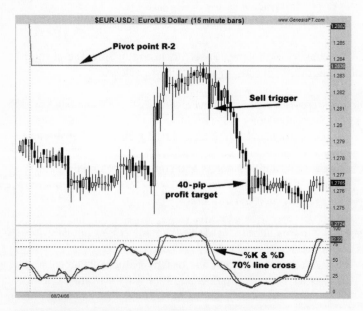

FIGURE 8.1   Stochastics and Pivot Trigger System
Used with permission of GenesisFT.com.

prices moved down, the 40-PIP profit target was elected. This sequence is based on a 15-minute time frame.

The results for this system, as shown in Table 8.2, produce a net profit of $41,240. The win percentage is pretty amazing at 67.3 percent. The net return on investment is 681 percent, based on a starting account size that requires $6,050, over a 30-month period. These results are not optimized by increasing lot sizes in accordance with increases in equity. I call this just a raw trading system, but it is great to see that the validity of stochastics signals integrate well at or near the predetermined pivot point support and resistance target price levels.

In Figure 8.2, we see that the equity curve has a pretty decent growth path with not a huge period of drawdowns or massive drawdowns against peak equity gains. By examining the drawdown from peak equity growth, you can evaluate how much capital is required to trade this system or methodology. It will also help you determine how much equity would be required to increase your position size. For example, if you decided to double your lot size and did so at a peak in equity, you would be able to sustain the

TABLE 8.2

Overall—Stochastics

Total Net Profit:	$40,400	Profit Factor:	1.86
Total Trades:	161	Winning Percentage:	67.1%
Average Trade:	$251	Payout Ratio (Average Win/Loss):	0.91
Average # of Bars in Trade:	205.31	Z-Score (W/L Predictability):	−0.6
Average # of Trades per Year:	101.0	Percent in the Market:	50.4%
Max Closed–Out Drawdown:	−$5,530	Max Intraday Drawdown:	−$6,050
Account Size Required:	$6,050	Return Percent:	667.8%
Open Equity:	$260	Kelly Ratio:	0.3106
Current Streak:	8 wins	Optimal f:	0.29

Winning Trades		Losing Trades	
Total Winners:	108	Total Losers:	53
Gross Profit:	$87,250	Gross Loss:	−$46,850
Average Win:	$808	Average Loss:	−$884
Largest Win:	$3,680	Largest Loss:	−$1,000
Largest Drawdown in Win:	−$990	Largest Peak in Loss:	$1,730
Average Drawdown in Win:	−$389	Average Peak in Loss:	$383
Average Runup in Win:	$1,027	Average Runup in Loss:	$383
Average Rundown in Win:	−$389	Average Rundown in Loss:	−$960
Most Consecutive Wins:	11	Most Consecutive Losses:	4
Average # of Consecutive Wins:	3.18	Average # of Consecutive Losses:	1.56
Average # of Bars in Wins:	218.01	Average # of Bars in Losses:	179.43

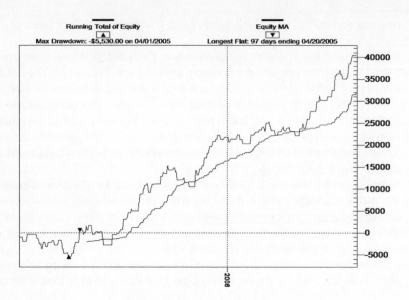

FIGURE 8.2   Equity Curve

position if the eventual drawdown occurs. One good rule of thumb is to double the maximum drawdown amount; and as your account grows by that amount, then increase your lot size by one more unit. With that said, here is what you would do: If the system starts with the suggested capital amount of $6,050.00, you do not increase your lot size until your account reaches $17,110.00. Here is how that is calculated: The maximum drawdown is $5,530.00; twice that amount is $11,060.00; add to that the initial start-up of $6,050.

This system is in reality a day trading program, and the look-back test period is 30 months (2.5 years). But that was a very good period for a backtest because it included several market phases; we had uptrends, downtrends, and choppy-sloppy congestion phases; and during that time period, it was a good representation of our current global economic environment. This shows that the method is rugged in all market conditions, rather than being a simple buy-and-hold long-only system. Overall, I believe it is a valid trading system with which you can build. You can add your own filters, change the parameter settings, or add discretionary trailing stop features based on the performance of each trade by scaling out of positions at the predetermined exit level and then letting the balance of your positions ride. One point I wish to make here is that the predetermined starting capital was based on a full $100,000.00 lot spot forex contract. Therefore, if you implement trading with mini-lots, you can trade a scale-out method with smaller start-up capital.

SEASONALITY PLAYS ON CURRENCIES

When evaluating systems, the power behind the software is certainly important in providing you with as many details as possible. One such aspect is determining if the performance of some months is better than others. Seasonality factors do have a tendency to influence price behavior in currency because money flows change at fiscal year-ends as multiconglomerate corporations move money to balance their books to tax season in April.

If you can determine which months perform best, you can enhance your performance or at least be aware that the system performs at it best or worst in various months. There are many analysts who contend that there are historic performances in currencies with a high degree of accuracy. I just want to review my back-test results to see how my system fairs at certain times of the year, and then I can look into each month to see if it was a situation that may reoccur (such as at the end of a fiscal year).

The graph in Figure 8.3 shows March as having a vicious drawdown period. Granted, there are not enough sample years to determine if there is a high probability that the same phenomenon will reoccur, but the results certainly will help me to look at trading during that time period the following year.

My philosophy on trading is to use a method that provides consistency and a better-than-normal degree of accuracy with a good risk/reward ratio.

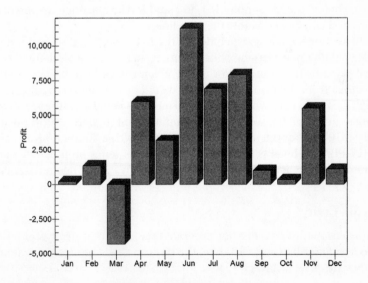

FIGURE 8.3   Profits by Month

The method should be built on time-tested strategies that are slightly complex yet simple. I believe this stochastics–pivot point method is one such method and a system that you can build on yourself. So as the song goes, "Shine on, you crazy diamond!"

Now let's examine the MACD Histogram Trading System. The moving average convergence/divergence indicator is based on a series of moving averages and, therefore, can be considered more of a lagging indicator than stochastics is. Since many forex traders use MACD, I wanted to run a system based on the same parameters, under the same conditions, and for the same length of time as the stochastics to see which one would produce better results or a more reliable system.

The parameters used in the MACD settings were 12- and 26-day exponential moving averages (EMA). To determine the two moving averages, the "fast line" is calculated out as follows: Take the 26-day EMA and subtract it from the 12-day EMA. The slow-line average is the 9-day EMA of the fast line. The histogram is figured out when the fast line is above the slow line; the bar will read above the zero level. Inversely, when the fast line is below the slow line, the histogram will cross below the zero level.

These crossover features are what trigger buy and sell signals. The time frame in which this system was performed was a 15-minute time period and for all trading sessions, meaning a 24-hour period from a 5:05 P.M. (EST) open and using a 5 P.M. (EST) close. The pivot points were calculated at the 5 P.M. (EST) Bank of New York settlement time. The parameters for the MACD system sell signals were programmed to trigger within 10 PIPs above or below the pivot point R-1, R-2, and R-3 levels, once the histogram bar crossed and closed below the zero line.

The testing signals are included at the R-1 level, but it does not define a wide enough price extreme or departure from the means as defined by the typical price or the actual pivot point. When prices have had an extreme price move from the prior session, R-1 would be calculated at a significant enough distance that I would consider a move as being in a short-term overbought state. Once the sell signal is generated and triggers a short position, we use a 100-PIP initial stop from entry price with a 40-point profit target. The 100-PIP risk level is mainly used as an emergency stop, which can be programmed to be trailed or moved as prices move in the desired direction.

Genesis Code

For this case study, we did not program this feature in the system. Using Trade Navigator by Genesisft.com, the trade sense language programming code is written as follows:

Trading System Code

IF Near (Low, NumPips, JP S1 Daily) Or Near (Low, NumPips, JP S2 Daily) Or Near (Low, NumPips, JP S3 Daily) And Crosses Above (MACD Diff (Close, 12, 26, 9, If False), 0) then Buy next bar at Market.

Default Values for Rule Inputs

Num PIPS = 10

IF Near (High, NumPips, JP R1 Daily) Or Near (High, NumPips, JP R2 Daily) Or Near (High, NumPips, JP R3 Daily) And Crosses Below (MACD Diff (Close, 12, 26, 9, If False), 0) Then sell next bar at market.

Default Values for Rule Inputs

Num PIPs = 10

If you examine Figure 8.4, it shows the same time period as we used in the stochastics system, but with the MACD indicator. In this example, prices did meet our criteria setting of hitting above or below 10 PIPs of the pivot point resistance R-2 level; and a sell signal generated as the MACD histogram crossed and closed back below the zero line. It just so happens this setup occurred at the same time and price as the stochastics system did, which you can compare to Figure 8.1.

FIGURE 8.4   MACD and Pivot System Work to Trigger Entries
Used with permission of GenesisFT.com.

TradeStation Code

Here is the code for the MACD system in TradeStation's EasyLanguage.
There are several companies that offer back-testing capabilities; but Genesis Software and TradeStation, the two I have used over the years, are very
powerful software programs.

Strategy: JP Piv MACD

```
Inputs: NumPIPs( 10 ), StpPIPs( 100 ), PrftPIPs( 40 ), FastLength( 12 ),
SlowLength( 26 ), MACDLength( 9 ) ;

Variables: S1( 0 ), S2( 0 ), S3( 0 ), R1( 0 ), R2( 0 ), R3( 0 ), PP( 0 ),
TodaysHigh( 0 ),
        YestHigh( 0 ), TodaysLow( 0 ), YestLow( 0 ), TodaysClose( 0 ), Yest-
Close( 0 ),
        MyMACD( 0 ), MACDAvg( 0 ), xMACDDiff( 0 ) ;

If Time = SessionFirstBarTime(1, 1) then begin
        YestHigh = TodaysHigh ;
        YestLow = TodaysLow ;
        YestClose = Close[1] ;
        TodaysHigh = High ;
        TodaysLow = Low ;
        PP = ( YestHigh + YestLow + YestClose ) / 3 ;
        R1 = PP * 2 – YestLow ;
        R2 = PP + YestHigh – YestLow ;
        R3 = R2 + YestHigh – YestLow ;
        S1 = PP * 2 – YestHigh ;
        S2 = PP – YestHigh + YestLow ;
        S3 = S2 – YestHigh + YestLow ;
end
else begin
        If High > TodaysHigh then
                TodaysHigh = High ;
        If Low < TodaysLow then
                TodaysLow = Low ;
end;

MyMACD = MACD( Close, FastLength, SlowLength ) ;
MACDAvg = XAverage( MyMACD, MACDLength ) ;
xMACDDiff = MyMACD – MACDAvg ;
```

If xMACDDiff crosses over 0 and
        (Low > S1 – NumPIPs points and Low < S1 + NumPIPs points) or
        (Low > S2 – NumPIPs points and Low < S2 + NumPIPs points) or
        (Low > S3 – NumPIPs points and Low < S3 + NumPIPs points) then
                Buy next bar at market;

If xMACDDiff crosses under 0 and
        (High > R1 – NumPIPs points and High < R1 + NumPIPs points) or
        (High > R2 – NumPIPs points and High < R2 + NumPIPs points) or
        (High > R3 – NumPIPs points and High < R3 + NumPIPs points) then
                Sellshort next bar at market;

SetStopLoss(StpPIPs points * BigPointValue);
SetProfitTarget(PrftPIPs points * BigPointValue);

Taking a preliminary look, it would appear that the MACD might have a chance to meet or beat our performance of the stochastics system. However, taking just one sample is not sufficient enough information to go and trade based on these results. That is where a charting software package will help uncover true performance. In fact, the MACD system did generate decent profits, but it is nowhere as effective as the stochastics signals. The first noticeable change, as shown in Table 8.3, is the recommended starting capital. The MACD system requires $10,820 to start trading. The win percentage is only 58.4 percent, and the return percent is 315.9 percent, based on a higher equity requirement at start-up.

As we dissect the performance summary and chart the performance as shown in Figure 8.5, we see significant drawdowns occur against peak performance. The conclusion here is that since MACD is a lagging indicator, although it is a valid and highly effective technical analysis tool, the overall performance in the signals is less than desired. If the system does lag or generate more signals later, we would be entering trades too late and perhaps not getting an opportunity to take a 40-PIP profit before a market reversal takes us out of the game with our stop-loss. That would indicate that we need to either trail stops with this system or rely on stochastics more than MACD.

Does MACD show seasonal influences? I would like to say yes. However, looking at Figure 8.6, it is extremely hard to gauge an opinion because the month-to-month performance is very volatile. Even though June 2004 saw a spectacular one-month wonder gain, it is highly unlikely that using the MACD to trigger signals at or near pivot point support or resistance levels is a system I would want to rely on for my trades.

TABLE 8.3

Overall—MACD

Total Net Profit:	$34,180	Profit Factor ($Wins/Losses):	1.35
Total Trades:	267	Winning Percentage:	58.4%
Average Trade:	$128	Payout Ratio (Average Win/Loss):	0.96
Average # of Bars in Trade:	193.18	Z-Score (W/L Predictability):	−0.3
Average # of Trades per Year:	102.8	Percent in the Market:	74.0%
Max Closed–Out Drawdown:	−$10,220	Max Intraday Drawdown:	−$10,820
Account Size Required:	$10,820	Return Percent:	315.9%
Open Equity:	$170	Kelly Ratio:	0.1521
Current Streak:	2 wins	Optimal f:	0.13

Winning Trades		**Losing Trades**	
Total Winners:	156	Total Losers:	111
Gross Profit:	$131,260	Gross Loss:	−$97,080
Average Win:	$841	Average Loss:	−$875
Largest Win:	$4,680	Largest Loss:	−$1,000
Largest Drawdown in Win:	−$990	Largest Peak in Loss:	$1,410
Average Drawdown in Win:	−$370	Average Peak in Loss:	$404
Average Runup in Win:	$1,136	Average Runup in Loss:	$404
Average Rundown in Win:	−$370	Average Rundown in Loss:	−$960
Most Consecutive Wins:	13	Most Consecutive Losses:	7
Average # of Consecutive Wins:	2.44	Average # of Consecutive Losses:	1.73
Average # of Bars in Wins:	213.73	Average # of Bars in Losses:	164.30

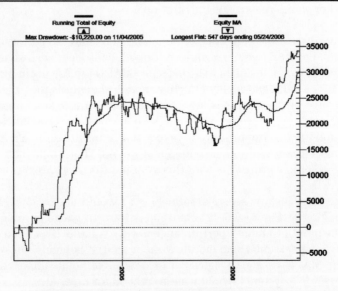

FIGURE 8.5   MACD Performance Lags Stochastics

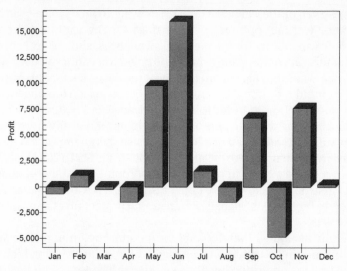

FIGURE 8.6   Profits by Month, 2004

THE PIVOT POINT MOVING AVERAGE SYSTEM

I call the pivot point moving average system the Defcon III system; its design was based mostly on pivot point theory. First, I use the pivot point moving average to help filter the projected support and resistance levels based on the closing price in relationship to the actual pivot point [(High + Low + Close)/3]. If prices settle above the pivot point by a certain percentage or PIP basis, then the market is determined to be in a bullish mode. Therefore, I look for the range of the next time period to be between S-1 and R-2. The opposite is true for a bearish outlook: If the market is bearish, then I look for the market to stay between R-1 and S-2; and that is what I look to be the projected range for the next time period. The next dimension I use to help determine trading signals is the use of two moving average components that generate buy and sell signals as prices cross and close above and below the averages. The moving averages are based on pivot points, and I use a short-term and a longer-term time period for these values. You can determine the best time periods and experiment with a pivot point moving average (H + L + C/3) of various time frames on the markets of interest you choose. You need to scan and test various markets to detect the ultimate time frame for that select market as a function of volatility.

Remember that a slower-moving, less-volatile market will respond better with lower time frame settings. A market with heightened volatility with shorter time frame settings will generate too many signals. Let's face facts: The euro and the British pound have larger swings on a daily basis than do the Japanese yen or the Canadian dollar. You want to mechanically and also visually back-test and optimize your settings for the various currencies. Genesis Software allows for the mechanical analysis; and just by setting up the parameters on your moving average settings, you can scroll back on the charts to see what the market did at these cross-over spots. This is what I consider a multidimensional trading method because I am looking for more than just one function in order to trigger a trade. As I stated earlier, I incorporate a moving average approach to help automatically filter out the projected support and resistance levels and use the pivot point value as a moving average. Next, I need one more criteria to confirm a sell signal at resistance or a buy signal at support. This is determined by the programming of a high close doji or a low close doji. I also have a few other patterns that help generate buy and sell signals at or near the project pivot support or resistance levels.

Generally speaking, I am looking for a confirmation of a shift in momentum by spotting a conditional change with a higher closing high for a buy signal or a lower closing low for a sell signal. The programming has filtered how many past time periods it will use for these signals. In other words, if the market is in a steep decline, with the pattern formation of lower closes than opens, lower highs, lower lows, and lower closing lows, a conditional change would be what? A conditional change would be a combination of those events to reverse, such as prices forming higher closing highs, with higher highs and higher lows as the closes of each candle are above the open. The sample trade signal shown in Figure 8.7 illustrates how prices drifted lower and then fell in a steep decline. You will see that this downtrend consisted of the sequence of lower closes than opens, lower highs, lower lows, and, most important, lower closing lows (the close was below the prior one or two time frames' lows). That is what really defines *bearish momentum*. Now as prices reach the projected pivot point support target level, the trained professional or candlestick aficionado will notice that the exact low was formed by a doji; then two candles later, an inverted hammer formed. The buy signal is generated as the moving average crosses; and we see, as I described earlier, a conditional change occurred.

The system kicks in a nice buy signal; and as Figure 8.7 shows, a bullish trend develops and gives significantly more than our 40-PIP profit target. This leads me to explain that a mechanical trading system can be enhanced by discretionary input if you have the discipline to follow through with trailing stops and to monitor the price action rather than forming an opinion based on greed with respect to increasing your expectations on the outcome for the trade. Let me be more specific: The system generates a buy signal, and you enter multiple lots. As the market moves in the desired direction, you scale out of half or two-thirds of your positions and then enter a trailing stop. What was intended to be a day trade might now be carried

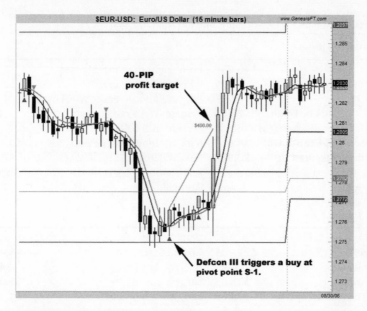

FIGURE 8.7 Pivot Point Moving Average Used to Trigger Signals
Used with permission of GenesisFT.com.

into an overnight or even a swing trade lasting several days. As long as you
do not start to build an opinion that the current trend might last forever and
stick with a risk mechanism, then you can milk the trade and increase your
performance. The trouble is—and the breakdown in a trading plan occurs—when traders stop following a system-driven plan.

Let's examine the performance statistics shown in Table 8.4 and see
how a moving average method fared compared to the previous two most
popular indicators, stochastics and MACD. The overall performance is
pretty good, with a 63 percent winning accuracy rate and a net return of
$46,750. The moving average system recommends start-up capital per posi-
tion based on a $100,000 lot size of $7,963. That is slightly more than the
stochastics system ($6,050), which had a winning percentage of 67 percent
and produced a net profit of $40,400, and less than the MACD system
($10,820), which had a winning percentage of 57 percent and a net profit of
$34,180. The best performer was, indeed, the moving average system, from
the standpoint of generating the most profits. It even ranked the best in the
profit factor category, with a reading of 2.03, as well as in the Kelly ratio,
with a ranking of 0.3191.

TABLE 8.4 Results for Pivot Point Moving Average System

Overall—Defcon III

Total Net Profit:	$46,750	Profit Factor ($Wins/$Losses):	2.03
Total Trades:	305	Winning Percentage:	63.0%
Average Trade:	$153	Payout Ratio (Average Win/Loss):	1.19
Average # of Bars in Trade:	79.63	Z-Score (W/L Predictability):	0.3
Average # of Trades per Year:	85.0	Percent in the Market:	77.4%
Max Closed-Out Drawdown:	−$4,063	Max Intraday Drawdown:	−$4,400
Account Size Required:	$7,963	Return Percent:	587.1%
Open Equity:	$313	Kelly Ratio:	0.3191
Current Streak:	2 wins	Optimal f:	0.64

Winning Trades / **Losing Trades**

Total Winners:	192	Total Losers:	113
Gross Profit:	$92,225	Gross Loss:	−$45,475
Average Win:	$480	Average Loss:	−$402
Largest Win:	$2,663	Largest Loss:	−$1,000
Largest Drawdown in Win:	−$1,663	Largest Peak in Loss:	$1,938
Average Drawdown in Win:	−$257	Average Peak in Loss:	$267
Average Runup in Win:	$726	Average Runup in Loss:	$267
Average Rundown in Win:	−$257	Average Rundown in Loss:	−$712
Most Consecutive Wins:	9	Most Consecutive Losses:	7
Average # of Consecutive Wins:	2.63	Average # of Consecutive Losses:	1.57
Average # of Bars in Wins:	78.80	Average # of Bars in Losses:	81.04

Looking at the equity curve shown in Figure 8.8, notice that the drawdown periods are less dramatic and that equity growth is on a steeper curve. One more item that stands out here is that the moving average system tends to not demonstrate as many nor as significant drawdowns against peak equity performance. Apart from a one-time maximum intraday drawdown in November 2004 of $4,400, this system shows decent consistency in profitable results, as well as fewer drawdowns.

Looking at the monthly performance statistics in Figure 8.9, we uncover the most profitable months and, best of all, the worst month. I say "best of all" because running a back-test as I reviewed earlier lets us see, at least from a historic perspective, what the weakest link in the armor is. In the moving average system we see that April is the worst month; and now we can draw a few conclusions and possibly defend our trading capital by dissecting the signals more closely when trading during April. Seasonality

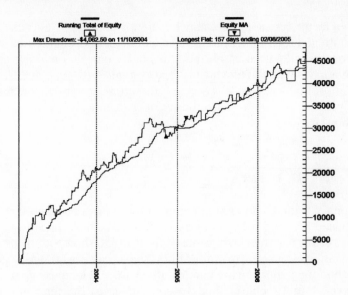

FIGURE 8.8 45° Trend on Equity Curve Growth Rate

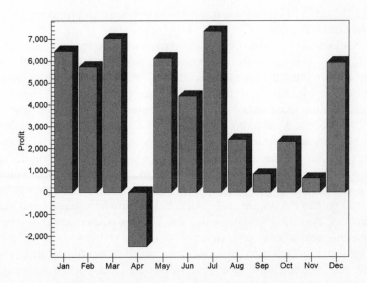

FIGURE 8.9 Avoid Trading This System in April

might be a factor, as the market may be choppy and sloppy because April is tax month and the first month of the second quarter. Capital flows may be a factor that influences the ebb and flow of the currency markets at that time as it applies with the moving average system. September and November, while profitable, seem less so; and, therefore, by studying a system, perhaps you will be able to make better decisions or decide not to trade during those periods.

TASTE OF REALITY

Discretionary traders can greatly benefit from a custom-tailored trading system based on solid rules and criteria that have been back-tested because the results can then be rigorously dissected to show the advantages, the disadvantages, and the overall results from a risk/reward basis. Creating a methodology that you are comfortable with will increase your confidence level, thereby eliminating (to some degree) the fear and greed factors. Trading requires strong discipline. With a trading system generating the indicator signals that advanced software can provide, you as an individual trader may not get caught up in the disastrous emotional pitfalls generated by fear and greed. By creating the closest thing to a fail-safe trading method using multidimensional confirmation signals based on trading signals from a multilayered sequence of events, you may see fewer trades but higher percentages of wins versus losses and bigger wins than those losses.

The reality is that most professional traders no longer rely on just one element, like a chart pattern or an oscillator signal. A highly effective executable trading signal comes from various confirming criteria, such as higher closing highs, closes above more than one moving average value, and confirmation from an oscillator such as stochastics, as I have covered so far in this book. Also, many systems try to filter buy and sell signals that are within various time frames, such as only taking buy signals when the next longer-term or predominant trend is in a buy mode or uptrend.

The harsh reality is that besides making money, the most important aspect of any system design is not just performance, but the risk exposure compared to the maximum and average drawdowns against peak equity performance and the measurement of risk-adjusted performance, that is, the measurement of expected returns minus the risk-free interest rate divided by the standard deviation of return on the investment. In laymen's terms, a good trading methodology should make money without giving you a myocardial infarction from massive drawdowns and exposure to extreme risk. Once you understand how and why a trade system works and you feel comfortable with the risk-to-reward parameters, having that information may help you overcome the fears and lack of confidence that plague many novice and experienced traders.

This chapter exposed you to three systems based on pivot points that you can implement immediately in your trading approach. I hope it helps you to expand your interest in this frontier of trading tactics. The next few chapters explain more on the subject of trade setups, risk management techniques, and the psychology of the game.

CHAPTER 9

Selecting Your Trading Window Frames

T echnical analysis is a picture or a window that reflects the attitudes of market participants as shown in the price behavior of a market. It helps us determine support and resistance points. Traditional charting shows us where prices have been (lagging indicators). Certain technical tools give us clues based on past tendencies of the direction in which prices could go (leading indicators).

As we have learned so far, the purpose for using technical analysis is to uncover and forecast market moves. Traders rely on technical analysis to give indications on the trend, support and resistance, trend reversal signals, potential price moves and objectives, and the distance the markets can move based on "measuring" techniques. But what do we do to pull the trigger to enter a position, and what can we do as traders to put the odds in our favor? For answers, we need to delve into one of the oldest and certainly the most subjective techniques in technical analysis—multiple time frame analysis. Longer-term time frames do influence the shorter-term time frames. But which time frame triggers action first? How do we determine which is the dominant time frame to follow, and what is the shortest time frame a trader should choose against a longer-term trend? More on this subject lies in how to choose the appropriate number of time frames. To find out where our window of opportunity lies, we need to ask ourselves:

- Which time frame do you use to trigger a trade?
- Which time frame do you use to set your stops?
- Which time period do you use to establish your profit objective?

225

TREAT TRADING AS A BUSINESS

Understanding what your objectives are by first having an understanding of what type of trader you are is critical to achieving success. Are you entering a trade as a scalp, a day trade, or a swing trade; or will you look to expand the trading opportunity as a position trade to ride a long-term trend? Another reason that I shared with you in Chapter 1 on the various forex investment vehicles besides the spot forex markets (such as the exchange traded funds (ETFs) and the futures and options markets) is so that you can decide which investment vehicle you may want to use to capture a profit within your risk-to-reward parameters and in the time frame you expect the market might take to reach those objectives based on decisions regarding what your objectives and your expectations out of the trade are or what the time horizon for the market might need to reach those price objectives. Then you will be able to determine which time frame to follow, and then you can monitor the shorter-term time frame as well. You may think of yourself as just a day trader; or maybe you are a long-term trend follower. Eventually you will encounter market phases that may dictate that you diversify your trading tactics. In periods or consolidation phases, as a longer-term trader, you may need to use short-term day-trading tactics to cover your operational business expenses. This is a great time to bring this to your attention because if you are reading this book to expand your knowledge to learn how to trade or if you are currently trading for a living, remember that this is a *business*. You need to treat it like a business. Therefore, some considerations need to be made, such as forming a corporation in order to deduct expenses such as your computer equipment, your quote feed, your DSL line, travel to various investment conferences, and continuing education seminars. You should seek advice from a tax specialist so that you can take advantage of all regular and necessary expenses as business deductions. This can help you save thousands of dollars each year. What matters most to every trader and investor is creating a positive cash flow. After all, it would be horrible to finally start learning to make money consistently in the market and find out that you cannot take any expense deductions that could literally save you thousands of dollars each year.

As a forex trader, let's see what your total expenses could be: Suppose your quote feed is $200 per month and your DSL is $50 per month. Renting a small one-room office could run $500 to $700 per month. Then there are equipment expenses, such as your desktop computers, a laptop for travel, monitors and printers and ink cartridges and general office supplies to purchase and upgrade from time to time, say $2,000. Attending an investment conference could mean $700 roundtrip airfare, plus $250 per night for hotel and meals. If you have business entertaining expenses and went to at least two conferences per year, you could be talking as little as $5,000 to as much as $25,000 in actual business expenses that can be deducted if you are running trading as a business.

If you are a first-time smaller investor and decide that trading for a living is something you have the financial resources, time, and emotional makeup to trade full time, what business plan do you have in place to protect the money you make in the market? Where will you put your profits as a short-term trader? As a longer-term trader, what will you do when market conditions change according to your system or methods? Not only do you need to cover your cost-of-living expenses, mortgage payments, or, for some, dockage fees for the yacht, but you need to cover the business expenses. The forex market offers an individual a bare-bones means to participate in the markets on a pay-as-you-go method because there are no commissions. Forex dealers do provide, as we covered, free charts, quotes, and news. There are, however, the considerations to cover the bid and the ask spread each time you trade. So if you are a day trader, consider that if you trade a minimum of twice a day at 3 PIPs (percentage in points) per transaction as your cost to enter a $100,000 contract value position, then if you trade 10 lots each trade, that amount would equate to $600 per day. At an average of 200 trading days per year (minus personal days, holidays, and vacation time away from the markets), you need to cover over $120,000 a year, not including covering the losses on bad trades. My point is that trading is not free. Therefore, it is important—more like critical—that you explore all your options and trading opportunities. Now with that said, let's see how to use various time frames in your analysis.

The first step is to identify the type of trade into which we will enter. Is it a day trade, is it a swing trade (which lasts two to five days), or is it a long-term position trade? Once we acknowledge what our objective is and what our goals are, then we can narrow our expectations. Let's assume I am a day trader. I will generally be able to identify what the average range for a day is and expect that if I miss 20 percent of the bottom and 20 percent of the top, then I can expect to capture 60 percent of the average daily range. My expectations are now for X amount of a given range. Now how do I start? First, I need to structure my computer and charts to a format that is conducive to day trading. As we went over in the previous chapter, using a system that earmaked 40 PIPs profit on a day trade system, some FX prop traders even set their goals on less that that, for instance, 30 PIPs, or within a specific time period, such as eight or six bars from entry. You need to determine whether you are day trading in order to use these parameters. Let me show you what I use in day trading.

DAY TRADING TIME FRAMES

For the FX currencies, I watch at least two markets in two time periods. Generally, I follow the euro currency, the yen, and the British pound. For day trading, I use the 15-minute time frame for my dominant trend and the 5-minute time frame for my short-term as a trigger to go with the 15-minute signal; and I use the 5-minute time period to exit a position in my day trading. I have my software preprogram, which automatically calculates and filters the pivot point lines on my charts. This software also comes complete with the monthly and weekly numbers, which are a tremendous help in identifying a confluence or layer of support (S) or resistance (R) levels in the various time frames. These are generally set with the R-1 and S-1 calculations. The graph in Figure 9.1 represents the euro on the left and the pound on the right. When I have a 5-minute trigger confirming a 15-minute time period signal, that tends to be the highest probability signal. This is the case especially when we have a sell signal based on a low close doji trigger when it coincides at or near the pivot point resistance numbers. If you look on the bottom left chart in Figure 9.1, you will see the arrow confirming a sell on the 15-minute chart confirming a textbook low close doji signal. Notice that the market moves sideways for 10 more consecutive periods, but the system is still identifying that the euro is in a sell mode. The top right

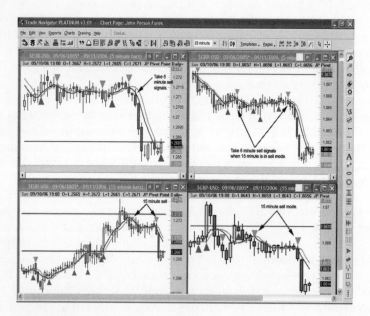

FIGURE 9.1   Use Multiple Markets and Time Periods to Confirm Triggers

TABLE 9.1   Day Trading

	Monthly Pivots	Weekly Pivots	Daily Pivots
Time Frames	60-minute	15-minute	5-minute

chart is a 5-minute period, and as you can see it generates buy and sell signals. The key thing to remember is that when the 15-minute time period is in a sell mode, take the 5-minute sell signals.

The chart on the bottom right in Figure 9.1 is the British pound; coincidently, it had generated the sell signals at the corresponding time period to the euro. Here we have a great example of how to take advantage of trading using a tandem, or like, market to help confirm a signal in a specific market sector. This shows that there was strength in the U.S. dollar at that precise moment, which should give you a higher degree of confidence that a bigger move or a sell-off may be in the works. As such, the market did indeed experience a nice day trade. Now notice that the corresponding 5-minute period in the upper right-hand corner generates buy and sell signals as illustrated by the triangles. If the 15-minute period is in sell mode (triangles point down), then take the sell signals in the 5-minute time period.

As a day trader, you can watch the 60-minute charts; but if you are in a trade based on the 5- and 15-minute periods, these are the time frames you need to continue monitoring for that specific trade. Keeping an eye on the 60-minute charts will help you identify the current trend and a potential change in trend if a moving average crossover occurs. Keep in mind your profit objectives and where you are in the trade as it relates to the average true range. If the euro is already down 50 PIPs when a sell signal is triggered, the odds favor that your potential for profits is only 36 PIPs or less if the average true range (ATR) is 86 PIPs based on the past 14 trading days. The breakdown in Table 9.1 may help guide you on what to watch for and the time periods to follow.

THE SWING TRADER

Swing traders are considered miniposition traders. They may have started out as day traders. As the market kept moving in the desired direction, either they scaled out of a portion of the position, set a stop-loss objective, and kept letting the trade ride; or they felt that there was a breakout of a period of consolidation and the market would continue in trend mode for three days or more. Regardless of how they initiated a swing trade, they

TABLE 9.2 Swing Trading

	Monthly Pivots	Weekly Pivots	Daily Pivots
Time Frames	Daily charts	240-minute	60-minute

need to focus on a higher-degree time frame and spend less time on the micromovements that 5- or 15-minute periods generate.

If you are a swing trader holding a position for more than one day, 5- and 15-minute charts will generate too many short-term signals. The most reasonable time frames to follow are the daily charts, the 240-minute charts (which break down to a 4-hour time frame), and the 60-minute charts. As far as using pivot points, it is important for swing traders to pay attention to the daily pivots as well as to the weekly and monthly numbers to help give a potential entry or exit target price but also to help be aware of any confluence of support or resistance for those various time periods. Table 9.2 shows the breakdown of the importance of which pivot points and time frames to follow.

In Figure 9.2, I have the daily chart on the euro on the left and the British pound on the right. If you examine the charts closely, you will see that the daily chart on the pound is in the bottom right-hand corner of the chart; it generates a sell signal first on September 5, 2006. The euro did not generate a sell signal until the following day. However, the 240-minute charts shown in the top windows show corresponding sell signals in the respective time periods, as the daily charts show. This method of taking trades in the shorter time frame when the signals line up (that is, take sell signals at resistance and buy signals at support, and use the higher time frames to confirm the triggers on the shorter time frames) will be instrumental in your trading results. Both charts on the daily time frame have the weekly and the monthly pivot lines across the screens, and the 240-minute charts in the windows at the top have the daily pivot points lining up to help illustrate where the sell and buy signals are in relation to the predicted support and resistance levels for those time periods.

This is the method I use to line up specific charting time frames with the proper pivot point time frames. Keep in mind that, as a day trader, you are not so much concerned with long-term macroeconomic situations as you are with riding a momentum wave; and the same is true for swing trading. Granted, it helps to have a good understanding of fundamental conditions, being aware of release times for economic reports; but for the most part, as a day trader and a swing trader, you are simply looking to ride a move and profit from it. That is your job. In short-term trading, conditions change; and you need to capture opportunities as they arise. Forex markets are ideal for momentum trades. The foreign currency market tends to trend

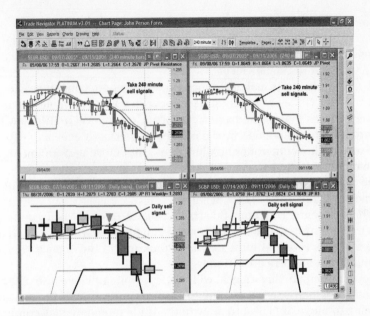

FIGURE 9.2 Trading Tandem or "Like" Markets Helps Confirm Signals

well over the course of 3 to 10 days, and this allows swing traders opportunities to capture larger price swings over a given period of time. One of the greatest benefits here is that you have access to the markets on a 24-hour basis, unlike the equity markets. Therefore, you can monitor your positions, place stops, and take action to exit a trade at any time, day or night.

BASIC RULES FOR SWING TRADERS

Because of the time frame involving several days in swing trading, the nature of this style of trading is slightly more advantageous in forex, mainly due to the fact that you have 24-hour access to monitor and to trade a forex position. Because of this constant market action, there are very few times that gaps occur. Therefore, I do not trade or use the gap-"fade" techniques. However, here are some basic rules that apply to swing trading and to which forex traders should adhere.

- If a day trade moves sharply in your favor, carry it through the overnight session, except for Fridays. Do not hold positions over the weekend unless you have a very well funded trading account or can manage a position that has a big profit built into the trade. When a market closes strong near the highs in the U.S. session (5 P.M. EST), odds favor the likelihood that there will be more upside potential in the European session. Tighten stops and look to exit the next day near a pivot point target resistance level.

- If your trade starts making money from the get-go, your entry was correct. Good trades generally start to move in your favor almost immediately. Prices may come back to test your entry level a little, but they certainly should not test your risk level. It's perfectly acceptable for the market to hover at your entry level for a bit before performing in your favor.

- Do not carry a losing position from one session to another. Exit the trade and look for a better signal.

- When you enter on a bona fide trading signal, don't get fancy and try to get a better fill by placing limit orders; go to the market. Other traders or systems (competitors) may also pick up on the signals, and you could miss out on a great trade.

- Never anticipate that a signal will happen. Wait until the close of the period for which you are trading to confirm the signal. If the market is going to move, it is best to go with the trade momentum as confirmed by the closing time period rather than guess and be too early on a long entry, only to watch the market crash and burn.

SUMMARY

When you are looking for a short-term day trade, focus on the 5- and 15-minute time periods for which a signal was generated. If you have time constraints that limit you to following the markets, such as work or bedtime, then scaling out of positions and trailing stops are great features. If you capture a strong-trending market condition and turn a day trade to a swing trade, then follow the 60-minute chart at the close of each 60-minute time period to see what the relationship of the close is to past highs and lows.

In addition, focus on the higher-degree time frame pivot points, such as the monthly and weekly support and resistance levels, as well as on the moving average values, to see where prices are in relation to both averages. If there is a crossover and prices close above a prior high and if the 60-minute chart closes above all of these variables, then you want to go long and/or look for buy signals on the shorter-term time frames, such as the 15- and 5-minute periods. For swing traders, watch the daily charts and the 240-minute time period in conjunction with the 60-minute period.

CHAPTER 10

Risk and Trade Management: Stop Selection, Scaling Out, and Setting Profit Targets

This chapter will walk you through the various types of stop orders and when and where to place them. It will also provide a great deal of important information on why and which stops should be placed at critical price levels and how to identify those price areas. If a trader is to maintain a degree of profitability over time, managing risk and using a system that helps evaluate price changes are critical. When you have finished this section, you will understand how to select stops to limit your potential losses and how to let profits ride. The process in selecting stop placement as a risk management tool starts with the price of where the trade was initiated. Here are some finer points on the rationale for using a risk method or for having a stop-loss system in place.

- Predetermined stop-loss orders help conquer emotional interference.
- Stops should be part of a system or included in a set of trading rules.
- Weigh the risk/reward ratio before entering trades; set a stop objective.
- When volatility is low, stops can be placed closer to an entry level.
- When volatility is high, stop-loss orders should be placed further away from the entry level.

One of my favorite bits of advice I give students and seminar attendees is that the first rule of trading starts with the premise that it is okay to form an opinion on a gut feeling; just act on a trade signal that substantiates that opinion. Write your rules down and have them posted on your trading screen on your computer. Before you enter the trade, check your rule list twice; and make sure you know why and where to place a stop. As you gain more experience in the business, you will undoubtedly get caught in a news-driven, price-shock event, if you have not already experienced one. These are unavoidable and are hard to escape unscathed. It is considered a cost of doing business and should not reflect on your abilities as a trader. Managing risk is your job, and capturing as much profit as possible from winning trades should be your utmost goal. The descriptions of the types of stops and the pros and cons of each should help you make the right decision for the various circumstances or market conditions. In Chapter 1, we did cover a lot of material, including economic reports. These news releases do cause price spikes; and I want to repeat, it will be inevitable that if you trade or have a position on before a report, some time in your career, you will experience an unfortunate adverse move against you. Remember, stops cannot be guaranteed. This chapter will give you the general knowledge of what to expect and which type of risk protection method you can use.

PLACING STOP-LOSS ORDERS

Stop orders are often placed to protect against losses. These orders can also be placed to enter positions. Specifically, a stop order is one that you place online in the FX market if the market trades at a certain price; then the order is triggered and becomes a market order to be filled at the next best available price.

- Buy stops are placed above the current market price.
- Sell stops are placed below the current market price.

I will focus on *protective* stops used to offset a position and to protect against losses and against accrued profits. Stops can also be used to enter a position. A variety of stops can be used depending on your situation, on the market you are trading, and on what you are trying to accomplish. Various types of available stops and several techniques can be used with them to help you manage your position and reduce your overall risk.

Dollar Limits

Stops can be based on a dollar amount per position, which is categorized under a strict money management system. If you are risking $250 per $100,000 lot position in a euro currency, then your stop level would be placed at a 25-point distance from your entry price. This method is used less frequently by professional traders because it has no relevancy from a mechanical trading model. However, there are benefits to this feature with setting a daily dollar amount on a loss limit for active day traders. Some electronic order platforms allow you to set a daily loss limit. Rather than per trade, it sets an overall loss limit on your account.

Percentage Figures

Most traders hear of using a stop of a certain percent of the overall account size. Generally speaking, that number can be from 2 percent up to as much as 5 percent of the overall account. Unfortunately, for most traders in forex, the average-size trading account is $10,000, which is $200 to $500 per trade. This leaves little room for error. Normally, traders want to use at least a two-to-one risk/reward ratio on their trades or have a statistical reason for a large risk amount that is consistent on each trade such as we have in our trading system discussed in Chapter 8.

Time Factors

After a specific time period, if the price does not move in the expected direction or if the velocity of such a move does not warrant holding onto the position, then exit the trade. If you see a low close doji (LCD) or a high close doji (HCD) trigger, you have experienced that the market generally demonstrates immediate reaction. If after a long period of time (which could be defined as three to five candles) the market does not respond to the signal, then liquidate the position. The timing of the trade did not correspond with the desired or historical past proven results. Another consideration in the art of stop placements using a time element is the aid of a moving average. If you are long and the market starts to close below a moving average value, then exit the trade.

Once again, moving averages are simply trend lines that are considered a time-driven price-direction tool. One time factor that you can use as a stop placement method is the crossover point of reference created when using two moving average values—once the shorter-term moving average crosses the longer-term, it reflects a value change in the market. In the chart in Figure 10.1, we have a spot FX euro currency on September 7, 2006, which shows a classic LCD sell signal near the projected daily pivot point resistance level. Combined with prices closing below both moving average values, this is a textbook setup. The stop would be initially placed as stop-close-only (SCO) above the high of the doji. Now, this would need to be a visual stop because most FX platforms do not accept intraday SCOs. So you need the discipline to exit as a market order, in other words, to buy back the short position at the market once prices close above the doji high.

We should see immediate results with this trade; and as prices respond

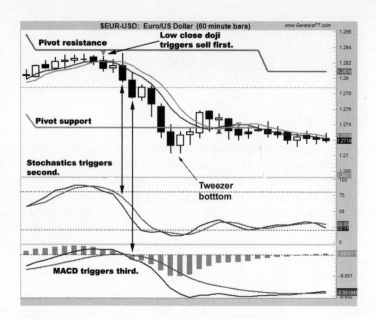

FIGURE 10.1 Initially, Use SCO Then Adjust the
Stops Accordingly
Used with permission of GenesisFT.com.

favorably and move lower. we can place a hard stop above below the doji
high. Once again, you would want to look at the point of crossover of the
two moving average values. If the market closes back above the high of the
doji or those moving average (M/A) values, then a trigger to exit the position would be warranted. As you can see, a bearish trend develops with the
golden sequence of events consisting of lower highs, lower lows, and lower
closing lows and closes below the opens. I want to point out that the indicator showed the sell signal first in this case, at 128.12; the stochastics gave
a signal with the %K and %D values crossing and closing back beneath the
80 percent level just one candle later at 127.97. But notice the zero-line
crossover of the moving average convergence/divergence (MACD), which
triggers the sell signal much later at 127.75. The stochastics was more in
sync with the LCD trigger.

The difference between the pivot points moving average method and
the MACD trigger was 37 PIPs (percentage in points), which on some days
is a decent trade all by itself. Granted, the market traded lower; in fact, see
how prices traded just below the daily projected pivot point support target
at 127.36. The tweezer bottom candles that look almost like an equal-and-
opposite pattern may have helped you decide to exit the trade had you
taken this sell signal. The point here is that a trade signal was generated, the

stop mechanism is in place, the market responded according to the tendencies of a particular pattern, and a profit objective was reached. When markets move into trend mode, there is only one way to trade them: You have to wait until each time period closes to see confirmation that prices are in fact following a specific course of action. In a downtrend, that would be lower highs, lower lows, and lower closing lows or closes near each time period's low and closes below each time period's open. The way to capture the most profits is to initially set your stop and then trail the stop as the market moves in the desired direction. Trailing stops can be placed automatically on some trading platforms. You need to do a little homework here to determine the settings of when you want the stop moved and at what price level. For instance, you can set the amount for every 30-PIP decline below your entry level; your stop will be moved lower by 10 PIPs. Market conditions warrant where you place your stops, such as if the market gives you an immediate windfall profit of 100 or 150 PIPs or so, it might be best just to take the money off the table.

 HOT TIP

Swing traders can use the automatic trailing stop feature from your FX dealers platform. This makes the decision-making process fully automated and reduces the chance that you will tend to let trades ride. Many traders tend to turn winners into losers as they get in the let-it-ride mindset. Measure the currency's average pullback range on an intraday time period during the most recent two or three past 24-hour trading sessions. Then, as the market moves in your favor, set your trailing stop order at that price amount multiplied out by 120 percent. If the average pullback is 20 PIPs, 120 percent expansion of that amount would be a trailing stop of 24 PIPs. However, as the currency moves closer toward your profit target, tighten the trailing stop amount so you capture the best possible profit margin.

Price Levels

Traders often use basic statistics to measure the degree of price volatility that can occur on a daily basis in a given market. These measures can then be used to place a stop or a limit order that takes into account these natural daily price movements. Statistics that are often used will be the *mean*, the *standard deviation*, and the *coefficient of variation*. The best trailing stop approach has been explored by many technicians. The various methods for this approach include placing a stop using a set price amount that could be as much as 150 percent of the average true range of a given time period either above or below the swing high and low point. Why is this method important? If you place a stop near a specific chart point of interest, such as an old high or an old low, those levels are obvious to every chart watcher. Markets do test and penetrate those levels from time to time. If you set your stop too close, such as setting a sell stop below an old chart low point or a buy stop above an old chart price high, chances are that your order may be executed if it is too close. So generally, a certain factor or distance should be calculated for your stop placement. Since most traders believe a market has reached a peak, they will place a stop slightly above an old high or below an old low. Depending on where you place your stop, the market may demonstrate a spike pattern that will hit your order and then proceed to move in the desired direction.

Generally, the market stops traders out and never looks back. In Figure 10.2, I have an example of how when the market is at major turning points, price spikes in the forex market are a common occurrence, especially right before some pretty big turns happen. Two stop methods can be employed that will help alleviate being prematurely stopped out. One is a stop-close-only, and the other is taking the average daily range of the past 10 periods or more and using a factor between 120 percent and 150 percent of that 10-day average daily range. On a buy stop, you would be looking to establish a short position and would place that stop-loss order by that calculation

FIGURE 10.2   Price Spikes Nail Stop Order
Used with permission of GenesisFT.com.

above the highest high of the preceding target swing high. For example, if you take the average daily range for the 10 trading sessions prior to the high back on July 5, which was the first peak, the sell signal was triggered by a low close doji pattern. The rules state to initially place a stop-close-only above the high of the doji. Stop-close-only orders do not guarantee where you will be filled, just that you will be filled if the market closes above that price point.

Check with your FX dealer to see if it has SCOs and the time it considers as the close. You want to be crystal clear on this point. As a position trader, you can use this method on spot FX, on futures, or on exchange traded funds, such as the FXE. Remember that the risk amount would not be absolutely defined, but the SCO would be placed at 1.2823; the sell was triggered at 1.2703. That would be a risk of 120 PIPs. Two days after you entered, the market prices did spike back and take out the high as shown at point B at 1.2862. The stop-close-only method saved you from the market's grips of getting bagged and tagged.

If you wanted to place a hard stop using the average daily range for the prior 10-day period, it worked out to 94.9 PIPs. Table 10.1 shows the breakdown of each session's high, low, and overall range. The spike top exceeded the prior high by 39 PIPs. By using the average true range of the prior 10 sessions and placing a stop above the initial high by that amount or even a factor of 120 percent, that would work out to 112 PIPs above 1.2823. You would be out of harm's way. The key is that you would need to place your stop at 1.29; and from your entry of 1.2724, that would be 211 PIPs, which is quite far away and certainly more than most traders would risk. Keep in mind that this is an initial risk order and that the next phase is to move the stops as the market moves in your favor.

Granted, depending on your risk tolerance, this may seem excessive; but you can select and back-test any percentage variable of an average daily

TABLE 10.1

Date	High	Low	Range (PIPs)
7-4-06	1.2823	1.2782	41
7-3-06	1.2822	1.2792	30
6-30-06	1.2796	1.2653	143
6-29-06	1.2671	1.2516	155
6-28-06	1.2584	1.2513	71
6-27-06	1.2618	1.2558	60
6-26-06	1.2603	1.2502	101
6-23-06	1.2588	1.2473	115
6-22-06	1.2679	1.2546	133
6-21-06	1.2679	1.2579	100

range stop placement. This method is used more for position traders, but
the concept can be adapted for day traders. The key idea here is to keep
your stops out of harm's way. If a trade is to become profitable, there
should be signs: In the case of selling short, you see immediate results with
lower highs, lower lows, and lower closing lows. Even in the days where
you see spike highs or spike lows, notice where the market closes in
relation to their respective highs and lows. The price penetrates the highs
but closes back below the prior highs. The reverse is true at the spike
lows. This is a good clue that the market has exhausted the trend and
is ready to reverse. Keeping a stop out of harm's way will allow you to
participate in the move using a variation of an average daily range stop
placement.

Conditional Changes

This is my favorite method, and here is how I define a *conditional change*:
It is the last higher closing high or lower closing low. Such as the case with
a spike top, the market does not close above an old high. Therefore, one
factor such as the SCO order will be of great use to a trader not looking to
get bumped out of a position. There is, as with any stop, the unknown risk
that there is not a guaranteed price at which your stop order will be filled.
This order has a negative connotation among traders as it spells out too
much risk. A buy stop will be elected and knock you out of a position if the
market closes above the stop price; and a sell stop will be elected and
knock you out of your position if the close is below your selected price
level. The unknown is how far away the market will close from the selected
stop price. The key benefit in using a stop-close-only is that it keeps your
risk defined to a conditional change and helps you from getting knocked
out of a position from intraperiod volatility. SCOs are for end-of-day trading
and can be placed on most trading platforms. The concept can be used for
day trading; however, it must be used manually because most platforms do
not accept intraday SCOs. Some consider this as a *mental stop*, which is a
predefined risk factor. However, many traders violate the rules once a signal gives an exit; they don't exit, and their losses are increased.

The challenge in selecting the right stop is to not be shaken out of the
trade by market volatility. A variable may be used to place trailing stops
that adapt to market volatility, which combines enough sensitivity to price
changes with flexibility to fit your trading needs. Using this combination, in
fact, may well provide an extremely profitable stop for the intermediate-
term trader. Trailing stops are used in an attempt to lock in some of the
paper profits that could accrue should the market move in the direction desired. Like an ordinary stop, the trailing stop is started at some initial value;
but then it is moved up (in a long trade) or down (in a short trade) as the

market moves in your favor. It is important to try to maximize your trading results and to stay in profitable trades as long as possible. Employing stop-losses and profit targets of the wrong sizes can ruin a trading strategy, making it perform significantly worse than it would have otherwise. Testing has demonstrated that a proper combination of even simple exit methods (such as placing sell stops below the low of the past two days when going long) can substantially improve the behavior of a trading strategy, even turning a random, losing strategy into a profitable one! Another less complicated method to use for a bullish trending market condition is to place a stop below the lowest low from the past 10-day period. Another one of my favorite methods is a trailing stop using the lowest low or the highest high from the last conditional change candle. I define the *last conditional change* as a higher closing high or a lower closing low. This is a much more important event than a higher high or a lower low since those price points are simply spikes. Buyers who stepped in on the open have a strong conviction that prices should expand to new higher territory once the market established a new high ground; and when the close is higher than the open and the market closes higher than a previous high, then the market is demonstrating significant strength. When you see a lower closing low as the lows are violated, then the market is demonstrating significant weakness. In turn, under these conditions, we should expect to see weaker or lower prices.

Let's examine this conditional change method on a day trade with a chart example using the spot euro currency from July 10, 2006, using a 15-minute time frame. Figure 10.3 shows a low close doji trigger to sell short at 1.2796. The initial stop per the LCD trigger states to use a stop-close-only above the doji high. That would be 1.2812. As you can see, the market stalls in a traditional sideways channel that the forex market is famous for; but it never really gives any pressure on the trade. As the sideways channel forms, at the end of the channel, notice that another low close doji sell signal materializes; and this time the market closes below the channel support trend line multiple times.

According to the trading rules, your stops should be placed initially above the doji high. If you were short from the first signal, then use the second doji as your stop point still using the SCO method. Once prices start to move lower, trail your stop above the highs of the candles that make new lower closing lows. At the end of the run, we want to trail the stop above the high of the last conditional change candle that made a lower closing low. If the market is to remain bearish and continue in a bearish trend mode, we should not see the high of a conditional change candle tested. Generally, when we do, that is a sign that the market condition will either enter in a consolidation phase or will reverse. Either way, it generally marks the time to exit the position.

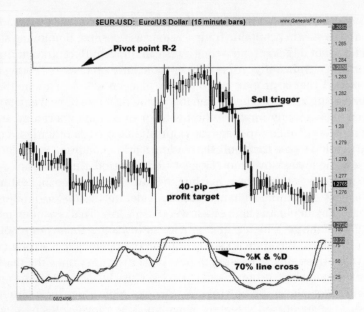

FIGURE 10.3   LCD Triggers a Short: Initially Use a SCO above
the Doji High
Used with permission of GenesisFT.com.

SCALE IN ENTRIES AND SCALE OUT EXITS

One of the single most important habits that some successful traders have
is that they possess a method that helps them define where the market
should go each day or they follow a game plan. They may possess a system
or use a method that provides an accurate daily forecast. They also may
have a set of rules for when to get in and out of the market, which may include a set of timing indicators to help them to pull the trigger at the key
areas. But above all, they possess discipline to follow through with these
rules. Trading is about making money, not about being correct in market
analysis or being a great prognosticator. Traders must be consistent in their
approach and strive to completely remove emotion from trading decisions.
This is often best achieved by having and sticking to a plan for every trade.
Trades are made in the current market, not in the *past* market. Hindsight is
always twenty-twenty; keep in mind that you will never trade as well in real
time with real money as you will by looking at or trading in the past. Trading in the past is an exercise in futility that will only harm your psyche
going forward.

You should view every trade you make as the best trade you could make at the time with the information available. That is why I like to scale out of a portion of my positions at key spots that guarantee money in my account while allowing me to participate in further gains. The reason I like to keep a portion of positions on is simple: As good as my triggers can be, I cannot predict the future. I do not know if a market will go into a consolidation phase or if it is simply pausing before continuing the trend or getting ready to reverse the trend entirely. Therefore, it is crucial to take money off the table when given the opportunity, while letting a trade mature and potentially develop into a larger profit.

There is only one way I know how to manage such a feat, and that is by scaling out of partial positions. The question some traders ask is, "What is the formula or percentage that I use to take positions off?" I normally use the 50 percent rule, but at times the one-third rule works as well. In order to define what the percentage figure is, I need to judge the condition of the current market environment. Ask and observe: Has the market been in a trend, a sideways range, a small-range low-volatile period, or a long-range extreme-volatility trading condition. Remember that trading requires you to ask questions and observe. The three critical stages for a trader are:

1. Gathering of information on which to make decisions.
2. Using that data to help formulate a trading idea.
3. Planning which actions to take.

The gathering of information involves collecting past data and then applying it to a specific means of market analysis, such as what I have covered using pivot point analysis. In formulating ideas, you may look at the pivot point moving averages to help determine a market's ability to trend by certain price direction. This step helps you to predict where the market might head, then gives you information so that you can decide where it should be going. Planning action involves thinking creatively about alternative courses of action, evaluating their feasibility, and making decisions on implementation of the plan. This step helps you decide if you should be in multiple contracts or if you should scale back on your normal position size. If the risk is not worth the reward, then trade with fewer positions; scale back your normal position size. Pivot point analysis helps give me a heads-up on the potential range of a session. The moving average of the pivot point helps give me a truer reflection of the market's value, and that helps me define the market's condition and possibly the correct direction. Candlestick charts help illustrate and define the trigger or the entry as well as the risk as indicated by past highs or lows. This enables me to carry out a systematic process of arriving at optimum plans and strategies for my trades.

   With that, I am now aware of the full range of issues to be considered in a systematic thinking process before entering a trade, I can formulate a trade with a clear, concise strategic plan by examining a set of relevant questions: How low can the market go? What is the next support target? How high can the market go? What is the next resistance?

   Exiting the positions and taking money off the table should be the easy part. However, as it turns out, that is the hardest part for most traders. Scaling out of positions is the most appropriate method when the market gives you a clue that the trend momentum is slowing. It allows you to capture a profit while participating in the market. The euro currency chart in Figure 10.4 demonstrates a nice day trading opportunity, and it shows how scaling out of half of your positions is a great mechanism to capture profits while staying with a potentially longer-term trend. As you can see, the sell signal triggers at 1.2872; immediately, we see the sequence of events, such as lower closes than the opens, lower highs, lower lows, and lower closing lows. This is what we want to see each time we place a short position in the market. I like to move my stops to just above the high of what I call a last conditional change (LCC).

   When a candle makes a lower closing low, that is the inflection point in time that causes a market to continue lower. If not then, there is another

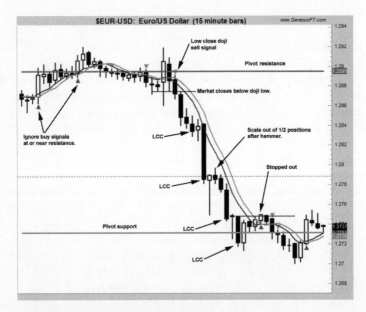

FIGURE 10.4   Watch Price Action at the Last Conditional
Change Candle to Determine Stop Placement
Used with permission of GenesisFT.com.

conditional change. In other words, a bearish trend would change to bullish, and I would want to be out of my short positions. Now, as we see prices decline, a hammer forms; and as you know, that is generally a clue that a market reversal is developing. In addition, notice that the low of the hammer is pretty close to the daily pivot support level. The candle right after the hammer does make a higher high, which would give you reason to scale out of half of your positions at 1.2785. That would be an 87-PIP gain on half of the positions—not a bad trade over 1 hour and 45 minutes. The market has truly not given any confirmation of a trend change; therefore, you would want to move a stop down on the balance of the positions to just above the high of the candle that made the most recent major conditional change of a lower closing low. Trading with scaling out of the balance of half of your positions, combined with the trailing stop method we went over in the previous section, will help you capture profits while participating in the majority of a trending market condition.

A day trader looking to capture a portion of a day's potential trading range has to use a plan. Scaling out of positions is such a plan of action. By setting stops at critical points and scaling out of trades, you can enjoy the best of both worlds: booking profits and letting trades ride. In Figure 10.4, we have our final trailing stop placed at the high of the LCC candle, and a bullish piercing pattern does form the low. Accordingly, the trade is stopped out at 1.2750 for a 122-PIP profitable move on the balance of positions. Even if you have a minimum of two lots on, that is 209 PIPs for a day. If you are a small-size equity trader and just starting out, this would be a great example of why you should trade mini-accounts; if full-lot-size positions are too much leverage, knock the trade size down. If your trades have merit, you will be rewarded. Building equity takes time; but by proper risk management and implementing scale-out trading techniques, you will increase your chances for continued success.

Take a look at Figure 10.5; we have a spot British pound (cable) versus the U.S. dollar from May 11, 2006. Notice that the market breaks below the targeted pivot point support several times; however, prices do not seem to decline very far or to carry any negative momentum. In fact, the market does what forex is notorious for—consolidates in a sideways pattern.

A doji pattern develops, which is actually the low of the session. Notice that the actual range of the doji (high/low) contains the majority of the price action. We do not want to take sell signals at support; so at this point, we need to wait for a definitive signal. There are two ways to enter the high close doji trigger: (1) using a stop-close-only below the low of the doji as indicated on the chart with the dashed line, or (2) a trade signal based on a momentum breakout of the sideways channel. In either case, your stops should be placed initially under the low of the doji as SCOs. Once the market breaks out of the consolidation pattern and the pivot support line at

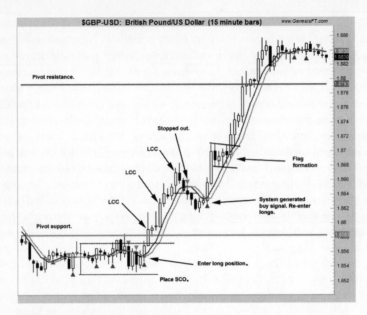

FIGURE 10.5 Take Buy Signals at Support and Trail Stops to Manage Your Position
Used with permission of GenesisFT.com.

1.8591, you can place a hard stop below the doji low and follow the developments as the trade matures. We see higher highs, higher lows, and higher closing highs. The market closes closer to the highs of each successive candle, and the closes of each candle are above the opens; all are very bullish signs. So far, you do not have a reason to liquidate the position or scale out of the trade. You can trail your stops below the low of the LCC candles. Here is an example in which if you are trading multiple lot positions, you can trail your stops on a portion of positions and put the portion at breakeven. If you choose to trail the stops in this example, notice the LCC candle: Not only does the market turn, but it also generates a sell signal. I would accept getting stopped out of the positions here, but I would not look to sell short for two reasons: (1) it is near support, and (2) the higher time frame 60-minute chart is still in buy mode.

If you entered late at 1.8569 and exited on your stop out at 1.8670, this is still a great day trade with a gain of 101 PIPs. As the saying goes, you can always reenter the market. As this chart shows, the system does generate a secondary buy signal, in which it gives you an opportunity to reenter a long position, which goes with the 60-minute dominant trend. The second trade would get you back in at 1.8656. Your stop should be placed below the reactionary low at 1.8615; and as prices forge higher, you can trail your stops below the low of the LCC candles. Follow the sequence of events that ensues: higher highs, higher lows, higher closing highs, and mostly higher closes than open candle patterns. The first clue to exit would be the projected daily pivot resistance level or once you see the first lower closing low. That happened at 1.8818, which is an additional 162 PIPs! This day gave two great signals; by following the flow of the market, you had the opportunity to take two trades using the LCC candle method to trail your stops. It ends a terrific, stress-free trading day.

I encourage you to explore any and all methods, but I will stick to what works for me. When I have a projected entry price based on pivot point analysis, I never have at any time a "guaranteed" profit until I liquidate the trade. By scaling out of a trade, it is the finest known method that puts cash in my account while allowing me to further participate in gains. Pivot points help target the entry and the exit on my trades.

CHAPTER 11

Game Psychology: Techniques to Master Your Emotions

F ear, ignorance, and greed are very destructive emotions that all traders need to conquer. These little demons wreak havoc on all traders' decisions from time to time. Do you quickly identify them and deal with them, or do you let them control your actions?

The bulk of your trading profits does not come from a few trades but rather from a string of consistent trades over a long period of time. Do not worry about losses; they will happen. Your success is influenced by how you react emotionally to the losses or the fatigue in trading, especially if you are simply focused on day trading. If trading is becoming monotonous or tiring, then change your time frame horizons; reduce your leverage or lot size, and change to swing trading. Many students I have mentored and worked with began trading on a steady pace but began to get in trouble once they prematurely started trading with way too many positions. When you discover a trading signal or a system that shows consistency, the one emotional element that will interfere with your success is greed.

If you find yourself asking, "How do I make serious money in this game?" as a small speculator, if you want to make big bucks, perhaps you need to expand on your interest and expertise in all aspects of the forex market. Diversify not only what markets you trade, but also what time frames you trade, such as day, swing, or position trading. Perhaps you should diversify in other avenues of currency, from exchange traded funds to options on the futures, as covered in Chapters 1 and 9.

Whatever style of trading you use, many of the techniques covered in this book can be applied and can help you improve your results if you apply proper risk management techniques. You may have a superior understanding of the fundamental developments, and now you can apply technical analysis tools such as Elliott wave, Fibonacci, and pivot point analysis to aid you in the timing of your entries and, most important, the exits.

Trading requires a disciplined approach toward risk management; most traders fail when they break their own rules. In fact, the famous speculator of our time, Jesse Livermore, was nearly broke and committed suicide. The main reason? He broke his own trading rules. Successful trading is all about diligence and hard work and having a winning attitude! Take the trades that were developed with thought and keen observations and that were triggered on predefined trading signals. This is what will help you develop the confidence to execute when a trading opportunity presents itself. Lack of confidence and fear are your enemies.

Trading on a rule-based system will help you overcome any issues as long as you are trading based on a signal or a bona fide trigger. Forget missing out on an opportunity that drives traders to a state of fearfulness. You cannot act on emotional impulse. That is why, if you wait until the actual close of the time period to trigger a trade, you will see a tremendous improvement in your trading results. Remember, your mind can and does play tricks on you when you are trading. You might see a signal; but if it is not confirmed by the close of the time period, then you could be setting yourself up for disaster.

It is always that little subconscious voice that tells you to just hang in there, just keep holding on to the loser, the market will bounce back. Traders who sit on a losing trade, hoping and praying that the market will soon turn around in their favor, are destined for failure. You need to identify these negative thoughts and start focusing on the condition of the market itself. Do not let these thoughts control your actions.

Table 11.1 is a list of the common negative traits and remedies that may help you as either a beginner or an experienced trader. There will be times when we all fall off the horse, so to speak. If you can identify and respond with a positive response or actions, you can overcome the way you respond to these negative emotions—and get back on the horse.

SIMULATED TRADING

It goes without saying that the more practice you have in any skill, the better you will be. But if you practice the wrong thing over and over, then there is little hope for improvement. It just so happens that this also applies to trading. Almost any forex dealing firm will give you a free trial to a simulated trading account for you to bang around on. With no real money on the line, you really are not putting your time to good use.

TABLE 11.1 Traders' Negative Traits and the Remedies

Destructive Habit	Remedy Exercise
Gets out of winners too early.	Trade multiple lots and scale out of half of the positions; setting stops on the balance just above breakeven.
Holds on to losers too long.	Implement hard stops rather than mental stop-close-only orders.
Is afraid to enter positions.	Cut back on your position size or on the lot value.
Doesn't act on signals; is always anticipating.	Accept the fact the market is better than you are. Learn to deal with trading with the flow of the market rather than trying to see who is smarter.
Gets too aggressive with lot size.	This tendency generally comes from pure greed and a feeling of invincibility. These are humbling times when you find out that no matter how great a system or trading signal is, it generally fails the morning you wake up and decide to go "all in."
Is not profitable enough, expectations too high.	Focus on a goal. Look to trade on a specific setup, strategy, or pattern. Set a goal for the trade even if it is only 20 PIPs per trade. Concentrate on that goal. When you achieve your daily goal after a period of at least two weeks, review your progress and equity balance. Write down your results and your evaluation. This will help solidify the purpose of your actions and eliminate unrealistic expectations.

If you have never traded or if you switch to a new company, it is extremely advisable to get accustomed to the trading platform that may be unique to that company. That makes all the sense in the world. The biggest concern is that a trader needs to take action when a trigger is generated rather than taking a wait-and-see attitude and then reacting to the market long after the market has moved. Hesitation is a trader's enemy; *plan your trade, and then trade your plan.*

Simulated trading is helpful in understanding the mechanics of a trading execution platform. However, putting real money on the line is what will test your trading skills. Here is a suggestion: If you want to really see if you have what it takes to be a professional trader who can execute a testable trading system, then trade with the smallest lot or position size for a period of six weeks or more until you develop a relaxed state of mind when you trade, until it becomes second nature to you. If you trade mini-lot-size positions in forex, you may not make lots of money if you are consistently right, but you will develop the confidence to act on your signals when your self-imposed training session is completed. Open an ultra-mini-sized forex account, and apply the trading signal to that market. This is a nifty idea for those who are beginners and still have day jobs. The markets trade 24 hours a day, you can afford to hold positions overnight, and you have money on the line so that you will be more realistic in execution of your trading plan. You can trade at night and execute trading signals in an extremely liquid market. If you have a system that works reasonably well based on statistical back-testing studies, the only confidence that should be in question is your ability to execute the signals. That is what trading a mini-FX account can do for you; it will get you to exercise your emotional intellect. You will learn that when you place a trade, it is based on an educated decision, not merely a guess. Developing that knowledge will give you the confidence to execute and to act on the trading signals. Building confidence in yourself and in your trading skills is extremely important in stimulating an optimistic winning attitude. Opening a mini-forex account just may help a newcomer using a technical based system. If you want to follow what the money makers do, have a good plan, method, or system; execute when a trigger presents a call to action; and maintain a winning attitude! One web site to visit so you can test trading platforms and trading signals based on my software is www.fxtriggers.com. The saying is old but very true: Practice does make perfect. In this business, you may not achieve perfection, but you will develop consistency.

Through the subjects covered in this book, you have learned a complete insight into pivot point analysis, trading signals, and trading systems. What I did not cover was how to help you overcome negative thoughts and feelings. As human beings, we react to current events from past experiences. If you have a hard time admitting defeat, that is one element based on ego that keeps you in losing trades. You must develop a robotic mindset. The key is to reduce such outside influences as events and even your trading surroundings so you are the most comfortable you can be in both state of mind and physical condition. If you go through a period where you are struggling in your trades and have the slightest doubts about how you feel, in my first book, *Technical Trading Tactics* (John Wiley & Sons, 2004, p. 199), I gave a great exercise to improve your mindset through positive visualization techniques or positive affirmations. Positive affirmations are extremely important to help improve self-confidence, especially in this business. This exercise requires real physical exertion. What you need to do is to pick up that 20-pound pen or pencil and write out these words 10 times a day: "I choose to be a positive, fearless, and successful trader" and "I choose to succeed in making money trading the markets." By doing this, you are reaffirming to your subconscious mind that you are a successful trader. You are then going to focus only on the positive forces and work on combating the destructive negative emotions that can and usually do interfere with being successful in trading.

RELAX: STRESS BUILDS ANXIETY

This job can be stressful, not from losing but from accumulating a winning position, which causes an increase in your heart rate. Take quiet times during the day to help you focus your attention on the business at hand; after all, not everyone can be staring at a quote screen all day without taking a breather. Relaxation techniques through yoga exercises actually work and are easy to do. Take in a few deep breaths through your nose. While doing so, tell yourself to relax, and say to yourself that you are in control and focused in the now. One more version is to take a long deep breath and hold it for about 10 seconds. You are going to *slowly* exhale and at the same time concentrate on saying to yourself: "I am calm and relaxed." You should repeat it at least six times.

Trade the Plan

When you have no plan of attack or specific plan of action before entering a trade, you are trading by the seat of your pants. This will invite negative emotions of fear and doubt because you don't know how much money may be made or lost.

Scared Money

It does not take a fortune to trade the markets with success. Traders with less than $3,000 in their trading accounts can and do trade futures successfully. And traders with $100,000 or more in their trading accounts can and do lose it. It all comes down to how you manage your risks and trades. Let the winners ride; and, for gosh sakes, get out of the losers when the signals turn on you. Don't get burned by not being able to admit defeat. There will be another trade. If you trade with money you cannot afford to lose, odds are you will lose it because you will accept small profits to build your account. Trade your plan.

Instant Gratification

Beginning traders, if you expect to quit your day job, don't! Use trading to supplement your income, and find out first if you can make a good living trading. Find out if trading is even fun for you after the first few months.

High-Risk Gamblers

Using protective stop mechanisms are crucial. Whether you use a stop-close-only, a hard stop, a timing stop, or a dollar amount, don't be a gambler who risks it all. No stop method is perfect, but at least you have a good idea of how much money you are willing to risk on the trade.

Patience and Discipline Go Hand in Hand

While patience and discipline are often discussed in this book, as are many other virtues, these are the essence of what trading successfully is about. You must wait for your setups and demonstrate the discipline to act on them. Getting bored is one great way to enter bad trades. You need to practice patience, otherwise you are setting yourself up for a loss.

Picking Tops and Bottoms

It's all about human nature. We all want to buy cheap and sell expensive. In trading, we discover new values that dispel our beliefs in what truly is cheap or expensive. That is why it is important to use a rule-based approach in the market and to trade on signals rather than depend on gut instincts.

Overtrading or Trading Too Many Positions

Oftentimes, traders are unclear about the word *diversification* and act by taking trading signals on similar markets simultaneously, such as the euro and the cable. To add to the stress, they trade with excessive positions. It goes without saying that if you find this happenening to you at this point in your trading career, ask yourself what the risk parameters of the trading strategy are and what aspect of the overall position you like. I have asked many traders when they are in this predicament if they begin a thought process on how the trade is working and if it is an acceptable position or size of position for the overall account. If the answer is no, that the trade is not acceptable, then action needs to be taken by eliminating a portion of the trade or cutting the trade entirely.

Is Your Trading Environment Conducive to Trading?

Is the place in which you are trading set up to allow you to concentrate or focus on your trading? If there are distractions, then the slightest interruption can cause a negative thought to interfere with a trading decision. Once you are in a trade, you cannot control the market—only your thoughts and actions. You have the ultimate power over your own thoughts and actions. If you have any distractions (loud neighbors, poor seating, bad lighting, or, my favorite, listening to a financial station and being subjected to someone else's opinion), these are the factors that may influence your thoughts and then your actions. Therefore, make sure your trading space or environment makes you comfortable and relaxed.

And remember, try to eliminate outside distractions that can spark emotional responses, especially something irritating, something that can invoke anger. If you are in a frustrated mood or simply anxious or impatient from sitting with a trade for too long, that emotional response could trigger inappropriate action, such as getting out of the market right before the move occurs. Stay calm, cool, and collected. Be the master of your emotions!

Postscript

From what we have gone over in this book and especially in Chapter 11, if there were any top suggestions that I would offer you, they are these:

- Never, ever, average a loss. Exit if you think you are wrong. Reenter the trade when you believe you are right or when the picture becomes clear again.
- Never listen to anyone else's opinion.
- Never pray when you are in a losing trade. God did not invent this game, and He has not informed me lately that He is trading. Just get out!
- Trading is not you against the market; egos have destroyed many a great trader. There is no room for ego when trading.
- Stay focused in the now. You can't change a trade you were in yesterday or the outcome of the trade tomorrow. So focus on what you are doing now.

I wish you well in your trading endeavors. I believe that if you can master your emotions, then you can master this game. Despite what the regulators and risk disclosure statements say—which, if you have not heard, is that "trading is risky"—I believe that you have the power to learn and the power to succeed.

After reading this book, I invite you to share with me your progress. Visit www.fxtriggers.com. Reply to the comment section.

All the best to you.

JOHN L. PERSON

Glossary

Appreciation Describes the strengthening of a currency in response to market demand rather than by official action.

Arbitrage The action of a simultaneous buy and sell of a similar or like commodity or futures product that may be made in different contract months, on different exchanges, and in different countries in order to profit from a discrepancy in price.

Arbitrage channel The range of prices within which there will be no possibility to arbitrage between the cash and the futures markets.

Ask The price at which a curency or instrument is offered.

Asset In the context of foreign exchange, the right to receive from a counterparty an amount of currency either in respect of a balance sheet asset, such as a loan, or at a specified future date in respect of an unmatched forward or spot deal.

Asset allocation Dividing instrument funds among markets to achieve diversification or maximum return.

At best An instruction given to a dealer to buy or to sell at the best rate that can be obtained in a given time period.

At or better An order to deal at a specific rate or better.

Backwardation The amount by which the spot price exceeds the forward price.

Balance of payments A systematic record of economic transactions during a given period for a country. (1) The term is often used to mean either (i) balance of payments on "current account" or (ii) the current account plus certain long-term capital movements. (2) The combination of the trade balance, current balance, capital account, and invisible balance, which together make up the balance-of-payments total. Prolonged balance-of-payment deficits tend to lead to restrictions in capital transfers and/or decline in currency values.

Bank rate The rate at which a central bank is prepared to lend money to its domestic banking system.

Base currency United States dollars; the currency to which each transaction will be converted at the close of each position.

Basis   The difference between the cash price and the futures price.

Basis point   For most currencies, denotes the fourth decimal place in the exchange rate and represents 1/100 of 1 percent (0.01%). For such currencies as the Japanese yen, a basis point is the second decimal place when quoted in currency terms or the sixth and seventh decimal places, respectively, when quoted in reciprocal terms.

Basis trading   Taking opposite positions in the cash and the futures markets with the intention of profiting from favorable movements in the basis.

Basket   A group of currencies normally used to manage the exchange rate of a currency.

Bear   An investor who believes that prices are going to fall.

Bearish   A downtrending market or a period in which prices are devaluing.

Bid   The price at which a buyer has offered to purchase a currency or an instrument.

Book   The summary of currency positions held by a dealer, a desk, or a room; a sum total of assets and liabilities.

Bretton Woods   The site of the conference that in 1944 led to the establishment of the postwar foreign exchange system that remained intact until the early 1970s. The conference resulted in the formation of the International Monetary Fund (IMF). The system fixed currencies in a fixed exchange rate system with 1 percent fluctuations of the currency to gold or to the U.S. dollar.

Broker   One who solicits, executes, or fills orders for customers or solicits funds on behalf of a brokerage firm.

Bullish   Referring to an uptrending market or to a period in which prices appreciate in value.

Bull market   A prolonged period of generally rising prices.

Bundesbank   Central Bank of Germany.

Cable   In the foreign exchange market, refers to the U.S. dollar/British pound rate.

Candlestick charts   Charting method that involves a graphic presentation of the relationship between the open, the high, the low, and the close. Color schemes are used to illustrate the real bodies of the candles, which is the difference between a lower close than the open (black or dark) and a higher close than the open (white).

Capital risk   The risk arising from a bank having to pay the counterparty without knowing whether the other party will or is able to meet its side of the bargain.

Carrying charges   The cost associated with holding or storing cash or physical commodities and financial instruments. Four variables are involved: storage, insurance, finance charges, and/or interest payments on borrowed monies.

Cash   Usually refers to an exchange transaction contracted for settlement on the day the deal is struck. This term is mainly used in the North American markets and those countries that rely for foreign exchange services on these markets because of time zone preference (i.e., Latin America). In Europe and Asia, cash transactions are often referred to as "value same day deals."

Cash market   The market in the actual financial instrument on which a futures or options contract is based.

Cash settlement   A procedure for settling futures contracts through payment of the cash difference between the future and the market price, rather than through the physical delivery of a commodity.

Central bank   A country's head regulatory bank, which is responsible for the development and implementation of monetary policy.

CFTC   Commodity Futures Trading Commission, which is the federal regulatory agency in charge of overseeing the futures and nonbank forex industry.

Closed position   A transaction that leaves the trade with a zero net commitment to the market with respect to a particular currency.

CME   Chicago Mercantile Exchange.

COMAS™   Conditionally Optimized Moving Average System, which incorporates two different time-period moving averages with two different variables, such as a simple moving average based on the close and a second value based on the pivot point.

Commission   The fee that a broker may charge clients for dealing on their behalf.

Commodity   A financial instrument or a product that is used in commerce and is mainly traded on a regulated commodity exchange. The types of products are agricultural (such as meats and grains), metals, petroleum, foreign currencies, stock index futures, single stock futures, and financial instruments (such as interest rate vehicles like notes and bonds).

Commodity trading advisor (CTA)   A registered individual or entity that advises others for compensation or profit in buying or selling futures contracts or commodity options; also includes one who exercises trading authority over a customer's account or who provides research and analysis through newsletters or other media.

Conversion   The process by which an asset or a liability denominated in one currency is exchanged for an asset or a liability denominated in another currency.

Conversion account   A general ledger account representing the uncovered position in a particular currency. Such accounts are referred to as "position accounts."

Conversion arbitrage   A transaction where the asset is purchased and buys a put option and sells a call option on the asset purchased, each option having the same exercise price and expiry.

Convertible currency   A currency that can be freely exchanged for another currency (and/or gold) without special authorization from the central bank.

Correspondent bank   The foreign bank's representative who regularly performs services for a bank that has no branch in the relevant center, e.g., to facilitate the transfer of funds. In the United States, this often occurs domestically due to interstate banking restrictions.

Counterparty   The other organization or party with whom an exchange deal is being transacted.

Countervalue   The dollar value of a transaction in which a person buys a currency against the dollar.

Country risk   The risk attached to a borrower by virtue of its location in a particular country; involves examination of economic, political, and geographical factors. Various organizations generate country risk tables.

Coupon   The interest rate on a debt instrument expressed in terms of a percent on an annualized basis that the issuer guarantees to pay to the holder until maturity.

Cover   To close out a short position by buying currency or securities that have been sold short.

Covered arbitrage   Arbitrage between financial instruments denominated in different currencies, using forward cover to eliminate exchange risk.

Credit risk   Risk of loss that may arise on outstanding contracts should a counterparty default on its obligations.

Cross rates   Rates between two currencies, neither of which is the U.S. dollar.

Current account   The net balance of a country's international payments arising from exports and imports together with unilateral transfers, such as aid and migrant remittances; excludes capital flows.

Day trader   A speculator who takes positions in commodities that are liquidated prior to the close of the same trading day.

Dead cross   A term used when a sell signal is generated when one or more shorter-term moving averages cross below a longer-term moving average.

Deal date   The date on which a transaction is agreed on.

Dealer   A person who acts as a principal in all transactions, buying and selling for his or her own accounts; opposite of *broker*.

Deal ticket   The primary method of recording the basic information relating to a transaction.

Deferred month   The more distant month in which futures trading is taking place, as established from the active nearby or front contract delivery month.

Deflator   The difference between real and nominal gross national product (GNP), which is equivalent to the overall inflation rate.

Delivery date   The date of maturity of a contract, when the exchange of the currencies is made; more commonly known as the *value date* in the forex or money markets.

Delivery risk   A term to describe when a counterparty might not be able to complete one side of the deal, although willing to do so.

Depreciation A fall in the value of a currency due to market forces rather than to official action.

Discount rate The interest rate charged on loans by the Federal Reserve to member banks.

Doji A candlestick term; used to describe a time period when the open and the close are nearly exact. It is a strong sell signal, but a cautionary warning at bottoms.

Easing A modest decline in price.

Economic indicator A statistic that indicates current economic growth rates and trends, such as retail sales and employment.

ECU European currency unit.

Effective exchange rate An attempt to summarize the effects on a country's trade balance of its currency's changes against other currencies.

Elliott wave Analysis theory developed by Ralph Elliott, based on the premise that prices move in two basic types of waves: impulse waves, which move with the main trend, and corrective waves, which move against the main trend.

Euro dollars U.S. dollars on deposit with a bank outside of the United States and, consequently, outside the jurisdiction of the United States. The bank could be either a foreign bank or a subsidiary of a U.S. bank.

European Monetary System (EMS) A system designed to stabilize if not eliminate exchange risk between member states of the EMS as part of the economic convergence policy of the European Union (EU). It permits currencies to move in a measured fashion (divergence indicator) within agreed bands (the parity grid) with respect to the ECU and consequently with each other.

Exchange control Rules used to preserve or protect the value of a country's currency.

Exchange for physicals (EFP) A transaction generally used by two hedgers who want to exchange futures for cash positions; also referred to as "against actuals" or "versus cash."

Exchange traded fund (ETF) Index-based investment vehicle that is traded as a share of a single security based on an entire portfolio of stocks or a set contract size of a given commodity or investment product, such as a foreign currency.

Exercise The process by which options traders convert an options position into the underlying futures or derivative market; e.g., buyers of a call option would convert their calls for a long position, and buyers of a put option would convert their option to a short futures contract.

Face value The amount of money printed on the face of the certificate of a security; the original dollar amount of indebtedness incurred.

Falling three methods A bearish continuation pattern similar to the Western version of a bear flag. It is a four- but mostly a five-candle pattern composition.

Fast market   Rapid movement in a market caused by strong interest by buyers and/or sellers. In such circumstances, price levels may be omitted, and bid and offer quotations may occur too rapidly to be fully reported.

Fed   The United States Federal Reserve System. Federal Deposit Insurance Corporation (FDIC) membership is compulsory for Federal Reserve members. The corporation had deep involvement in the savings-and-loan crisis of the late 1980s.

Federal Reserve System   The central banking system of the United States.

Fed fund rate   The interest rate on Fed funds. This is a closely watched short-term interest rate because it signals the Fed's view as to the state of the money supply.

Fibonacci numbers and ratios   An infinite series of numbers such that any number in the series is the sum of the preceding two numbers. The ratios are the math calculations, which are the sum of the relationships between the numbers derived either from dividing the series numbers or, in some cases, taking the square roots of the numbers. The common ratio numbers are 0.38%, 0.618%, 0.50%, and 1.00%.

Fill or kill   An order that must be entered for trading, normally in a pit, three times; is immediately canceled if not filled.

Financial instrument   One of two basic types: a debt instrument, which is a loan with an agreement to pay back funds with interest, or an equity security, which is a share or stock in a company.

First notice day   According to Chicago Board of Trade (CBOT) rules, the first day on which a notice of intent to deliver a commodity in fulfillment of a given month's futures contract can be made by the clearinghouse to a buyer. The clearinghouse also informs the sellers of whom they have been matched up with. Each exchange sets its own guides and rules for this process.

Fixed exchange rate   Official rate set by monetary authorities; often permits fluctuation within a band.

Flexible exchange rate   An exchange rate with a fixed parity against one or more currencies with frequent revaluations.

Floating exchange rate   An exchange rate determined by market forces. Even floating currencies are subject to intervention by the monetary authorities.

FOMC   Federal Open Market Committee, which sets U.S. money supply targets, which tend to be implemented through Fed Fund interest rates, and so on.

Foreign exchange (forex)   The purchase or sale of a currency against sale or purchase of another.

Forex market   Usually referred to as the over-the-counter market where buyers and sellers conduct foreign currency exchange business.

Forward margins   Discounts or premiums between the spot rate and the forward rate for a currency; usually quoted in points.

Forward operations   Foreign exchange transactions on which the fulfillment of the mutual delivery obligations is made on a date later than the second business day after the transaction was concluded.

Forward outright   A commitment to buy to or to sell a currency for delivery on a specified future date or period. The price is quoted as the spot rate plus or minus the forward points for the chosen period.

Forward rate   Quoted in terms of forward points, which represent the difference between the forward rate and the spot rate. To obtain the forward rate from the actual exchange rate, the forward points are either added to or subtracted from the exchange rate. The decision to add or to subtract points is determined by the differential between the deposit rates for both currencies concerned in the transaction. The base currency with the higher interest rate is said to be at a discount to the lower interest rate quoted currency in the forward market. Therefore, the forward points are *subtracted* from the spot rate. Similarly, the lower interest rate base currency is said to be at a premium, and the forward points are *added* to the spot rate to obtain the forward rate.

Free reserves   Total reserves held by a bank minus the reserves required by the authority.

Full carrying charge market   A futures market where the price difference between delivery months reflects the total costs of interest, insurance, and storage.

Fundamental analysis   A method of anticipating future price movement using supply and demand information; also a method to study the macroeconomic factors (including inflation, growth, trade balance, government deficit, and interest rates) that influence currency and financial markets.

G7 (Group of Seven)   The seven leading industrial countries: the United States, Germany, Japan, France, the United Kingdom, Canada, and Italy.

Gann, William D.   An early pioneer in technical analysis who is credited with a mathematical system based on Fibonacci numbers and with the Gann Square and Cycle studies.

Gap   A mismatch between maturities and cash flows in a bank or an individual dealer's position book. Gap exposure is effectively interest rate exposure.

GLOBEX   A global after-hours electronic trading system used on the Chicago Mercantile Exchange (CME).

Golden cross   A bullish term used when one or more shorter-term moving averages cross above a longer-term moving average; generally generates a buy signal.

Gold standard   The original system for supporting the value of currency issued. This is where the price of gold is fixed against the currency; it means that the increased supply of gold does not lower the price of gold but causes prices to increase.

Good until canceled   An instruction to a broker that, unlike normal practice, does not expire at the end of the trading day; usually terminates at the end of the trading month.

Gravestone doji   A long-range day where the open and the close are near the low of the range.

Gross domestic product (GDP)   Total value of a country's output, income, or expenditure, produced within the country's physical borders.

Gross national product (GNP)   Gross domestic product plus "factor income from abroad," i.e., income earned from investment or work abroad.

Hammer   A candlestick pattern that forms at bottoms. At market tops, the same construction is called a "hanging man." The shadow is generally twice the length of the real body.

Harami   A two-candle candlestick pattern that can be seen to mark tops and bottoms. The second candle of this formation is contained within the real body of the prior session's candle.

Hard currency   Any one of the major world currencies that is well traded and easily converted into other currencies.

Head and shoulders   A pattern in price trends that, according to chartists, indicates a price trend reversal. The price has risen for some time, at the peak of the left shoulder; profit taking has caused the price to drop or to level. The price then rises steeply again to the head before more profit taking causes the price to drop to around the same level as the shoulder. A further modest rise or level will indicate that a further major fall is imminent. The breach of the neckline is the indication to sell.

Hedging   The practice of offsetting the price risk inherent in any cash market position by taking an equal but opposite position in the futures market. Hedgers use the futures markets to protect their businesses from adverse price changes.

High wave   A candle that has a wide range with a small real body that develops in the middle of that range. It has significance as a reversal formation, especially if several of these form in succession.

Horizontal spread   The purchase of either a call or a put option and the simultaneous sale of the same type of option with typically the same strike price but with a different expiration month; also referred to as a "calendar spread."

IMF   International Monetary Fund; established in 1946 to provide international liquidity on a short and medium term and to encourage liberalization of exchange rates. The IMF supports countries with balance-of-payments problems with the provision of loans.

IMM   International Monetary Market; part of the Chicago Mercantile Exchange that lists a number of currency and financial futures.

Implied rates   The interest rate determined by calculating the difference between spot and forward rates.

Implied volatility   A measurement of the market's expected price range of the underlying currency futures based on the traded option premiums.

Indicative quote   A market maker's price that is not firm.

Inflation   Continued rise in the general price level in conjunction with a related drop in purchasing power; sometimes referred to as an excessive movement in such price levels.

Initial margin   The margin required by a foreign exchange firm to initiate the buying or the selling of a determined amount of currency.

Interbank rates   The bid and offer rates at which international banks place deposits with each other; the basis of the interbank market.

Intercommodity spread   The purchase of a given delivery month of one futures market and the simultaneous sale of the same delivery month of a different, but related, futures market.

Interdelivery spread   The purchase of one delivery month of a given futures contract and the simultaneous sale of another delivery month of the same commodity on the same exchange; also referred to as an "intramarket spread" or "calendar spread."

Interest arbitrage   Switching into another currency by buying spot and selling forward, and investing proceeds in order to obtain a higher interest yield. Interest arbitrage can be inward (from foreign currency into the local one) or outward (from the local currency to the foreign one). Sometimes better results can be obtained by not selling the forward interest amount. In that case, some treat it as no longer being a complete arbitrage because if the exchange rate moved against the arbitrageur, the profit on the transaction may create a loss.

Interest rate swaps   An agreement to swap interest rate exposures from floating to fixed or vice versa. There is no swap of the principal. It is the interest cash flows, be they payments or receipts, that are exchanged.

Intermarket spread   The sale of a given delivery month of a futures contract on one exchange and the simultaneous purchase of the same delivery month and futures contract on another exchange.

Internationalization   Referring to a currency that is widely used to denominate trade and credit transactions by nonresidents of the country of issue. The U.S. dollar and the Swiss franc are examples.

Intervention   Action by a central bank to effect the value of its currency by entering the market. *Concerted intervention* refers to action by a number of central banks to control exchange rates.

Introducing broker (IB)   A person or an organization that solicits or accepts orders to buy or sell futures contracts or commodity options but does not accept money or other assets from customers to support such orders.

Inverted market   A futures market in which the relationship between two delivery months of the same commodity is abnormal.

Island chart pattern   A pattern formed when the market gaps in one direction and then in the next session gaps open in the opposite direction, leaving the prior day's bar or range seeming like an "island" on the chart. At tops, this is extremely bearish; and at bottoms, it is extremely bullish. This is a rare chart pattern and is similar in nature to the Japanese candlestick pattern called the "abandon baby."

J trader   An independent electronic trading order entry platform provider by Pats Systems that routes orders to such exchange trading systems as the Chicago Board of Trade's E-CBOT system and the Chicago Mercantile Exchange's GLOBEX system.

Kelly ratio   Money management tool used to determine how much money to place on each consecutive trade based on a methematical formula using a past win probability and win-loss ratio to help a trader determine what to risk to maximize total returns.

Lagging indicators   Market indicators showing the general direction of the economy and confirming or denying the trend implied by the leading indicators.

Last trading day (LTD)   The final day on which trading may occur in a given futures or options contract month.

Leading indicators   Market indicators that signal the state of the economy for the coming months. Some of the leading indicators include average manufacturing workweek, initial claims for unemployment insurance, orders for consumer goods and material, percentage of companies reporting slower deliveries, change in manufacturers' unfilled orders for durable goods, plant and equipment orders, new building permits, index of consumer expectations, change in material prices, prices of stocks, and change in money supply.

LEAPS   Long-Term Equity Anticipation Securities; options that have an extended life as long as five years; generally used for options on stocks.

Leverage   The ability to control large dollar amounts of a commodity with a comparatively small amount of capital.

Liability   In terms of foreign exchange, the obligation to deliver to a counterparty an amount of currency either in respect of a balance sheet holding at a specified future date or in respect of an unmatured forward or spot transaction.

Limit order   A request to deal as a buyer or a seller for a foreign currency transaction at a specified price or at a better price, if obtainable.

Liquidation   Any transaction that offsets or closes out a previously established position.

Liquidity   The ability of a market to accept large transactions.

Long   The condition of having bought futures contracts or owning a cash commodity.

Long-legged doji   A specific doji that forms when the open and the close occur near the middle of a wide-range trading session.

Maintenance margin   A set minimum margin that a customer must maintain in his or her margin account. If the cash amount in a trading account drops below the margin level and a margin call is generated, then a trader must either send additional funds to get the account back to the initial margin level or liquidate positions to satisfy the call.

Make a market   The action of a dealer quoting bid and offer prices at which he or she stands ready to buy and sell.

Managed float   The regular intervention of the monetary authorities in the market to stabilize the rates or to aim the exchange rate in a required direction.

Managed futures   Represents an industry comprised of professional money managers known as commodity trading advisers who manage client assets on a discretionary basis, using global futures markets as an investment medium.

Margin   The amount of money or collateral that must be initially provided or thereafter maintained to ensure against losses on open contracts. Initial margin must be placed before a trade is entered. Maintenance or variation margin must be added to initial margin to maintain against losses on open positions. The amount that needs to be present to establish or thereafter maintain is sometimes referred to as "necessary margin."

Margin call   A claim by one's broker or dealer for additional good faith performance monies, usually issued when an investor's account suffers adverse price movements.

Market maker   A person or firm authorized to create and maintain a market in an instrument.

Market order   An order to buy or to sell a financial instrument immediately at the best possible price.

Market profile   A method of charting that analyzes price and volume in specific time brackets.

Mark to market   The daily adjustment of an account to reflect accrued profits and losses; often required to calculate variations of margins.

Microeconomics   The study of economic activity as it applies to individual firms or well-defined small groups of individuals or economic sectors.

Midprice or middle rate   The price halfway between two prices, or the average of both buying and selling prices offered by the market makers.

Minimum price fluctuation   The smallest increment of market price movement possible in a given futures contract.

Momentum   The measure of the rate of change in prices.

Morning doji star   A bullish three-candle formation in which the middle candle is formed by a doji.

Moving average   A way of smoothing a set of data; widely used in price time series.

National Futures Association (NFA)   The self-regulatory agency for forex and for futures and options markets. The primary responsibilities of the NFA are to enforce ethical standards and customer protection rules, to screen futures professionals for membership, to audit and monitor professionals for financial and general compliance rules, and to provide for arbitration of futures-related disputes.

Nearby month   The futures contract month closest to expiration; also called the "spot month."

Net position   The amount of currency bought or sold that has not yet been offset by opposite transactions.

Offer   The price at which a seller is willing to sell; the *best offer* is the lowest such price available.

Offset   The closing out or liquidation of a futures position.

Offshore   The operations of a financial institution that, although physically located in a country, has little connection with that country's financial systems. In certain countries, a bank is not permitted to do business in the domestic market but only with other foreign banks; this is known as an "offshore banking unit."

One cancels other   A contingency order instructing a broker to cancel one side of a two-sided entry order.

Opening range   A range of prices at which buy and sell transactions take place during the first minute of the opening of the market for most markets.

Open interest   The total number of futures or options contracts of a given commodity that have been neither offset by an opposite futures or option transaction nor fulfilled by delivery of the commodity or option exercise. Each open transaction has a buyer and a seller; but for calculation of open interest, only one side of the contract is counted.

Open outcry   Method of public auction for making verbal bids and offers in the trading pits or rings of futures exchanges.

Option   A contract that conveys the right, but not the obligation, to buy or to sell a particular item at a certain price for a limited time.

Out-of-the-money option   An option with no intrinsic value; i.e., a call whose strike price is above the current futures price or a put whose strike price is below the current futures price.

Overbought   The condition of a specific move when the market price has risen too far too fast and is set up for a corrective pullback or a period of consolidation; the opposite of *oversold*.

Overnight   A deal from today until the next business day.

Overnight limit   Net long or short position in one or more currencies that a dealer can carry over into the next dealing day. Passing the book to other bank dealing rooms in the next trading time zone reduces the need for dealers to maintain these unmonitored exposures.

GLOSSARY

Oversold   The condition of a specific move when the market price has fallen and is in a position for a corrective rally or a period of consolidation; the opposite of *overbought*.

Par   The face value of a security; e.g., a bond selling at par is worth the same dollar amount for which it was issued at which it will be redeemed at maturity.

Parity   The value of one currency in terms of another.

Pegged   A system where a currency moves in line with another currency; some pegs are strict while others have bands of movement.

Piercing pattern   A candlestick formation involving two candles formed at bottoms of market moves. The first candle is a long dark candle; the second candle opens lower than the dark candle's low and closes more than half way above the first candle's real body.

PIP (percentage in points)   One unit of price change in the bid/ask price of a currency. For most currencies, it denotes the fourth decimal place in an exchange rate and represents 1/100 of 1 percent (0.01%).

Pit   The area on the trading floor where futures and options on futures contracts are bought and sold. It is customary for Chicago markets to refer to the individual commodity trading areas as "pits," whereas in New York, they are referred to as "rings."

Pivot points   The mathematical calculation formula used to determine the support or resistance ranges in a given time period. These formulas can be used to calculate intraday, daily, weekly, monthly, or quarterly ranges.

Point and figure   A charting style that tracks the market's price action by representing increases with plotting Xs on a chart and downside corrections with Os. Time is not an issue with this method; rather, it is concerned with pure price movement.

Position   The netted total commitments in a given currency; can be flat or square (no exposure), long (more currency bought than sold) or short (more currency sold than bought).

Premium   The dollar value amount placed on an option.

Prime rate   Interest rate charged by major banks to their most creditworthy customers.

Producer Price Index   An index that shows the cost of goods and services to producers and wholesalers.

Profit taking   The unwinding of a position to realize profits.

Put option   An option that gives the option buyer the right but not the obligation to sell an underlying futures contract at the strike price on or before the expiration date.

Quote   An indicative price; the price quoted for information purposes but not to deal.

Rally   A recovery in price after a period of decline.

Range   The difference between the highest and the lowest prices of a future recorded during a given trading session.

Rate   (1) The price of one currency in terms of another, normally against the U.S. dollar (USD); (2) assessment of the creditworthiness of an institution.

Reaction   A decline in prices following an advance.

Real body   The section of a candlestick defined as the area established between the opening and the closing of a particular time period.

Reciprocal currency   A currency that is normally quoted as dollars per unit of currency rather than as the normal quote of units of currency per dollar. Sterling is the most common example.

Relative strength index   A technical indicator used to determine a market in an overbought or oversold condition; was developed by Welles Wilder Jr. to help determine market reversals.

Resistance point or level   A price recognized by technical analysts as a price that is likely to result in a rebound but if broken through is likely to result in a significant price movement.

Revaluation   Increase in the exchange rate of a currency as a result of official action.

Revaluation rate   The rate for any period or currency that is used to revalue a position or book.

Rickshaw doji   A doji that has an unusually large trading range.

Risk management   The identification and acceptance or offsetting of the risks threatening the profitability or existence of an organization; with respect to foreign exchange, involves consideration of market, sovereign, country, transfer, delivery, credit, and counterparty risk, among other things.

Risk position   An asset or liability that is exposed to fluctuations in value through changes in exchange rates or interest rates.

Rollover   An overnight swap; specifically, the next business day against the following business day; also called "tomorrow next" (Tom-next).

Round trip   Buying and selling of a specified amount of currency.

Same-day transaction   A transaction that matures on the day that the transaction takes place.

Scalper   A trader who trades for small, short-term profits.

Selling rate   Rate at which a bank is willing to sell foreign currency.

Settlement date   The date on which foreign exchange contracts settle.

Settlement price   The last price paid for a commodity on any trading day. The exchange clearinghouse determines a firm's net gains or losses, margin requirements, and the next day's price limits, based on each futures and options contract settlement price; also referred to as "daily settlement price" or "daily closing price."

Shadow The area on a candlestick between the high or the low in relation to the open or the close.

Sharpe ratio Calculation used to determine trading system's or method's stability to individuals trading in order to determine the risk-reward profiles of a system.

Shooting star The candle that forms at tops of markets where the shadow is at least twice the length of the real body and the real body forms near the low for the session with little or no shadow at the bottom. This candle resembles an inverted hammer.

Short The position in a futures market where a trader sells a contract with the intention of buying it back at a lower price for a profit or if at a higher price for a loss. Option traders would be considered "short the option" if they were writers of that option.

Short sale The sale of a specified amount of currency not owned by the seller at the time of the trade; usually made in expectation of a decline in the price.

Slippage Refers to the negative (or depreciating) price value between where a stop-loss order becomes a market order and where that market order may be filled.

Speculator An investor who is looking to profit from buying or selling derivative products with the anticipation of profiting from price moves by trading in and out of his or her positions.

Spinning tops A candle where the real body is small in nature with a large range and with shadows at both ends.

Spot price The price at which a currency is currently trading in the spot market.

Spread (1) The difference between the bid and the ask prices of a currency; (2) the difference between the price of two related futures contracts.

Spreading The simultaneous buying and selling of two related markets with the expectation that a profit will be made when the position is offset.

Sterling British pound; otherwise known as *cable*.

Stochastics A technical indicator created by George C. Lane that gives an indication of when a market is overbought or oversold.

Stock index An indicator used to measure and report value changes in a selected group of stocks.

Stop-close-only (SCO) Orders that are elected only if the close of the time period is at or below your sell stop or at or above your buy stop. This order can be used to enter a position or exit a position if a certain price level is breached on the close of the day.

Stop-limit order A variation of a stop order in which a trade must be executed at the exact price or no worse than a specific price. The limit side of the order limits the slippage. It also does not ensure execution if the next best price is beyond the limit side of the stop order until the limit or stop price is reached again.

Stop order   An order to buy or to sell when the market reaches a specified point. A stop order to buy becomes a market order when the futures contract trades at or above the stop price. A stop order to sell becomes a market order when the futures contract trades at or below the stop price.

Strike Price   The price at which the futures contract underlying a call or put option can be purchased or sold.

Support   A price level that attracts buyers.

Swap   The simultaneous purchase and sale of the same amount of a given currency for two different dates against the sale and the purchase of another. A swap can be a swap against a forward. In essence, swapping is somewhat similar to borrowing one currency and lending another for the same period. However, any rate of return or cost of funds is expressed in the price differential between the two sides of the transaction.

Technical analysis   The study of price and/or volume to anticipate future price moves. Studies can include price patterns, mathematical calculations, and data regarding the open, the high, the low, and the close of a market.

Thin market   A market in which trading volume is low and in which bid and ask quotes are wide and the liquidity of the instrument traded is low.

Three crows   A candlestick pattern consisting of three dark candles that close on or at their lows. After an extended advance, this formation can be a strong reversal pattern.

Three white soldiers   A candlestick pattern consisting of three candles that close at their highs and can indicate a continued advance. This pattern is a reliable indication that prices are moving higher, especially if they develop after a longer period of consolidation at a bottom; opposite of *three crow's* formation.

Tick   A minimum change in price, up or down.

Tomorrow next (Tom-next)   Simultaneous buying of a currency for delivery the following day and selling for the spot day, or vice versa.

Transaction   The buying or selling of currencies resulting from the execution of an order.

Transaction date   The date on which a trade occurs.

Uncovered   Another term for an open position.

Undervaluation   The condition of an exchange rate when it is below its purchasing power parity.

Uptick   A transaction executed at a price greater than that of the previous transaction.

Volatility   A measure of the amount by which an asset price is expected to fluctuate over a given period.

Volume   The number of purchases or sales of a commodity futures contract made during a specified period of time; often the total transactions for one trading day.

Wash trade   A matched deal that produces neither a gain nor a loss.

Windows   A Japanese candlestick term referred to as the Western gap.

Working day   A day on which the banks in a currency's principal financial center are open for business. For forex transactions, a working day occurs only if the banks in both financial centers are open for business (all relevant currency centers in the case of a cross are open).

Yield   A measure of the annual return on an investment; also referred to as the "amount of interest on a debt instrument."

About the CD-ROM

INTRODUCTION

This appendix provides you with information on the contents of the CD that accompanies this book. For the latest and greatest information, please refer to the ReadMe file located at the root of the CD.

SYSTEM REQUIREMENTS

- A computer with a processor running at 120 Mhz or faster.
- At least 32 MB of total RAM installed on your computer; for best performance, we recommend at least 64 MB.
- A CD-ROM drive.
- Internet access.

USING THE CD WITH WINDOWS

To install the items from the CD to your hard drive, follow these steps:

1. Insert the CD into your computer's CD-ROM drive.

   Note: The interface won't launch if you have autorun disabled. In that case, click Start@@-->Run (for Windows Vista, Start@@-->All Programs@@-->Accessories@@-->Run). In the dialog box that appears, type **D:\Start.exe**. (Replace D with the proper letter if your CD drive uses a different letter. If you don't know the letter, see how your CD drive is listed under My Computer.) Click OK.

2. The CD-ROM interface will appear. The interface provides a simple point-and-click way to explore the contents of the CD.

WHAT'S ON THE CD?

The following sections provide a summary of the software and other materials you'll find on the CD.

Content

There six separate tutorials totaling more than 40 minutes of one-on-one instruction.

Along with the actual Pivot Point and Fibonacci calculators, this CD covers:

- How to use the Fibonacci calculator and apply correction and extension studies in your trading analysis
- How to use analysis and calculation to identify Pivot Points

The tutorials are included as follows:

- First Tutorial (12:57)—Fibonacci Corrections Tutorial
- Second Tutorial (3:44)—Instructions on Fibonacci Calculator Corrections
- Third Tutorial (6:50)—Fibonacci Corrections and Extension Tutorial
- Fourth Tutorial (2:51)—Instruction on Fibonacci Calculator Extensions
- Fifth Tutorial (4:56)—Instruction on Pivot Point Analysis
- Sixth Tutorial (9:16)—Instruction on Pivot Point Calculation and Identifying Confluence of Pivot Points

In order to activate the Pivot Point and Fibonacci calculators, users need Internet access. Any Internet speed will work. Users do not need high speed DSL.

Shareware programs are fully functional, trial versions of copyrighted programs. If you like particular programs, register with their authors for a nominal fee and receive licenses, enhanced versions, and technical support.

Freeware programs are copyrighted games, applications, and utilities that are free for personal use. Unlike shareware, these programs do not require a fee or provide technical support.

GNU software is governed by its own license, which is included inside the folder of the GNU product. See the GNU license for more details.

Trial, demo, or evaluation versions are usually limited either by time or functionality (such as being unable to save projects). Some trial versions are very sensitive to system date changes. If you alter your computer's date, the programs will "time out" and no longer be functional.

Troubleshooting

If you have difficulty installing or using any of the materials on the companion CD, try the following solutions:

- Turn off any antivirus software that you may have running. Installers sometimes mimic virus activity and can make your computer incorrectly believe that it is being infected by a virus. (Be sure to turn the antivirus software back on later.)
- Close all running programs. The more programs you're running, the less memory is available to other programs. Installers also typically update files and programs; if you keep other programs running, installation may not work properly.
- Reference the ReadMe: Refer to the ReadMe file located at the root of the CD-ROM for the latest product information (if any) at the time of publication.

Customer Care

If you have trouble with the CD-ROM, please call the Wiley Product Technical Support phone number at (800) 762-2974. Outside the United States, call 1(317) 572-3994. You can also contact Wiley Product Technical Support at **http://support.wiley.com**. John Wiley & Sons will provide technical support only for installation and other general quality control items. For technical support on the applications themselves, consult the program's vendor or author.

To place additional orders or to request information about other Wiley products, please call (877) 762-2974.

Author's Disclaimer

Stock, futures, forex and options trading involves substantial risk. The valuation of futures, forex and options may fluctuate, and as a result, clients may lose more than their original investment. In no event should the content of this presentation be construed as an express or an implied promise, guarantee or implication by John Person, or John Wiley & Sons, Inc., that you will profit or that losses can or will be limited in any manner whatsoever. Past results are no indication of future performance. Information provided in this presentation is intended solely for informative, educational purposes and is obtained from sources believed to be reliable. Information is in no way guaranteed. No guarantee of any kind is implied or possible where projections of future conditions are attempted. There is a risk of loss in trading stock, futures, forex and options. One's financial suitability should be considered carefully before placing any trades.

Index

**For more information regarding the CD-ROM,
see the About the CD-ROM section on page 275.**

John Wiley & Sons, Inc.